MURDER WITH A DOUBLE TONGUE

MURDER

WITH A

DOUBLE TONGUE

The Enigma of Clarissa Manson

Peter Shankland
and
The Rt. Hon. Sir Michael Havers, QC

For murder, though it have no tongue, will speak
With most miraculous organ.
                    HAMLET, Act 2, Scene 2

SOUVENIR PRESS

To David Peter Shankland

Contents

		Page
	Foreword	11
1	Premonitions	15
2	A House of Ill-Fame	23
3	The Woman in the Alcove	40
4	Two Women Pray	61
5	The Trial Opens	71
6	Clarissa tells her Story	87
7	A Cloud of Witnesses	97
8	Murder Without Motive?	110
9	'You are a liar, Madame!'	125
10	The Verdict and Appeal	137
11	Clarissa Captive	146
12	Truth Veiled	163
13	A Corner of the Veil Lifted	183
14	Witnesses Persecuted	201
15	Bastide's Defence	220
16	'These you are to Believe!'	238
17	Clarissa's Triumph	253
18	The Veil Torn Aside	267
	Bibliography	281
	Index	283

List of Illustrations

	Between pages
Clarissa Manson	96–97
Monsieur Fualdès	96–97
Madame Bancal	96–97
Monsieur Clémendot	96–97
Didier Fualdès	96–97
Rose Pierret	96–97
The Bancal children at the Hospice	96–97
The Maison Bancal	96–97
Bastide	128–129
Jausion	128–129
Bastide and Jausion	128–129
A sketch of Jausion, Bastide, Madame Bancal and Bousquier on trial	128–129
Bax	128–129
Missonier	128–129
Bousquier	128–129
Colard	160–161
Anne Benoît	160–161
Théron, the miller	160–161
Maître Romiguière	160–161
The Court Scene at Albi	160–161
The prison at Albi	160–161
Clarissa Manson in court	160–161
Clarissa Manson in prison	160–161

All photographs are the copyright of the British Library Board

ILLUSTRATIONS IN THE TEXT

	Page
Plans of the Maison Bancal and of the Maison Fualdès	31
Plan of Rodez	48–9

Foreword

In France a man may be arrested on suspicion and then have a case built up against him, whereas in England the investigation takes place first and, except in special circumstances, he cannot be held without being charged. In France a citizen who believes himself to have been injured financially by a crime may join in the prosecution: it is perhaps a good thing that the family of a victim should be awarded damages after a crime has been proven, but their intervention during the hearing of a case may not always be in the interests of justice as they are likely to be prejudiced against the accused. Witnesses are allowed to give second-hand information and to repeat rumours: in England they would be stopped immediately by the judge and told that they must only say what they know from their own experience.

It seems strange to us to find a judge questioning the witnesses and the accused: the example of the Fualdès trials strengthens us in our belief that it is easier for him to be impartial if he does not take part in the discussions but listens to the arguments of the prosecution and the defence and holds the balance even between them. If he intervenes, in England, it is usually to reject or admit a piece of evidence or, on rare occasions, to call someone to order. Finally he sums up the case for both sides, clarifies the legal issues for the jury and explains to them the questions they have to decide.

Some of the proceedings described in the following pages seem unjust to us, but we have to remember that these trials took place about 160 years ago. Many important reforms have been introduced both in England and France which have gone far to establish and safeguard the rights of the accused. One aspect has not changed; a criminal trial in France is more dramatic, more akin to the theatre, than in England, both in its setting and in the display of emotion.

Note on a Special Source

If we did not have an eye-witness account of the Fualdès trials and what led up to them, written by a sensitive observer, it would be hard indeed to understand and explain the tragic and sinister events of 1817 that focussed the attention of the whole of France, and beyond, on the little town of Rodez in Provence. The book was published anonymously (in French) in 1819 but from interior evidence it is clear that it was written by Monsieur Amans Rodat, known as Auguste by his family, who was connected by ties of blood and friendship to several of the characters concerned. This intimate record, which we found in the London Library, has opened up resources not usually available to an historian, and enabled us to describe, often in detail, Monsieur Rodat's states of mind and emotions as he followed the unfolding of the drama in which Clarissa Manson, to whom he was passionately attached, became more and more deeply involved – without it we should have been unable to do this.

We express our grateful thanks to the staff of the British Library and the London Library, who have been unfailingly helpful.

Never, in the whole course of criminal justice, has there been an incident like this. Only a concourse of the most extraordinary circumstances, and a woman like Madame Manson, could bring it about.

Maître Romiguière,
Avocat de Toulouse

Celebrity is the reward not only of great virtues and heroic deeds : it is associated also with great crimes and great criminals. If history honours eternally the men who have earned the gratitude and the veneration of peoples, it perpetuates also the memory of the monsters who have defiled the earth and dishonoured the human race. The names of Jausion, Bastide-Grammont and their accomplices therefore will descend to posterity.

Complete History of the trial relative
to the assassination of Sieur Fualdès
Paris, 1817

CHAPTER ONE

Premonitions

In March 1817 Auguste Rodat left Paris very much against his will
to return to his native town of Rodez which he had not seen for sixteen
years, because his father had died and his mother had sent for him
to manage their estate. As he took his place in the stage coach he was
filled with regrets for the life he was being forced to give up and for
the many friends he was leaving behind him. In Paris he had lived
through momentous days, witnessing the glory of the Empire and its
fall, the occupation by Allied troops and the restoration of the
Monarchy: he had been at the centre of affairs. He felt that Rodez
was in a backwater, far from the mainstream of history: it lay in a
fertile valley shut in by wild and barren mountains, an isolated community cut off from all centres of enlightenment because of the almost
impassable roads. With much bitterness he describes its people who
have always been different, he says, from the other inhabitants of
Provence: he despises them because of their ignorance and brutality,
and he dislikes them also because of some unhappy memories of his
youth that he has almost forgotten but which have left a painful
impression.

Centuries ago, he recalls, according to Julius Caesar, they had
worshipped the goddess Rhea, wife of Chronos, all-devouring Time,
who demanded human sacrifices: they still called themselves Rhutenians
in consequence, and it seems to Rodat in his dejected mood that their
character has changed little in the past two thousand years. This is a
résumé of what he has to say about them:

In medieval times the Rhutenians were ruled by bishops who kept
them in a condition of grossest superstition. Though there are only
six thousand inhabitants they have their own cathedral and four
large monasteries. As a result of the Revolution most of the monks
have gone but nothing else has changed: the people still observe
the outward forms of the Catholic religion while continuing to

believe in witches and werewolves and sorcerers, and in a local deity known as Drak, and they are haunted, or so they imagine, by the spirits of the dead. They think that to confess their sins regularly is the only way to escape eternal damnation : women are esteemed not for their virtue nor for the good management of their households, but for the number of times they confess their sins – but they confess only peccadilloes : the sins that lie heavy on their consciences they reserve for their last dying confession, and this they take very seriously. The mountaineers, generally tall with long faces and black eyebrows meeting in the centre, are smugglers or solitary morose hunters of wolves and deer : their women are ill-favoured and always dressed in black, their favourite colour. The villagers live by making cheese which they store in vast natural caverns, and by breeding mules which they export to Spain : the townspeople keep pigs and turkeys in vast numbers which roam about the streets feeding in the open drains.

Perhaps if there were some other industries the Rhutenians might develop more diversified tastes and aptitudes, but these are lacking. Because their fields are productive they work little and eat well, regularly consuming four large meals a day. The pleasure of making love has little part in their lives : they believe that sex is a sin but that indulgence in it is necessary; therefore it has to be taken as quickly and as secretly as possible; any romantic preliminaries might lead to discovery. Eating and gossiping about their neighbours are their main sources of entertainment. There is a small educated class of merchants and landowners who regularly send their sons to Paris or Toulouse to study law; and there are a few aristocrats living on their estates who consort only with each other and consider that they are sufficiently well educated if they can read their own pedigrees.

Rodat was oppressed by these thoughts. In his sixteen years of absence he had grown, he thought, from a Rhutenian to a Parisian : he contrasted almost in despair the life he would have to lead in the future with the life he had become accustomed to in Paris. He arrived, at eight a.m. on 28th March, at Saint-Flour in the Auvergne, about fifty miles from Rodez; and there, as if an evil hand was stretched out to welcome him, he learned that one of the leading citizens of Rodez, Monsieur Fualdès, who had had a distinguished career as a magistrate and as Public Prosecutor, had been murdered. He felt this tragedy keenly because he was well acquainted with Monsieur Fualdès and all his family and he had been educated with his son, Didier, who was then in Paris : but as he had been on the road all night he was tired and wanted a bed. He asked at the hotel if there was a room free, but no one would listen to him or talk of anything but the death of Monsieur Fualdès.

'Take any room you please,' said the manageress. 'We don't know where we are since we heard the terrible news. Can it really be Monsieur Bastide who murdered him? If so, whom can one ever trust again?'

He was astonished to hear Bastide named as a suspect: he was a man, very highly esteemed, who farmed his own domain close to Rodat's country home. He had known him, therefore, but not very well as they belonged to different generations. The only unusual circumstance he recalled about him, rather inconsequentially, was that Bastide's uncle, the Chevalier de Grammont, a Gentleman of the King's Bodyguard, had been torn to pieces by the mob at Versailles during the Revolution.

Finding all the hotel rooms occupied, Rodat applied to an old family friend who lived at Saint-Flour, Monsieur Dupré, and asked to be put up for the night; but here too there was talk only of the murder, and he could get no sense out of anyone. When his servant arrived with the horses he couldn't get near him: he had to push his way through a jostling crowd who were absorbed in his no doubt exaggerated account of what had happened. He asked the fellow if he had brought a letter from his mother: he seemed scarcely to understand what Rodat was saying. When at last he extricated the letter from his pocket, it contained nothing but expressions of horror instead of the loving words of welcome he had expected. He decided to leave at once. The servant, who was enjoying a kind of celebrity as the bearer of the latest news from Rodez, reluctantly trailed after him.

Towards sunset they reached the village of Chaudes-Aigues in the mountains of Layole. Here, he was relieved to find, the people were normal: there was no talk of murder, and everyone was busy about his daily task. The women pleased him: he thought they looked fair and fresh, quite different from the women of the other villages whom he had found dark, gross and dirty. He was made welcome at the inn, and here at last he was able to rest.

When he awoke next morning, having slept well, he was charmed by the beautiful situation of the place and by the pine forests spreading up the hillsides. He decided to stay there for a few days. After breakfast he went for a walk; and in spite of himself he began speculating about the Fualdès affair and all he had heard at Saint-Flour. While walking deep in thought he found himself by a garden wall with a broken gate in it. Somehow it seemed to him that he knew this garden. He pushed the gate open, and went in.

There was a large walnut-tree with a seat under it, and beyond it a spring whose waters fell into a rippling pool surrounded by willows intertwined with ivy. He certainly didn't feel that he was a stranger there. He sat down and tried to recall why it seemed so familiar. A light wind from across the valley brought the sound of a rustic voice singing the charming old song of Languedoc :

> I love you and I love you my shepherdess,
> I shall love you as long as I shall live.
> If I see you even for an hour
> I am happy all day.

Then he remembered Clarissa. How could he ever have forgotten her? They had played together as children in a garden just like this one, planted with walnut-trees and with willows and ivy; and beneath the fairest tree there was a bank of green turf where they used to sit and tell each other stories and listen to the sound of the tinkling water.

She was rather a lonely and neglected little girl. Her mother had been arrested during the troubles and for much of Clarissa's childhood had been held in prison in Lyons as a suspected Royalist; her elder brother had his own interests; and her father, with whom she passed much of her time, had such strict rules about how children should behave that his wayward daughter frequently transgressed against them. 'My father doesn't love me,' she would say; and he had suffered with her and tried to comfort her, but he had also pointed out her faults which she was always ready to admit, though she took little trouble to correct them. Being neighbours and cousins, they met almost daily and were nearly always alone together.

One day – they were both about fourteen at the time – she showed him a book she had taken from her father's library : 'Come,' she said, 'We'll look at this where no one can see us.'

They ran down to the meadow, and there hidden in the long grass they read to each other the magic verses of Jean Second* which opened a new world for him of chivalry and romance :

> I recalled with intense emotion the effect of reading this book : I could actually hear Clarissa's voice again, and see the strange expression on her face – it was the first time I had seen tenderness for me in a woman's eyes : I owe that to her. . . . We experienced all the feelings of love without solving its mysteries. With Jean Second to guide us we learned to make each

---

* This was a translation from the love poems of Joannes Secundus, 1511-1536. He broke away from the classical tradition and sang of the joys of love.

kiss sweeter than the last. If anyone had told me then that there existed a woman more beautiful than Clarissa, more gracious, more worthy to be loved, I should have taken him for a fool.

They read together all the books they could find about love. They read the heroic legends of Old Provence : and he like a true knight worshipped her and respected her innocence.

When they were about sixteen there came a change in their relationship or, at least, in her attitude to Rodat : she became more reserved in her manner, and more mysterious. She was late sometimes for their rendezvous, and sometimes she didn't come at all :

> Accustomed to read in her eyes her most secret thoughts and emotions, I no longer saw in them the same warmth of affection that had accompanied our reading of the romances : her smile was more full of meaning, but less tender, our discussions were less intimate . . . I suffered in silence.

Once when he was late because his father had sent him on an errand to a neighbouring village, and he was riding past her garden wall, impatient to be with her, he saw her playing with another lad, who kissed her : she ran away from him laughing : he quickly caught up with her, took her in his arms and held her fast : she abandoned herself, apparently with delight, to his embrace. At first Rodat was stupefied, then he realised that his world had fallen in ruins, and he began to suffer a thousand torments.

Next day he found her alone in the garden. He told her what he had seen, and how he suffered :

> She sat impatiently crushing some leaves in her hands she had plucked from the walnut-tree, while I implored her with tears to love no one but me : I promised to forget that cruel kiss that had been so lightly taken, and I begged her to marry me.
>
> When I had finished she threw away the crushed leaves and took my hand in hers. 'Auguste', she said, 'You should have spoken like this to me two years ago when I thought only of you. Ever since we came upon the beautiful verses of Jean Second my imagination and my blood have tormented me, but with you everything was calm and tranquil. We knew very well that what we were reading did not tell us everything, but you never satisfied my desire to know more. Because I was piqued by your reserve, I turned to your cousin Louis. He gave me other books : from

them, and from him, I learned everything. (She blushed.) You talk of our being married : I know how gladly our parents would consent to it, but my heart would not be satisfied. You can make your own way in the world, you are self-sufficient : I want a man who would be lost without me, if I didn't help him. I must have obstacles to surmount, risks to run, great sacrifices to make : I should have to be the sole source and creator of his happiness. I love you like a brother, but that is quite different. I am like one of the people in the romances we have read together : I too feel in myself the courage and the desire to be a heroine !

He listened with a sinking heart. He knew that she was lost to him and that it was his own fault : he had delayed too long, he had missed his opportunity. A week later he had started on his travels, intending never to return; but now in this other garden he was feeling her memory sweet in spite of the bitterness of their parting, and the dismal prospect of having to live in Rodez was being lightened by the hope of seeing her again.

Because he had asked his parents never to mention her in their letters, he did not know what had become of her, whether she had married his successful rival, young Bessières-Veynac who had kissed her in the garden, or whether she had attempted to be the sole source of his happiness or of anyone else's. He still thought of her as he had left her, brilliant in her youth and grace, her eager spirit waiting to be fulfilled, looking forward to her heroic destiny with confidence in her childish dreams.

The garden gate creaked, an old woman entered and asked if she could serve him in any way : he recollected where he was, muttered his apologies for intruding, and returned to the inn.

Now everything had changed for him. He no longer looked back regretfully to his life in Paris and to the charming friends he had made there : Clarissa had become more real to him than they were. He no longer wished to linger at Chaudes-Aigues : he called for the reckoning and set off at once for Rodez.

When they were clear of the village, his servant following respectfully at a distance, he abandoned himself entirely to his new-found memories of Clarissa and let his horse pick its own way along the rough track that led southward and wound endlessly up a narrow valley increasingly overshadowed by the steep barren slopes of mountains. He recalled perfectly now the sound of her laughter and the delicate modulation of her voice speaking in their local patois that he thought so becoming for a woman, and he felt again the magic of her presence perhaps more intensely now than before he had lost her. For a long time he was

completely unconscious of his surroundings; he was living in the past.
When he looked about him again they were in the most desolate part
of the mountains, the savage volcanic region of Gévaudan where the
high basalt cliffs are riddled with grottoes and caverns, traditionally the
haunts of outlaws and malefactors. As they approached a gorge that
was deep and gloomy and fearful to gaze into, he had a strange
experience :

> This region without human habitation, without trees or any kind of
> vegetation is terrifying : it reminded me of the dreadful catastrophe of
> the murdered Fualdès and, I do not know why, it was associated in my
> mind with my dream of Clarissa, making her less beautiful and less lovable.
> I shuddered with horror. I attributed this funereal impression to my sur-
> roundings and the approach of darkness.

He fought this impression with all the strength of his will, but he could
not regain his former happiness or shake off the foreboding of disaster.
He could think of no reason to associate her with the crime; until he
recalled that her lover in the romantic little scene he had witnessed in
her garden was the nephew of Bastide de Grammont, the principal
suspect according to the manageress of the hotel at Saint-Flour : it was
probably this, he decided, that had been niggling at his mind. There
was indeed a connection between Clarissa and the Fualdès case, though
a very tenuous one, and only if she had kept up with Bessières-Veynac
which, he had to admit, was quite possible, to judge from the warmth
of the scene he had accidently witnessed. She might even have married
him for all he knew.

They quickened their pace to get away from that oppressive neighbourhood and entered the head of a valley that gradually opened out
and broadened as they descended. Soon they had left the wildest part
of the mountains; boxwood, holly and birch appeared in the ravines;
then there were long groves of chestnut-trees, and paths hewn out of
the rock above narrow intersecting valleys : they passed several ruined
watch-towers on the spurs of hills, and at last saw the open plain
beneath them in the soft evening light. He drew rein when he caught
sight of the old town of Rodez crowning a hill in a bend of the River
Aveyron : it was there that he would find Clarissa.

The ancient walls and cluster of Gothic church towers were black
against the setting sun : a brown mist was hanging over them like the
stigma of the crime that had been committed there, for even in its
weather Rodez was unlike its neighbouring towns, and it was frequently
enveloped in cloud and rain when the sun was shining on the mountains

surrounding it. On a low plateau to one side there were some farms and country houses, and he knew that his beautiful domain was among them at Olemps with the Château Perier close to it where Clarissa lived, or had lived, with her parents: it was really a large farmhouse to which a square tower had been added, giving it the appearance of a small medieval fortress.

Like most of the landowners in the district, his family had lodgings in the town as well, and his mother was awaiting him there. Night had fallen by the time they reached the steep cart-track that led up to the walls, and the moon was bright. They left their horses at the stables of Père Larouche and walked on into the narrow winding streets – just as he remembered them. The tall stone houses huddled close together cut off the light of the moon and plunged them into deepest shadow except while they were crossing the Cathedral Square.

All around them were the sounds of footsteps and the dimly sensed forms of passers by, some like themselves with a lantern, some with a flickering candle in cupped hands, some with no light at all. An incredible number of bats squeaked and swirled about their heads. Every now and again the flash of their lantern, or the glow from a shop or a tavern, or from a window abruptly opened for a chamber-pot to be emptied indiscriminately into the street, picked out a staring white face from the surrounding night.

CHAPTER TWO

A House of Ill-Fame

For the first few days after his return, Rodat was too pre-occupied with the thought that he would find Clarissa again, and with her his almost forgotten youth, to be over-critical of his surroundings : it was a thread of gold in the grey pattern of provincial life that lay before him. He wondered if he would meet her once more in her garden, or perhaps casually in the street, or at the house of some mutual friend where, in a crowded room, he would suddenly hear her voice with its grave sweet tone that made it so different from the voices of all other women : he decided that he would not look round at first, once he was sure that she was there, in order to postpone for as long as possible the exquisite moment when he would see her face to face; but she did not appear and no one mentioned her. He didn't like to make enquiries, fearing to hear from a perhaps prejudiced or uniformed acquaintance something that would mar the charming picture he had formed of her in his mind. Disappointed in his expectations, he began to find fault with everything – the voices of the local women were monotonous, their manner of dressing was unbecoming, their rooms were small and encumbered with outmoded furniture.

He had expected his mother to give a small entertainment to their friends and relations to welcome him home, but when he asked her about it she was profoundly shocked : by common consent, she said, all entertainments had been cancelled, and anything of the kind would be considered very frivolous and out of place when the whole town was in mourning. Of course many old friends dropped in to see him; but to such an extent had the Fualdès affair entered into and dominated all their minds that they seemed intent only on the pleasure of inflicting upon his unwilling ears their own particular theories about it. No one thought of enquiring what he had been doing all the time he had been away, or wanted to hear the latest news from Paris, or even asked whether he had had a pleasant journey : it was as if they were well-informed men of the world and he was an ignorant stranger who had to be enlightened.

Among those who came to wish him well was Monsieur Jausion, a small alert figure who looked exactly what he was – a keen business-man and an active agent on the Exchange : he was Bastide's brother-in-law and had been associated with him and the late Monsieur Fualdès in many of their transactions; he also acted as business manager for several landowners, Clarissa's father among them. He greeted Rodat warmly, and evidently wanted to speak with him alone – but he was already under suspicion : voices were hushed while he was in the room, and the general feeling of uneasiness communicated itself to Rodat who was deliberately unresponsive. It was not that he suspected him in any way but he knew he would be one of the key witnesses in the approaching trial and he didn't want to be involved at all or to be the recipient of his confidences. He felt profoundly relieved when Jausion left.

One evening, tired of the hot rooms and the incessant chatter, he went out by himself and walked upon the ramparts, the only place in the town where the air was pure and fresh : a row of young trees newly planted and a few seats showed that some attempt had been made to provide amenities. He was alone. The moon was now at the full, and the dimly-discerned view across the fields and broken hills to the mountains attracted him : he scrambled down the steep slope descending from the ramparts so that he could walk in the open country.

Soon he came to the edge of an escarpment. Below him he could see the little hamlet of La Mouline surrounded by woods and fields, and there was a little winding stream near it that showed here and there like a ribbon of silver. He sat down beside a clump of trees that hid a cavity in the face of the cliff, and began thinking about his situation and wondering if he should ever be able to reconcile himself to provincial ways.

Gradually he became aware of a rustic song coming from a distance and, just as in the garden at Chaudes-Aigues, the thought of Clarissa stole into his mind, and with it peace : his boredom and irritation melted away and he saw clearly what to do. As she was evidently not in Rodez he should leave early in the morning for his country domain near the Château Perier where he would either find her or learn from her mother what had become of her. Only her mother, he felt, was worthy to tell him, for she loved them both.

All at once he heard footsteps approaching the other side of the clump of trees where there was a path : they stopped, and he heard a man's voice saying, 'Goodbye – and above all, guard the secret. You have already been indiscreet. It is my life that is at stake.'

A woman's voice replied, and it electrified him : although he had not heard it for sixteen years, he was sure it was Clarissa's. 'No need to worry,' she said. 'I am as embarrassed as you are.' Then there was silence.

Rodat quietly withdrew and joined the path farther up the hill. A few minutes later the sound of approaching footsteps began again : he left the path and hid behind some bushes. Soon Jausion passed with his head down, deep in thought. A minute later the woman appeared : he could not discern her face because of the low brim of her hat and the large shawl that enveloped her. It was difficult in the moonlight to estimate her height, so he had nothing to go on except that her movements were easy and graceful although she was hurrying, and the distinctive sound of her voice which, it seemed to him, had grown rather deep and rough for a woman, but was still grave and melodious. She followed Jausion at a distance, and soon both were out of sight. The night was silent again.

He went home and lay down on his bed. He felt no desire to sleep. Before that chance encounter in the moonlight he had refused to take a serious interest in the Fualdès case; he had listened only with his ears, determined not to be emotionally involved although assailed on all sides. Now it seemed he had to face the fact that Clarissa and Jausion shared a dangerous secret, and that Jausion was the partner of Bastide who would shortly be on trial for murder. If she was involved, however innocently, she would need his help, and therefore he had to piece together all the information he had picked up about the affair, and try to understand it.

He let it all run through his mind and came to the conclusion that he, as a reasonable man, could reject outright most of the stories he had heard. Although everyone was prepared to discuss innumerable theories and suppositions day after day and all day long, as far as he could make out only four things could definitely be established : Monsieur Fualdès, who was in his sixties, had left his home at about 8 p.m. on 19th March carrying a heavy package under his arm that was believed to contain money : next morning his body had been found floating in the Aveyron River : the cause of his death was a deep wound in his throat about three inches long : his stick and his handkerchief had been brought in by a woman who said she had found them in the rue de Terral near the corner of the rue des Hebdomadiers. All the rest was conjecture.

The rue des Hebdomadiers, once occupied by the priests who were doing their weekly service at the cathedral, was now the most sordid street in the town : the public imagination had seized upon this fact to assume that the murder had been committed there, and had picked on the most sordid house in it, the Maison Bancal, a brothel, as the actual scene of the crime; and this view persisted although the police had searched the place and found nothing incriminating.

When in their frequent discussions Rodat had pointed out that the stick and the handkerchief could have been planted there to lay a false trail, or that the woman who said she had found them there was possibly not a reliable witness, his objections had been brushed aside as absurd. It was being said openly in the bars and cafés that the affair would be hushed up; and it was being whispered darkly, 'It's the work of the nobles,' meaning the landed proprietors – Rodat's own class – as well as the aristocracy : 'No one can touch them,' they said. 'There won't be any arrests.' Obviously this was a dangerous situation.

The Chief Superintendent, Monsieur Teulat, who had of course to show his superiors in Paris that something was being done, had gone himself to the Maison Bancal, and after a careful search had found a blanket and some rags with traces of blood on them. Madame Bancal had assured him that it was menstrual blood, one of the girls having given birth there, but he had arrested her and her husband together with several *habitués* of the house. It was true that the Bancals had a motive for disliking Monsieur Fualdès, for two years ago he had acted as prosecutor when a woman was being tried for killing their son in a street fracas.* They thought she should have been executed, but she was sentenced only to three years in prison and ordered to pay 2,000 francs in compensation : Monsieur Bancal had frequently been heard to complain that as his son was the only one of his children capable of supporting him in his old age, the compensation should have been 3,000 francs. It didn't look like a strong enough motive for Bancal to have murdered the prosecutor.

The other suspect, Bastide de Grammont, seemed to have had no motive at all for killing Monsieur Fualdès who was his closest friend and also his godfather : he was a comparatively wealthy man with a fair domain at Gros, and he had recently purchased another. At the news of the murder he had hastened to the Fualdès home, where he was always welcome, and with Jausion he had carefully checked all

---

* 'A woman named Besse, known as de la Bessote, a butcher of Rodez, had just celebrated the marriage of her daughter. It is the common custom in several towns in the Midi to hold what they call *charivari* at the door of a newly-wedded couple. The woman Besse, irritated by the noise . . . dashed out to chase them away. They laughed in her face, which increased her anger. She lost her temper, seized a knife from her shop and struck the first person she met with – the son of Bancal.' *Quotidienne*, 20th March 1818.

the papers to make sure that nothing had been stolen : they had done this in full view of the family and the servants, never dreaming that anyone would associate them with the crime.

Why, then, was Bastide arrested? It seems that while he was being interrogated at police headquarters, Monsieur Teulat had suddenly turned on him and said, 'Bastide! You are the man! You killed your godfather!'

He had replied with great indignation, 'You! a magistrate! You dare to accuse me of this crime? You are mad!' and he was promptly clapped in jail.

A night in the cells is no doubt a suitable punishment for losing one's temper with a Chief Superintendent of Police, but he had not been released. The arrest of a wealthy landowner, connected by marriage to half the influential families in the neighbourhood, for the murder of his godfather caused a sensation : it was meat and drink for the editors of newspapers who had to find dramatic headlines, and the excitement in Rodez was intense : it would have been difficult for Monsieur Teulat to admit that he had acted rather hastily, so he held on to Bastide waiting for the excitement to die down, hoping, no doubt, that a more suitable suspect would be found : meanwhile he said nothing, and it was generally assumed that he had some weighty evidence against his prisoner that he would produce at the trial.

The most extraordinary rumours were flying about. It was suggested that there was a political motive for the crime, and the rivalries and hatreds engendered by the Revolution and the troubled times that followed it began to revive : this sinister development Rodat argued against and did his best to discourage : it was absurd anyway, for it was well known that Monsieur Fualdès and Bastide had always agreed about major political issues and that both belonged to the same masonic lodge of which Monsieur Fualdès had been Master.

Then it was said that Bastide was in the pay of a secret ultra-Royalist society seeking revenge for the part Monsieur Fualdès had played in the affair of the Queen's necklace – but he had played no part in it : at the time of that celebrated affair he had been living quietly in Rodez. Then the murder was supposed to be the work of the old Girondist resistance movement to exact retribution for the death of Charlotte Corday : this was equally improbable because, although Monsieur Fualdès had been a member of the Revolutionary Tribunal that sent her to the guillotine, it was on record that he had, with great courage and at considerable risk to himself, opposed the verdict and refused to subscribe to it.

In all this there was really nothing to connect Bastide in any way with the crime, or with any of the *habitués* of the Maison Bancal. It was only some time after his arrest that it occurred to someone that he and Jausion had gone through the Fualdès papers on the day following the crime, not to see whether they were in order but to extract from them anything of value : then it was immediately clear to everyone, except Rodat who protested against this assumption unwarranted by the evidence, that their motive for committing the crime had been robbery, that Bastide had given the victim a rendezvous that night in the Maison Bancal to discuss business and had employed some ruffians there to cut his throat.

Rodat considered all this as complete nonsense because Bastide had plenty of money, and had he needed any his godfather would have been the first to supply him with it, and why should he suggest discussing business in a brothel when they were in the habit of meeting and discussing business almost daily in their own homes? He was assured, however, that the suspicion was well founded because an hotelier named Albene, returning home late that night, had seen a mysterious group of men moving in the dark shadows under the trees of the boulevard d'Estourmel between the Maison Bancal and the river, and he was certain that they were the assassins of Monsieur Fualdès disposing of the body. It is most probable that the hotelier had created this shadowy group of men out of his own fear of the darkness – which is only too easily done.

That was about all the information, fact and fantasy, that Rodat had at the time, and from whatever angle he considered it he could see nothing that had a bearing on Jausion and Clarissa's secret. If he had not overheard their conversation he would probably have arrived at a very simple explanation for the death of Monsieur Fualdès : it was not difficult to guess why a man who had been a bit of a gay galliard in his youth should go out one night without a lantern, without telling his wife where he was going, and carrying a bag of money under his arm, on an expedition that had landed him in trouble – but by this time it had become almost sacrilege to breathe a word against his reputation for unblemished virtue.

Next morning Rodat got up early to go to Olemps. When his horse was already saddled, one of his oldest friends, Talliarda, a man of considerable charm but the biggest gossip in town, came and told him that Jausion had been arrested. This troubled him and made him more anxious than ever to make contact with Clarissa or at least to get a complete account of her from her mother. Talliarda saw that his news had affected him, and seemed pleased. He was very glad, he said, of an opportunity to speak with him alone for he had observed that he was frequently irritated by what must appear to be the rather facile theories and conclusions of their friends; but he should understand that this was entirely because he was not as well informed as they were about certain aspects of the case, aspects that were almost too horrible to think about, let alone discuss in public, and that he had been out of touch with life in Rodez for so long that he had lost his instinct for discerning the truths behind all their suppositions.

Talliarda obviously had a great deal more to tell him, so Rodat, anxious not to be delayed, suggested that he should ride with him out to the country: he readily agreed: but first he insisted on taking him to the Aveyron River to show him the exact spot where the body had been thrown in. As the distance was not great he could not very well refuse.

They went first to the Maison Bancal, silent and shuttered; it was certainly an ideal setting for a crime. People avoided the street, or passed hurriedly by with averted eyes; but apart from its melancholy associations the appearance of the house was not unpleasant. It had a solid stone façade, round-arched casement windows with heavy sills, a tiny attic with pointed dormer window in the pantiled roof, and a door opening directly onto the cobbled street: there was a board above it bearing the number 605. Centuries of neglect had made the house look venerable rather than dilapidated, although the shutters were broken and some were missing.

They crossed the Cathedral Square, went along the tree-lined boulevard d'Estourmel and then struck out across some waste land that had large outcrops of rock in it. Talliarda led the way along the monotonous and unfrequented bank of a section of the river where the sluggish stream had been damned to provide a head of water for a mill wheel, and pointed out a small bay, deeply indented into the land, covered with weed and overshadowed by trees; the banks were high and steep with jutting roots and blackened trailing branches.

Rodat looked at it in surprise, and asked why he thought the assassins had deposited the body there: the water was perfectly stagnant, and yet he was asking him to believe that, although there was no perceptible current, it had been found some distance away eight hours later, having somehow passed through the sluices of two barrages.

'It's impossible,' he exclaimed, 'that a body thrown in here should turn up next morning at the Moulin de Bress!'

'That's evidently what the assassins thought,' Talliarda coolly replied, 'but it seems that Providence discovered a way to confound them.'

Although his reason rejected this explanation, Rodat had to admit that the pool had made a powerful impression on him : it was a most mournful spot : its brooding spirit invited tragedy. It seemed to have been waiting for centuries for this tragic event to happen there, waiting for the heavy tread of the funeral cortège and the dull splash of the body in its still waters. He was glad to turn his horse's head towards the open road where he could breathe again.

'Although you have been absent for a long time,' Taillarda continued, 'you were born here, and you have returned. You belong to us. You are a Rhutenian. Therefore I shall tell you all I know, though had you been a stranger I should not have done so, because of the shame it has brought upon us.'

He drew a long breath and began, 'When the deed had been done, Bastide needed men to help him to carry the body to the river: naturally he called upon the smugglers who congregate in La Féral's tavern – they're all compromised anyway in the eyes of the law – and whom he thought he could rely upon to keep silent about it; but one of them, Bousquier, has confessed. We know exactly the route they took from the Maison Bancal to the river. It was the route we followed today.'

Rodat was impressed by this, but not convinced : 'And did he identify Bastide ?'

'He described the leader as a tall man carrying a shotgun; it could only have been Bastide. He threatened them with death if they talked.'

'But Bastide isn't tall,' Rodat protested : 'About five foot six, I should say, not more.'

'I admit that's a difficulty,' Talliarda replied, quite unperturbed, 'No doubt he looked tall in the uncertain light.'

Naturally Rodat rejected this explanation and told him that so vague a description would never be accepted in a court of law; that he would need something much more definite.

'Ah! but we have it!' he rejoined. 'We know all about what happened that night from the Bancal children whom everybody thought were in bed upstairs and fast asleep.'

'Weren't they afraid to say anything ?' Rodat asked.

'Afraid!' he exclaimed. 'Not in the least! You should have seen the horrible little guttersnipes, offspring of the dregs of society, with people crowding round them, offering them sweets and halfpennies to describe all the gruesome details. No one had ever troubled about them before, or ever given them anything. They were delighted to be courted and made a fuss of. No, it wasn't difficult to make them tell all they know. They have also made a statement to the police that

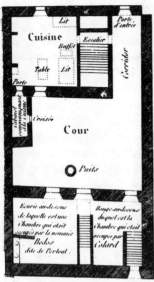

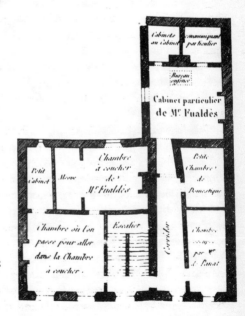

Plans of the Maison Bancal and of the Maison Fualdès

hasn't been published yet. Madeleine, aged nine, kept awake by the sound of a hurdy-gurdy in the street, heard voices in the kitchen. She crept down on tip-toe and found that the room was full of people none of whom she recognised except her father and mother. No one noticed her, so she slid into a curtained bed by the wall, and through a chink in the curtains saw all that happened.

'An elderly gentleman was dragged into the kitchen and made to sit down at a table. Some papers were put before him, and he was told he must sign them, or die. In great fear he signed them. Then Bastide brought out a black-handled bread knife from under his cloak. The man was stretched out on the table and held fast. He begged for time to make his last confession, but Bastide shouted, "You can make it to the Devil!" Then the man's throat was cut. He was stabbed first by Jausion, then by Bastide, then by a man named Missonier who gave him several thrusts. A woman of easy virtue, Anne Benoît, held a bucket to catch the blood, and Madeleine Bancal saw her own mother stir it with her hand as it poured in.'

There were several points in this story that Rodat might have questioned, but the circumstantial details were terribly convincing and his immediate reaction seems to have been one of horror that an innocent and tender child should have witnessed and described so terrible a scene, particularly one in which her father and mother were involved: but worse was to follow. Taillarda continued the story as Madeleine had described it to him:

'Just as the poor victim was giving a choking death-rattle, the murderers heard a sound coming from an alcove or cupboard at the far end of the kitchen. Bastide asked who was there. No one answered, so he ran to it, opened the door, and found someone hiding in it, dressed as a man. He tore open her shirt and found that it was a woman. He pulled her out and would have killed her also as she knelt at his feet begging for mercy, but Jausion stopped him, saying they already had one body to get rid of, and what would they do with two? So they put her hand on the still warm body and made her swear a terrible oath never to divulge what she had seen. Then Jausion took her away. They wrapped the body in a blanket and tied it with cords so that it looked like a bale of tobacco: then her father and some other men carried it out, and her mother washed the table and all the things that were covered with blood.'

At the end of this terrible story Rodat couldn't speak: he was possessed by an idea so dreadful that he could formulate it only with difficulty, even to himself: was Clarissa the woman? Recalling her brief conversation with Jausion at their moonlight rendezvous it seemed just possible. His heart was torn by pity at the very thought of it, and he blamed himself for ever having left her and gone to Paris.

At last he recovered his composure sufficiently to ask, 'Who was it?'

'The woman? Nobody knows. That's the great unsolved mystery of the year.'

He felt slightly relieved. Surely if it had been Clarissa, who was well known to Taillarda, he would long ago have ferreted out her secret.

He was puzzled by the ferocious picture Madeleine had painted of Bastide, and he asked Taillarda if it could possibly be true.

'I am inclined to think so,' he replied. 'Very soon after his arrest, extraordinary stories were in circulation about him. I suppose no one had dared to mention them before because, although he is an educated man and has studied law at the university, he had the reputation of being violent and revengeful. Even as a youth, I'm told, he delighted in cruelty. At the age of fourteen he killed a wounded partridge by cracking its skull with his teeth, and he flayed a fox alive that he had caught in a trap. He had some excellent hunting dogs: it is said that when one of the bitches whelped he trampled the puppies to death under the heels of his boots so that she would be able to work sooner – but the poor animal died of grief. Later on he threatened to kill his aged father if he didn't immediately hand over to him his inheritance, and he used his knowledge of the law to cheat his brothers and sisters out of their share. There are innumerable stories of him raping village girls: when one of the fathers protested he fired a blank charge in his face. Gambler, debauchee, leader of a gang of highway robbers, there is no crime on the calendar of which he is not accused. He is even supposed to have practised the bestial vices of the solitary mountaineers.'

Rodat listened aghast to this recital of his misdeeds: it seemed as if all the sins of the community had been personified in this solitary figure whom he had known only as a pleasant and kindly neighbour. Even making the greatest possible allowances for exaggeration, he had an uneasy feeling that he could have been mistaken in his estimation of his character, formed upon rather slight acquaintance when he was a youth: evidently there was a darker side to his nature of which he had been unaware.

When they reached Rodat's domain at Olemps which he was now seeing again after so long an interval, the beauty of his garden so worked upon him that, he tells us, he immediately felt all his fears had been groundless and he had just awakened from a nightmare: he saw how impossible it was to associate Clarissa with anything evil. This garden was part of their world; they had nothing to do with the sordid world outside that Talliarda had so vividly described. These were his thoughts:

> Everything delighted me as I walked through the garden where as an infant I had first taken my faltering footsteps. Before leaving Clarissa I had made her swear never to love anyone but me because I was certain no one else could secure her happiness, that no one else's love for her could be as deep as mine. Now I asked the flowers, the clear spring, the whispering breeze, the moving shadows of the trees, if she had kept her oath: for a moment the wind stopped, the trees stood still, the flowers seemed to hold their breath: could I have had a clearer answer? I felt that whatever she had done she had been true to me in the still depths of her heart and that in the end all would be well. In my garden there was perfect peace, and in my heart also. For the first time I freely pardoned her for the kisses so wantonly bestowed upon my rival. I even blamed myself, for if, while we were still all in all to each other, I had declared my passion, she would not have had to turn to others for her experience of life, she would have loved only me. Exalted by this vain thought, I swore to love her and to serve her in whatever situation I should find her, and that my love would be so entirely without self-interest that it should never be an embarrassment to her.

It was an oath in the spirit of the knights of Old Provence through whose chivalry and love of beauty culture had been re-born and civilisation had flourished again in Europe after the dark ages.

In the evening, when he had received the congratulations of the peasants on his return, and when he had enquired into their circumstances and welfare, he rode over to the Château Perier. Madame Enjalran, Clarissa's mother, received him with great affection and told him she was in Rodez with her brother Edward who had been miraculously restored to them after being missing for two years following the disastrous retreat from Moscow. He found the old lady very much changed. Her smile was as tender as he remembered it, but prolonged anxiety for her son had veiled the brightness of her gentle features.

Only when they spoke of the return of the legitimate king that had brought the long wars to an end, joy burnt in her eye: 'It means that my Edward will never leave me again,' she said. 'He is covered with wounds. He will need all his mother's care.'

Then she chided Rodat for not having written to her all the time he had been away. 'When you know my motives,' he told her, 'you will not only pardon, you will pity me.'

She smiled happily, took his hand and led him to a bower of

honeysuckle where they had often sat before : there he told her the whole story of his love for Clarissa, and he described the scene in this same garden when young Bessières-Veynac's kisses had destroyed his happiness; and how he had gone away, as he thought, never to return.

'If only you had come to me first!' she sighed. 'I cannot think, if we had been in touch with you, she would have behaved as she has done. How often we have talked of you! And how earnestly I have hoped that one day you would marry her and be my son! She always insists that she loves no one, and yet she is impetuous and romantic. The scene you described in the garden was not the end of it. When you had gone she continued to see Bessières-Veynac, more and more frequently. She visited the château where he lives and passed whole days there. Then she told us that his parents had invited her to go and stay with them, and she begged me to persuade her father to consent to it as it was necessary for her happiness. I did so with some difficulty, for there was a certain coolness at the time between our families.

'Then, to our astonishment, we received a formal visit from a Lieutenant Manson whom we hardly knew : he declared his love for Clarissa and asked for her hand in marriage. This was not at all what we had expected. It seemed to my husband that because of the difference in their temperaments and in their circumstances, the union he proposed held no prospect of happiness for either of them and he refused to consent to it : in any case the young man was hardly in a situation to support a wife and family : his army pay barely covered his expenses : his father, a wig-maker, a worthy man but living in humble circumstances, was unable to assist him.

'In vain Monsieur Manson pleaded that with Clarissa to inspire him he was certain he would make a success of his career in the army : he was sent away. What had gone wrong between her and Bessières-Veynac she never told us. She was still staying with his parents, and they sent me word that she was seriously ill with fever and a haemorrhage : I brought her home and nursed her back to health.

'The effect of her father's opposition to Monsieur Manson was to make her insist that she wanted him. After a year of trouble and argument the marriage took place under the worst possible auspices : her father declared that he never wished to see her again. All this time the news of the war was becoming more and more terrible; my days were full of sorrow and I trembled for my Edward's life. Three months after her marriage Clarissa wrote to me saying she could no longer put up with Monsieur Manson, which was just what I had expected : he had gone back to the army and she begged to be allowed to return here. For a long time her father would not hear of it, but he finally relented, and I had her with me again. For three months she was so ill with fever and hysteria that I feared for her reason. Once more she recovered, and she was a very great comfort to me at the time of the retreat from Moscow when we didn't know if Edward was alive or dead: she constantly tried to distract my thoughts, and if she couldn't, she cried with me. I owe to her the only alleviation of my misery until the Colossus fell, until the Empire of Nebuchednezzar crumbled and my Edward was restored to me.

'But a long time before this happened, when Clarissa had been with us for about a year, her attitude changed; she became distant and secretive and spent little time with her parents. I feared some new indiscretion, and so did her father. He searched the house, convinced that she had a lover – and so she had: it was Monsieur Manson, hidden in a garret! You may well look surprised. He had been with Junot's army in Spain – a land that had always fascinated Clarissa. She looked upon it as the most romantic place in the world. His letters from there had interested her, and it seems she had replied to them rather warmly. Then he ceased to write. Some time later she received a desperate note from him saying he had been wounded and captured, but had escaped and was in France again, in fear of being arrested as a deserter.

'It was a situation that appealed to her. Without saying a word to us she had brought him to our house, hidden him and fed him, often going without nourishment herself to do so. Both her father and I were delighted and relieved: we thought her marriage might be a success after all. Fortunately for him, but unfortunately for their marriage, we were soon notified that he was on the official list of prisoners of war: there was no longer any danger, no more need for secrecy, no romantic role for her to play. She sent him away.

'Monsieur Manson, however, had learnt a few things in Spain. He went away only as far as the next farmhouse where he took a room; and he sent her presents and little messages by carrier pigeon. Her father was exasperated: "If he is your husband," he told her, "live with him as a wife. If he is your lover, send him about his business. A married woman shouldn't have a lover." He forbade him to enter the house.

'She began to find him interesting again. Every night he came and played his guitar and sang under her window: she began to steal out and meet him in the garden. They made love in this summerhouse. But at last, the nights growing chilly, he suggested that they would be more comfortable if they moved into the château: at once she turned against him, called him a miserable bourgeois who didn't understand women, and sent him away again. This time he had had enough : although he had got her with child he applied for an annulment of the marriage. Her son was born three years ago : she leaves him here for me to look after. When she visits us she plays with him affectionately, calls him her Kleinking [Little King] and covers him with kisses, but then she goes away and takes her pleasure far from her mother and her child. I don't know where she gets her ideas : she lives in a constant ferment, her heart and her imagination need to be stimulated all the time : she is always being impelled by some extraordinary motive : no one can understand her.'

Rodat listened to Madame Enjalran with mingled relief and sorrow, reflecting that if she had married him none of these misfortunes would have happened to her, and feeling, of course, that he was the one person in the world who could really understand her : she was still seeing herself, as in their childhood days, as the heroine of a romance, longing to run risks and triumph in dramatic situations over enormous difficulties. He flattered himself that by offering her the counsels of a true friend he would be able to calm her and restrain the excesses of her imagination. He took her dear mother's hands in his and promised that from then on he would share her anxieties, for he still loved Clarissa and he was sure he would be able to help her.

'Please try,' she said. 'You are a man of the world, and she loves you dearly. She will listen to your advice.'

He hesitated for a while whether to tell Madame Enjalran what he had overheard at the moonlight rendezvous and finally decided not to mention it for fear it should serve no purpose and only add to the worries of one who had suffered enough already. Instead he asked casually if she had heard of Jausion's arrest : she replied that she had and that her husband was very uneasy about it. Jausion was a capable man of business and they had always trusted him.

'Does Clarissa like him?' he asked.

'Oh yes,' she said, 'and he is kind to her also. He frequently tries to persuade her father to increase the very small allowance he pays her, and he has several times acted as mediator in the family disputes occasioned by her betrothal and marriage to Monsieur Manson.' Rodat let the matter rest there, not liking to say any more.

He stayed at Olemps for nearly a fortnight. During that time, while Taillarda was going the round of his acquaintances in the neighbourhood, he frequently visited Madame Enjalran. One day her son Edward rode up on his splendid charger that had borne him safely through the

Battle of Wagram : he brought a letter from Clarissa to her mother in which she mentioned she had twice called at Rodat's house hoping to see him and had been disappointed : then he remembered his mother had told him a Madame Manson had called, but the name had meant nothing to him.

Edward was a graceful and athletic figure on his horse, but he limped painfully when he dismounted. Rodat hardly knew him because during their halcyon days he had been a student in Paris; he was very friendly, however, and addressed him with great good humour. He explained with disarming ingenuousness that he was in love with the dearest and most beautiful girl in the world, and that she returned his affection.

'Then you will soon be married?' Rodat asked.

A cloud passed over Edward's handsome face. 'I feel that in her own interests she ought not to marry me,' he said, 'because I have come back so damaged from the wars. I spend half my time trying to persuade her to marry me, and the other half advising her not to. When my suit is prospering I have a stab of conscience and retire to the country, and as soon as I get there I find I can't live without her, so I go back and try all over again.' He hurriedly embraced his mother and rode away. She watched him go with tears of pride and happiness. 'Rose is a sweet girl,' she said. 'She will be another daughter to me.'

Now that it was clear Clarissa was willing and even anxious to see him, Rodat decided to go back to town also. He set out with Talliarda on the following day.

We find a significant change has come over him : he describes a visit they paid on the way to one of his relations as follows :

> When we had exhausted the universal topic of conversation, the Fualdès affair, passed in review the usual thousand and one conjectures, expressed our opinion of the accused, of the victim, of his bereaved family, we at last spoke a few words about ourselves. I had grown accustomed to this routine : not only was I not shocked by it, as I had been at St Flour, but I was generally the first to talk of the crime and never dreamt of enquiring about anyone's personal interests until we had exhausted the subject. I even reproached myself now for being vexed with my mother and sister for having, upon my arrival, shed tears of sorrow for the tragedy instead tears of joy for my return.

He was no longer an outsider capable of independent judgement and criticism : he had been absorbed by the community. It was remarkable, he thought, that Madame Enjalran's household was the only one in the district in which the Fualdès murder was not almost the sole topic of conversation : he mentioned to Talliarda that he had expected as a matter of course to give her the latest news about it, and to learn from her any scraps of information she might have picked up, but she had been unwilling to discuss it.

'That is because her mind is preoccupied with Clarissa,' Talliarda commented. 'It must be a great worry to her that she is so friendly with Madame Pons.'

He was puzzled for a moment by this remark, and then recalled that Madame Pons was the name of one of Bastide's sisters, all of whom were celebrated for their beauty, and two of them, Madame Jausion and the widowed Madame Galtier, for their piety and benevolence as well. He knew nothing of Madame Pons except that she was married to a wealthy man who neglected her and spent most of his time in Paris.

'It's true, I assure you,' Taillarda went on. 'They're most intimate friends : she's a most lovable person and a great friend of mine also.' For once he had spoken simply and sincerely. Then in his usual mocking tone which his companion was beginning to dislike, he went on, 'You heard all about Clarissa's marriage, of course? She had played around with so many young officers that her father in desperation told her to marry one of them. She dutifully did so, but she couldn't bear him. She responded to his ardour by telling him that if he hadn't been a fool he'd have seen that her heart belonged to another, and that she had married him only because her father had told her to, just as if he had ordered her to take a spoonful of medicine.'

This account of Clarissa's marriage differed so drastically from her mother's account of it that Rodat commented ironically, 'You seem to know a lot about her.'

'Yes,' he agreed, 'Madame Pons showed me her letters,' and oblivious to the pain he was causing his lovesick friend he proceeded to give him all the scandal about her – that she gave private parties to the officers in her bedroom where there was an enormous bed decorated with carved cupids, and when the wine had flowed freely they pulled out her bath, which she kept handy behind a curtain, and filled it for her : then she bathed naked before them : this, and much else of the same kind. Rodat let him run on, thinking it was important for him as her champion to know all that was being said about her, however ridiculous it might be.

CHAPTER THREE

The Woman in the Alcove

Rodat decided to postpone his visit to Clarissa until the following day, and to choose a time when he would probably find her alone and have all her attention. Early next morning, as he wished neither to surprise nor to inconvenience her, he sent his servant to ask if he might call. She sent back this charming note :

> What a pleasure it will be to see the friend of my youth again ! The companion of my childish games ! Dark clouds have obscured the horizon since those wonderful days – but I shall find them again with you !

She was waiting for him at her casement window. As soon as she saw him she ran down and embraced him : he took her in his arms, he says, with as much tenderness as if she had been a long-lost and much-loved sister :

> I found her still beautiful in spite of her tears, and I could not hold back my own. It was only later when we were sitting in her room and our first emotion had passed I realised how much she had changed : the Clarissa before me was not the Clarissa of the walnut-trees in her mother's garden : her once perfect figure had grown thinner and straighter, some of the brilliance had faded from her eyes; and, worst of all, when her mouth was in repose it had a resentful expression as if she had been deeply wounded and suffered many disappointments : but while we were talking of old times her eyes were bright, her cheeks glowed and she looked young again. Of my exquisite Clarissa whose picture I had cherished in my heart, only her hands and her feet had retained their perfect beauty; but judged by ordinary standards she was still strikingly handsome. Her voice had certainly roughened and matured, and I was troubled by its resemblance to that of the woman I had heard talking with Jausion : it was a disagreeable thought; but faithful to the memory of my sixteen-year-old Clarissa, I swore eternal friendship to the Clarissa of thirty-three, and that I would devote my entire existence to her happiness.

To encourage her to talk he asked if she had ever regretted sending him away. She hastened to assure him, 'Of course I have! But I was relieved also that you had left me. I was a spoiled and selfish little girl then. You stood between me and so many things I wanted to do.' 'What sort of things?' 'Love, of course! Long before I experienced it myself I was consumed with curiosity, and listened avidly to the village girls with their boys, to their words, their songs, their familiarities: then, when my turn came, I experienced intense pleasure from all the intimate words addressed to me, and from the proposals as well, though I accepted none. You saw how Bessières played with me in the garden: he was very persistent. At last I had to go and complain about him to his parents: it was there I met Monsieur Manson: he was poor, he was despised by my father, he was nothing at all without me. I decided to overcome all obstacles and be the sole source of his happiness – that was my system, you remember? It worked out very badly, I'm afraid.'

He found it hard to reconcile the different versions he had been given of why she had married Monsieur Manson, from her mother, from Talliarda, and now from herself; but they were perhaps not as contradictory as they at first appeared: it was at least clear from them all that she had been imprudent and that she regretted what she had done. As he had understood from her mother that her romance with Bessières-Veynac had been very serious indeed, he asked if she had not wished to marry him.

'Marry him!' she exclaimed. 'But the same objections applied to him as to you: it was the sort of marriage everybody expected me to make. I wanted to be different, to break away, to be myself!'

He smiled understandingly; 'Is he married now?' She said she thought not. For the first time he felt a little sympathy for his rival and added half to himself: 'It seems no one having loved Clarissa can ever love again.'

She chided him for growing too serious, reminding him that they were all children at the time. Suddenly she became agitated: 'I shall be very glad of your friendship, but no more talk of love, please.'

He was profoundly sorry for her. Her whole manner of life was unsatisfactory; separated from her child, estranged from her husband, a disapproving father, a bewildered mother, living alone in furnished apartments and letting the whole town gossip about her. This was what her fine dreams had brought her to.

She did indeed to confess to him that she was uneasy about her position in society: 'My father tells me that being a married woman I shouldn't go out at all, and I tell him he shouldn't blame me – but he's right, of course. I try to stay within doors, but then I feel a disquiet I can't define, and I go out to amuse myself. My favourite distraction is the theatre, but I always leave the play just as dissatisfied.'

How typical of her, Rodat mused to himself, to be attracted to the theatre and yet not be content to play the role of a simple spectator! But perhaps she was merely alluding to the poor performances of the actors in the touring companies that reached that out of the way part of France.

She felt she had said enough, and broke off with, 'One day I'll tell you everything. You shall be the first to advise me. If my conduct displeases you I shall endeavour to correct it and to be more worthy of your friendship.' This seemed to imply that there was indeed something troubling her, but although they spent the whole day together she would say no more about herself or her problems.

In the evening Edward joined them, and they dined with Rodat's mother. When it was time for Clarissa to leave, he offered to accompany her, but she refused to allow him to.

'I have Edward,' she reminded him. 'He'll take me home. You seem to have forgotten that the women of Rodez make a scandal out of everything, and I have to be particularly careful just now. And please do not go on using the little endearments we were accustomed to use to each other as children, except when we are alone together.'

He protested in vain that everybody knew they had been friends all their lives: instead of allowing him to get closer she seemed to be pushing him away.

Still, he was not unhappy: he had found her again, and it was clear she needed him. Before going to sleep he thought for a long while about what he should advise her to do, and he concluded that the only way out of her predicament, as he understood it, would be a reconciliation with her husband. He decided to endeavour to bring it about.

During the next few weeks he saw a great deal of her, and he was presented to Edward's lady-love, Rose Pierret: she was just nineteen and as fresh and fragrant as the flower whose name she bore, but she was not, in his opinion, as beautiful as Clarissa had been in her youth: he saw at once that she was as deeply in love with Edward as he was with her.

He also met another of their friends who pleased him less, Monsieur Clémendot, a brother officer: he too had lived through the terrible retreat from Moscow and had been wounded several times, so naturally Edward treated him as a boon companion and thought the world of him. He was a handsome man, endlessly polite and very patient, but some of his expressions, and his attitude to Clarissa, indicated that his place was in the camp rather than in society. His favourite subject was his knowledge of women and the many successes he claimed to have had with them : his second was the Fualdès case which, like the rest of them he was never tired of discussing, but he, of course, always boasted that he knew more about it than everyone else.

Clarissa seemed to be flattered by his attentions, and they spent several cheerful evenings all together. Edward tried to make them talk of anything but the Fualdès case :

'It's the folly of the day,' he insisted. 'If, like me, you had taken part in great battles and seen men die in hundreds you would agree that we should salute the passing of this good man and then go on with our own lives, instead of continuing day after day to discuss the story of his assassination though it is sordid enough and sinister enough to amuse the Rhutenians.'

Then, to distract them from it he would tell them of his experiences in Russia, of how he had been wounded and stripped by the Cossacks, and left lying in the snow with nothing on but his boots, and how a Russian pillager had come along and torn them from his broken legs, causing him more agony than anything he had ever imagined.

'How I survived, I know not. My mother thinks it was her prayers that saved me. I am assured that for two whole years she never spoke a word except to pray.'

It was astonishing how Edward's terrible experiences had not changed him : he was gay and generous, always laughing, particularly at his own follies. He would buy dozens of bottles of beer and set them up in ranks in front of Clémendot, begging him to tell them about his adventures in the campaign, but he would not : nothing would distract him from giving them his theories about the murder.

There had been, as it happened, some sensational developments. Monsieur Bancal, who must certainly have known a great deal if the crime had been committed in his house, had died in prison, probably of gaol fever : it was not certain whether this or the remedies applied by the gaoler had actually caused his death. The public felt cheated when the days passed and they realised that no disclosures would be made. The gaoler had nothing to say. There had been a priest in attendance, but the secrecy of the confessional was strictly observed.

Soon the inevitable happened : an anonymous document appeared and was circulated purporting to be Bancal's death-bed confession : it had been written down by someone who claimed he had been eavesdropping in the cell without the knowledge either of the priest or of the dying man. The text of this alleged confession was virtually the same as the stories already told by his daughter Madeleine; the only additional piece of information it contained was that they had fed the blood of Fualdès to their pig, but it had not been able to drink it all : it also confirmed that there had been a woman, 'a veiled woman', hiding in the alcove who had witnessed everything.

Rodat observed Clarissa closely during their discussions and was relieved to find that she displayed no special knowledge of the case; she seemed on the contrary to be anxious to find out every detail of what had actually happened. He began to feel that his fears were groundless and she couldn't be involved in any way :

> The months of April and May we spent in the country, and there I rediscovered Clarissa as I had known her in our youth. There was no longer any incoherence in her conversation, no mystery in the way she turned a phrase, no thoughts half expressed that set me wondering : we rambled in the woods and meadows that had witnessed our former happiness. We were content also to be with our families : Edward was in high spirits, a constant source of merriment. With pleasure we visited our friends and neighbours; only Clarissa refused to go to the Bessières-Veynacs although they had called on us : she said it was because they had been the cause of her marriage. I was charmed to find in her the youthful gaiety of earlier years, the same warm feelings and irrepressible high spirits : I thought her as beautiful as she had been at sixteen. What sweet illusions happiness brings !

But one day at Olemps with a group of friends when they were discussing Bousquier's deposition – the smuggler who had turned King's evidence – she plucked Rodat by the sleeve and said in a confidential tone, 'You believe his deposition is true, don't you?' He replied it was too soon to form an opinion. 'Oh, for my part I believe him,' she affirmed. 'It is true.' A casual remark perhaps – or did it indicate that she did indeed know more about crime than the rest of them? Or had her friend Madame Pons perhaps told her something that she would have been wiser to keep to herself?

Meanwhile Clémendot was ardently pressing his suit, and Clarissa instead of sending him about his business was encouraging him. One evening he showed the unpleasant side of his character : they were all walking together outside the walls in the direction of a ruined monastery, the Annonciade, when he suggested they should go down to the river.

'What an idea !' exclaimed Clarissa, 'you don't mean it surely ! Everything there recalls the unhappy Fualdès. I should imagine I could see him, hear his despairing groans. . . .' There was real fear in her expression, but it was succeeded by a quiet smile as she concluded, 'No. The only reason I could have for going there would be to say a *de profundis* for his soul.'

Clémendot bowed with his customary politeness: 'Pardon me, Madame. I honestly didn't think that my proposal to go to the river would offend you, considering that on the morning after the crime you went there to see them take the body out of the water.'

'It is true,' she confessed, turning pale and concealing with difficulty the emotions that were agitating her.

Rodat, who had been looking at her enquiringly, was shocked by her reply. She seized his arm: 'Let's go, Auguste, let's get away from Clémendot. I can't stand him!'

As they walked away together, he told her he was surprised she had had the courage to look at the body. She shrugged her shoulders: 'Everyone was going. I dared not refuse when my friends suggested it. And besides, I have courage. I have a great deal, in fact, as you shall see.'

Although he regretted she had gone down to the river he was not sorry to see this resentment springing up between her and Clémendot: she had been going out with him rather frequently, usually with Edward and Rose as well: they made a handsome quartet. Had he not known Clarissa better he would expected that soon they would be two united couples, but he consoled himself with the thought this would have been too ordinary for her, it was happening all over the country, provincial girls accepting returning heroes. The fact that he was her brother's friend made it all the more inevitable, and therefore all the more impossible for Clarissa; never, he was convinced, would she do anything so normal or so obviously expected of her. The four of them used to hire a carriage and go for long moonlight drives together, laughing and singing, and knocking up the landlords of village taverns to provide supper for them at two or three in the morning. Her troubled spirit needed this relaxation, and he was confident that Clémendot's hopes, whatever they might be, were doomed to disappointment. Meanwhile, finding himself *de trop,* he returned to Olemps.

On 1st August he received from Clarissa this distracted note: 'Clémendot is a monster! Come my friend, come and console me and give me courage.' That was all. Troubled, and at a loss to know what had happened, he went at once to her mother and found her in tears.

'I have a letter from my husband,' she told him, 'saying that Clarissa has become involved in the Fualdès case. She is so imprudent always!

No doubt some careless words of hers have been picked up and reported to the authorities. How will she ever get out of it?' Suppressing his own forebodings he consoled her as well as he could, and then set out for Rodez.

He found Clarissa alone in her lodgings. At first her agitation was so extreme that she could not tell him what had happened: All that he could make out between her stifled sobs was that she had been summoned to appear next day before the Prefect. She implored him not abandon her. Society had always treated her unkindly, and now she would become an outcast, and what had she done to Clémendot for him to treat her like this? She who had never broken her word had been forced to break it and the severity of the law would descend upon her.

'He's a monster!' she cried. 'I shall have to kill him! What else can a woman do who has lost her honour and her reputation?'

He made her sit down, wiped away her tears, and at last she composed herself sufficiently to tell him that one night, returning home late, she had found Clémendot in her rooms – he had been drinking heavily at a regimental dinner, and he refused to leave.

'How was I to get rid of him without calling for help and letting it be known that I had a man with me? In desperation and to restrain his amorous advances, I decided to shock him by saying I was the veiled woman in the Maison Bancal. He was so taken aback that he gave me no trouble for the rest of the night. He cried, he groaned, he pitied me. I had no idea, he said, how interesting that made me in his eyes: he swore he would never betray my secret. Now he has done so, and I am ruined.'

Rodat was appalled by her words: although she had not admitted the truth of what she had told Clémendot, she had not denied it either: was this the secret that Jausion had warned her not to divulge because his life depended upon it? It was the fear that had been lurking at the back of his mind ever since he had learned that a woman had been there. It would explain a great deal in her behaviour that had puzzled him – her reticence, her nervousness, her sudden depressions, her changing moods. Being the daughter of a magistrate she was well aware that it was her duty to tell all she knew so that the assassins could be brought to justice, but in doing so she would lay herself open to their vengeance.

He tried to get her to tell him if it was true – what she had told Clémendot – but she only sobbed and said she couldn't talk about it, it was too horrible. He warned her that as she had to see the Prefect next day she must get control of herself, for the law would not only take note of what she said but of her every hesitation, of every inflection of her voice. He spoke to her quietly but very firmly, telling her that if it was not true she had only to deny it, and although the harm would be great she would be able to live it down : if it was true she must make up her mind to assist the cause of justice at whatever cost to herself or to her family and friends. He was, however, greatly alarmed :

> She made me swear that whatever happened I would be true to the friendship that had united us since our childhood and that I would never divulge anything that she told me : 'Let the stricken Clarissa have at least the consolation of being able to talk to you with more security than to myself,' she begged, 'for in my folly I have betrayed and sacrificed myself.' Her words, the promises demanded of me, filled me with fear. I dared to ask myself whether she was guilty or had only been imprudent : but it made no difference. She was my friend, my sister, the earliest object of my affections. . . . I promised all she asked of me. She seemed more calm. 'I know,' she said, 'that your promise is sacred. I believe in it as the sinner believes in eternal truth. Now you will see if Clarissa lacks courage ! You will learn the most profound secrets of my heart.'
>
> It was late so I took my leave. I was dissatisfied both with her and with myself : only the thought of our friendship and pity for her distress consoled me. I had not found in her that firmness which is the sign of innocence.

When he got home to his mother's house he found Edward waiting for him and was startled by his pale face and the intensity of his fury : 'Auguste !' he shouted as soon as he saw him, 'Into what abyss has my sister thrown us ! Of what use now are my cross of honour and my sixteen years of service ? She was in that infamous Maison Bancal ! She was the woman hidden in the alcove ! She saw and heard it all ! What could have been her motives in going there ? Only two are possible – a sordid rendezvous, or connivance with the assassins ! What horror ! My hair stands on end ! If I were sure, she would perish by my own hand ! If it was a liaison, what an odious one that she must go to the Maison Bancal to conceal it. How could she so have forgotten herself ? Doesn't she know that one must love ? And this infamous Clémendot, without any regard for us, or for me who was his friend, he forgets he was a soldier, forgets his honourable wounds and the battles in which he risked his life for his country, to become a public informer ! Doesn't he know that an officer's sole concern is to defend his native land ? I shall avenge the honour of my family and the shame he has imprinted on my forehead. I shall not be satisfied until my sword is red with his blood !'

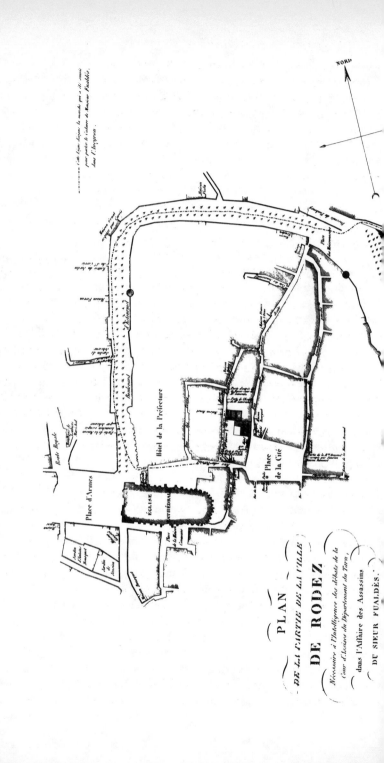

PLAN
DE LA PARTIE DE LA VILLE
DE RODEZ

Nécessaire à l'Intelligence des débats de la
Cour d'Assises du Département du Tarn,
dans l'Affaire des Assassins
DU SIEUR FUALDÈS.

Place d'Armes

Route Royale

Hôtel de la Préfecture

ÉGLISE
CATHÉDRALE

Place de la Cité

NORD

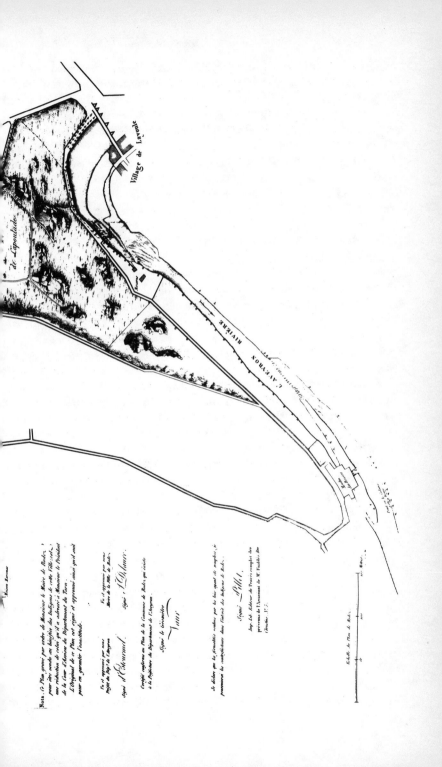

Rodat's attempts to reason with him only increased his fury, so he temporised by assuring him he was in entire agreement with everything he said : it was the only way to calm him.

Next morning they went together to see Monsieur Enjalran : his calm demeanour contrasted very favourably with the emotional outbursts of his children. He was pacing up and down, but his face was as grave as that of a Roman senator, and he spoke as solemnly : 'The misfortune is great. I regard her presence in that infamous place as an afront and a dishonour; but if she saw everything that passed, if she can assist the authorities to see that justice is done and the authors of that terrible crime punished, I shall not complain.' Then, turning to Edward, he added, 'You will kindly restrain your anger and do nothing to make matters worse. I am as jealous of the honour of our house as you are, but before all I am a citizen and a magistrate.'

He listened attentively to Rodat's account of his visit to Clarissa and of what passed between them : he thanked him for his devotion to the family, and he accepted him as a friend and ally. They arranged to meet later in the day and call upon the Prefect. Then Rodat took his leave, and left him remonstrating with Edward who was again giving vent to his rage.

Outside in the street he found Clémendot waiting for him who evidently wished to put his case. He approached and saluted. 'Sir,' he said, as a friend of the Enjalran family and also related to them, no doubt you are offended with me; but listen, and judge my conduct for yourself. On 28th July, while we were walking with some friends, I had the honour to offer my arm to Madame Manson : I always savour with delight the charm of her conversation. While we were discussing the tragic death of Monsieur Fualdès, she told me that she was the mysterious woman hidden in the alcove. I vow to you, sir, I was struck with astonishment. I took the liberty of getting her to repeat it several times, and I was convinced of her truthfulness by the sincerity of her manner. I knew how important the discovery of this precious witness would be to the authorities. I could not decide whether I should go at once to the Prefect and make my deposition, or whether I should apply to the general commanding the garrison for a transfer to another part of the country and carry my secret away with me into oblivion.

'I had not yet come to a decision when, returning to my quarters for lunch, I met a brother officer, Monsieur Ginesty : I was sorry for the poor devil because the woman he was about to marry was being accused on all sides of being the woman in the alcove. Indeed I could not help myself, I could not resist the pleasure of clearing her name and of helping him out of his embarrassment: I told him everything that Madame Manson had said. Then we went to the Café Coq where I repeated my story, and soon it was the common talk of the town, but. . . .'

Rodat had no desire to listen further. He bowed coldly, assured him he understood perfectly what he had done, and left him. It seemed impossible now to believe that Clarissa had merely been lying to Clémendot: she had been in the Maison Bancal, and he shared the grief she had inflicted upon her respectable family that was so closely allied to him by blood and friendship. He wrote:

My narrative is about to take on a more sinister tone, but I shall endeavour to bring out the upright character of Monsieur Enjalran and his family: Clarissa alone seems to detach herself from this picture; but when she is judged by the emotions that impelled her to act as she did, all will pity her as I do, and wish to share the burden of her sorrow. She has been unfortunate and very unhappy, both because of what is known to the public and because of what is unknown. When they read the details I shall give they will excuse and pity her. Is it reprehensible to have a sensitive heart? Clarissa was born to lead a virtuous life: long misfortune, an exalted imagination and great confidence in herself, have combined to make her imprudent – but never guilty.

In the afternoon Rodat and her father, anxious to know how she had fared at her interview, waited upon the Prefect, the Marquis d'Estourmel, a member of one of the three great families in the neighbourhood: he was elderly, urbane, quiet-spoken and gracious – exactly the kind of paternal figure who might be expected to gain Clarissa's confidence. After a few formalities they asked if she had made a statement.

'Indeed she has,' the Prefect replied. 'In fact she has made several, and unfortunately they all contradict each other.'

'Impossible!' said her father frowning.

'Here they are,' the Prefect went on, 'You may look at them.' He picked up several documents from his desk. 'In the first she says she scarcely knows Monsieur Clémendot and denies she ever confided to him anything about the affair that concerns us. In the second she admits she did in fact tell him she was the veiled woman in the Maison Bancal, but she hadn't meant it seriously; she had made up the story to see how it would affect him. I read his deposition to her: she admitted it was substantially correct. Her third statement is the most significant:

she implies she was there, but that nothing will induce her to talk about it.'

Monsieur Enjalran, controlling his indignation with difficulty, asked if she was still in the prefecture, and if so, might we speak to her alone. The Prefect bowed and left us : in a few minutes Clarissa was sent in.

'What's this I hear about you?' her father demanded as soon as she appeared, 'a daughter of mine who is not sure where her duty lies? Haven't you brought enough shame upon us already?' She looked at him defiantly, and said nothing.

'It appears to me, sir,' Rodat interposed, 'that Clarissa has been the victim of circumstances. She is confused and frightened. I'm quite sure that when we know. . . .'

'How can she be frightened,' he asked, 'here, surrounded by the forces of justice?'

She broke down and sobbed, 'If I tell what happened, you'll take Kleinking from me. I'll never see him again.'

'No, no,' he protested, 'I haven't even thought of doing so.'

'And you'll stop my allowance,' she went on, 'I shall be destitute.'

He seemed relieved to have discovered so easily what was troubling her. 'If I promise not to take your child from you, and not to stop your allowance, will you tell all you know?'

'Yes, father.'

'Then I promise. And I shall never reproach you again, provided you tell the truth and do everything you can to help the investigation.' He walked to the door and opened it.

When the Prefect came in again, he announced, 'My daughter has something to tell you.' Clarissa was now perfectly calm, and the words tumbled out as if she were in a hurry to give him the information he wanted : 'I was in the Maison Bancal, but it was not of my own free will. I was thrust into an alcove from which I heard everything that passed.'

'My dear young lady,' the Prefect bowed courteously, 'Providence has placed you in a situation where you can be of the utmost assistance to the cause of humanity. You will be our most important witness. We will go now to the scene of the crime, so that you can describe to us exactly what happened.'

'To the Maison Bancal?' she turned a shade paler. 'But surely every-thing is known already?'

'It is our duty,' he assured her, marshalling us out of the room, 'to establish the facts so clearly that the malefactors will not be able to escape justice.' No doubt his real reason was to make sure that this time she was telling the truth : if she displayed any ignorance of the place she would immediately be shown up as an imposter.

The examining magistrate, Monsieur Julien, was sent for, and they all made their way to the rue des Hebdomadiers. The sad little winding street was almost deserted because no one passed through it who could possibly avoid doing so by making a detour : the sinister Maison Bancal was still silent and shuttered. A gendarme unlocked the door, and they entered. Just inside there was a narrow corridor with stairs on the right : on the left was the kitchen which was in semi-darkness although there was bright daylight outside. There was nothing in it except a large wooden table with ominous dark stains upon it : the police, or creditors, had taken everything else.

The closed alcove was there, as the children had described it, at one end of the room : Clarissa told them it had a small window in it, about a foot square, with a large barrel standing under it. Monsieur Julien opened the door of the alcove – and the barrel was there under the window. He closed the door, remaining inside, and he informed the Prefect that he could still hear everything they said.

Clarissa gazed at the table as if she was seeing the whole scene re-enacted before her eyes : she started to tremble, evidently from extreme fear : then she grew as white as a sheet and fell over backwards in a dead faint. They carried her outside. When, after a few minutes she recovered, she told the Prefect she would withdraw her statement unless he promised she would never have to enter that fearful place again. He assured her it wouldn't be necessary, and she was taken home.

The Prefect and the examining magistrate were very pleased with themselves : they needed Clarissa's evidence badly, and they felt that now they could count upon her. Bousquier's deposition, useful as it was, covered only the transporting and disposal of the body : the only eye-witnesses of the actual murder were the Bancal children, and they had drawn rather too freely on the details of another murder that had been committed only two years ago on an outlying farm : in the district of Aveyron everyone kept pigs, and the ceremony, dating from pagan times of killing the pig was always celebrated with feasting and rejoicing. The children usually watched it with fascinated delight. In this case the farmer had objected to some liberties his guests were taking with his wife, and this provoked her to suggest they should bleed the farmer as well as the pig : they did so, and then carried on a drunken orgy for several days – but there had been too many witnesses : the wife was guillotined with several of her boon companions.

This story was, of course, familiar to the Bancal children, and their own stories were suspiciously like it : the farmer's wife had stirred her husband's blood with her hand, just as Madeleine Bancal had alleged her mother had done to the blood of Monsieur Fualdès – it was part of the ancient ceremony of the sacrifice of the pig. There were other reasons for not accepting Madeleine as an entirely reliable witness : she said she had entered a room full of people without any of them noticing her; she said she didn't recognise any of them and then proceeded to name Bastide, Jausion and others; she said that several of the assassins struck Monsieur Fualdès in turn, one of them several times, but there was only one wound on the body; she described extraordinary cruelties for which, if the motive for the crime was robbery, there could be no reason.

The green ribbon, which one of the children had said the mysterious woman wore, was evidently transferred from the hat of a 'Miss Gipson' which must have fascinated them – it was an example of the kind of fantasy they had been using. 'Miss Gipson' was an eccentric English spinster who lived in Rodez, no one knew why. But if the children's stories could be corroborated by an adult witness, the prosecution would be on sure ground at last.

Clarissa's testimony, therefore, was all-important for the authorities, but the fact that more than four months had passed since the murder and she had not come forward of her own accord, showed that she would have to be handled with care. If it was true what Madeleine had said, that the mysterious lady had been made to swear not to betray the assassins or they would kill her, she would have to be constantly reassured and protected or she would be afraid to speak.

That evening Rodat called on her to see if she had recovered from her ordeal : her landlady, Madame Pal, told him to his great surprise that she had just gone out to the theatre. He followed her there, and met her as she was hurriedly leaving the auditorium, although the play had not yet begun, followed by the angry shouts and jeers of the audience. He quietly gave her his arm and accompanied her home. She appeared to be more exalted than distressed by this hostile demonstration. He was hoping she would now tell him exactly what had happened on the night of the crime, but she was too conscious that all eyes were upon her, and she would not let him enter the house : she said, however, she would meet him at the end of the street in a few minutes so that they could go for a walk together as she wanted to talk to him.

Soon she joined him, dressed as a man, enveloped in a large cloak and with a hat pulled down over her eyes. He gives us a full account of what happened. In silence they descended from the ramparts and made for the open country. As they passed the extensive ruins of the Annonciade Monastery she glanced at them and shuddered – they were evidently associated in her mind with some tragic experience. When they passed the place where he had witnessed her meeting with Jausion on the night before his arrest, he told her he had overheard their conversation and discovered they shared a secret. She seemed startled, but made no comment.

They walked on, Clarissa preoccupied with her thoughts, until they came to a large boulder lying in the open where they had a clear view all round them. The moon was low, the night brilliant with stars. Enveloped in a great silence, they seemed to be the only inhabitants of the earth. He had never felt closer to her since their youthful days together. 'Oh my friend,' she said at last, 'I see I must tell you everything. Why cannot there be perpetual night to hide me in its protecting shade? I regret that I must trouble its peace with a recital of my sorrows, but you are entitled to the truth in its entirety, and it will be a relief to me to uncover my inmost thoughts. I don't want to excuse either my conduct or my motives. I look upon you as my other self, and your friendship protects me from its reproaches.'

This assurance that he had gained her confidence, filled him with gratitude, and the incredible sweetness of the low tones of her voice brought back to him the magic days of their youth. In spite of his distress for the terrible situation she was in, he counted that evening one of the happiest of his life. 'Only those who have experienced true friendship,' he wrote, 'will understand how I felt.'

'After the break up of my marriage,' Clarissa went on, 'when I was again living at the Château Perier, there was in the village a Spanish refugee, a very charming youth : his name was Ferdinand. I gave him no encouragement, but he took it upon himself to be jealous of everyone I spoke to. One evening at a gathering of friends he made a violent scene because I had danced several times with another youth : I tried to reason with him, but he ran out of the room shouting that he would know how to avenge himself. I saw that his behaviour on this, and on similar occasions, was linking our names together and making us talked about, so I decided to go away secretly and live for a while with an elderly lady, my cousin, in the mountains.

'To my great astonishment, when I arrived there I found him waiting for me – and I experienced love at last as I had always dreamed it would be; real, passionate, all-consuming love. He had learned in Spain how to make love to women, and for several weeks I could not tear myself away from him although I knew that my child needed me. At last I appealed to my elderly cousin to save me from this son of hers who had so captivated me : she sent him off for a few days on some pretext or other, and I ran away during the night. I returned to Rodez where I took lodgings in the rue Neuve because my father had no room for me.

'I had little regard for Ferdinand as a man, I felt no particular friendship for him – my passion was a weakness I was determined to overcome. By leaving him I had satisfied my conscience – but not my heart. Ferdinand, tormented by love, as I was, soon found out where I was living, through my dear friend Madame Pons to whom he was related, but I would not return to him. I wanted peace now from the storms of love, not to experience them all over again. However, I agreed to meet him once a week, but only for two hours at a time, at the home of my old nurse, Victoire Redoulez.

'It was about this time that Jausion began to pester me with his unwelcome attentions : he began by telling me that as he had had a hand in arranging my unhappy marriage he wanted to make some amends; therefore, as my father's agent, he would see that my allowance was increased. I rejected this insidious proposition, but he must have suspected I had a lover for he began to watch me, and to follow Ferdinand so that he had to change his lodgings several times and it was no longer simple for us to meet at my old nurse's house : she told us Jausion had called there under the pretext of seeking lodgings for himself.

'The fear of this unobtrusive but relentless pursuer haunted us like a phantom. We burnt all our letters. We enveloped our love in the profoundest secrecy. Alas! it was at this fatal time that Ferdinand arranged for us to meet at the Maison Bancal because it was the last place in the world where anyone would expect to find us. I knew neither the street nor the house : I only knew that Ferdinand awaited me there, and that was enough. On 19th March, the day that ended our happiness, I had at last decided to tell him what he most longed to hear – that I would return with him to the mountains. I am embarrassed to confess this to you, my Auguste, because I know your affection for me, but I want to hide nothing; I want you to know my whole soul.

'I changed into man's clothes at my nurse's house and went slowly towards the rendezvous, agitated and trembling because I was about to entrust my whole future to Ferdinand : I was surprised to see people in the rue de Touat because it is usually deserted. When I turned into the rue des Hebdomadiers there were two hurdy-gurdy players in it churning out raucous music, which I thought very strange. I reached the house : the door was half open.

'As I entered, Madame Bancal stood in front of me and said she could not possibly receive us that evening. "Impossible?" I cried, "and why?" and without paying any atention to her I walked into the kitchen, insisting that if my friend had not yet arrived I must wait for him. She seemed very upset. She kept on saying that she could not receive us, but I refused to leave. Suddenly there was a disturbance outside, and she cried in desperation, "They're here! Why wouldn't you listen to me? Now I am lost, and so are you!" She pushed me violently into the alcove near the entrance and shut the door. "Don't move," she hissed, "and don't make a sound!" Astonished and frightened I remained leaning helplessly against the wall where she had thrust me.

'Before I could collect my wits, I heard many people trampling into the kitchen. All my concern was for Ferdinand – my first thought was that Jausion had followed him with a crowd of layabouts and dragged him into the kitchen : I was about to rush out to protect him when I heard frightful oaths and threats of death, and I recognised the voice of the terrible Bastide. Through a chink in the door that was not quite closed I saw the unhappy Fualdès surrounded by his executioners : Bastide was holding his hand to force him to sign his name to some papers, and at the same time threatening him with a knife. I stood petrified with fear.'

Here she paused and rested her head on Rodat's shoulder. Her tears flowed freely. She drew her breath with difficulty. She cried in long shuddering sobs. 'Come, my dear,' he encouraged her. 'Be brave and hide nothing. Am I not your friend?' She went on with her story, her head still resting on his shoulder : 'Oh night of terror and horror! Cruel night! These eyes that had always looked on beauty now saw the agonies of death. On his knees the victim begged for life, offering his whole fortune : Bastide replied only with the mocking smile of the homicide. The unhappy man broke away from his grasp, but the murderers quickly recaptured him and laughed at his torments, using most horrible oaths that I cannot repeat. Bastide was like a tiger gorged with blood who for an instant leaves the prey that he has rent but not quite killed : he enjoys its feeble efforts to escape, then seizes it again with murderous claws. I had a mad impulse to go to the rescue of the victim : I grasped the alcove door-handle and was about to hurl myself among them when I heard the last cry of his life burst out with the blood that I heard flowing and dripping almost beside me.

'I saw Bastide looking at his victim with unholy joy as if to detect some spark of life or some drop of blood that could still be squeezed out of him. I looked away, and for the first time noticed there was a small window behind me : I was struggling to open it to escape when the door behind me was violently thrown open and I was dragged out. "I am a woman!" I cried, trying to avert my fate : Bastide tore my shirt open and passed his blood-stained hand over my breasts : I tried to push him away : the murderous knife he was still holding cut my hand and my blood mingled with that of Fualdès.

'The ferocious eyes of the assassin seemed to be demanding more blood, and I felt I was doomed – but Jausion dragged me away from him. I was thrust down onto my knees among a group of men and made to put my hand on the body that was still warm – it seemed to me in my bewilderment that I felt his spirit flow into mine, demanding I should take vengeance, and I silently promised I would – but at the same time my lips were repeating without understanding it a terrible oath dictated by the assassins which I had to repeat word for word.

'Then Jausion took me out of that terrible house. He hurried me through the streets. Many people passed us in the darkness : I shrank away from them, seeing assassins everywhere. I didn't know where we were going until I found myself on the broken steps of the Annonciade ruins. "I have saved your life," he said, "so now you will understand how much I love you!" "Wretch!" I cried, "You are more odious to me than death! Can I ever forget what I have seen? This life you have saved is henceforth nothing but a torment to me. I shall always see Fualdès. . . . Look! There he is!" I shrieked, for it seemed to me his ghost was standing beside us. Jausion started back, I fled into the ruins and he pursued me : burning tears forced themselves from my staring eyes, I heard stifled cries that must have been my own : I doubled back, I hid, I held my breath – and at last I was alone. My principal sensation was that I was parched with thirst. For hours, it seemed, I wandered about aimlessly, and then found my way back to my nurse's house and told her everything that had happened.'

Rodat waited to make sure she had finished, then, 'Should you not have gone at once to the police?'

'I wanted to, but she dissuaded me, saying that it would be disastrous, that I should find myself accused as an accomplice or find death at the hands of the assassins. Also that I should remember I owed my life to Jausion and ought not to give him away to the police. She helped me to change into more becoming clothes, and I returned home.

'Ferdinand was there waiting for me. He explained he had tried to meet me, but on his way to the rendezvous had run into a crowd of men dragging another : they had seized him by the collar, thrown him down, beaten him and said, "If you betray us, you'll answer for it!" "Naturally," he said, "I went home at once. No doubt you heard the disturbance and went back also?" I gazed at him in bewilderment. This coolness was not what I had expected after all I had suffered. He looked pale and drawn. An age seemed to have passed since I had set out so romantically, only a few hours ago, to put my life and destiny into his hands. When I told him I had seen the murder, he put his face in his hands and cried bitterly : he said he was ruined, he must fly, he must leave the country, for I would be called as a witness and it would become known he was to meet me there, and he would be accused also and he would die on the scaffold and his mother would die of a broken heart, and all because of his fatal obsession, and he cursed the day he had met me and seen the love glowing in my eyes that had made me irresistible, and he cursed all women who lured men to their destruction.

'When he paused in his tirade, I said coldly, "You have misjudged me. You don't know what I am capable of when I love. I pity your weakness, but because you were dear to me, once, I shall protect you. Have no fear. I shall tell no one of our rendezvous." "Will you swear it?" he asked, kneeling and covering my hand with kisses. Profoundly wounded by his cowardice, I picked up a holy book and holding it in my hand I cried in a solemn voice, "I swear that even if my life should depend upon it, the name of Ferdinand shall never again pass my lips." He stood up and looked searchingly into my eyes : "Adieu!" he said coldly. "I believe you. Never attempt to see me again," and he went out.'

The moon was down. Clarissa was tired and cold. As they made their way homeward in the darkness, she took his arm and clung to it. 'You are my greatest need,' she said, 'a friend who is always calm and strong and will never fail me, a friend to console me. I want to find again the dream that I cherished in my childhood. In the midst of the storms that threaten me, you are the haven that I long one day to reach.'

Rodat accepted her story without question. He tells us he was profoundly moved by it, and that her ordeal in the Maison Bancal had been so terrible that she was pale and trembling at the mere recollection of it : but what did he think of Ferdinand? He expresses no doubt about this part of her story either – but we can accept it only with qualifications. She had promised to tell him everything, and she had indeed done so, but on two levels; not only what had happened to her, but her inmost fantasy. In the real world Ferdinand did not exist, had never existed, and yet in another sense he was very much alive. He was her own creation, a dream lover, handsome, proud, cruel, self-centred and passionate : with him she could reach the heights of ecstasy and the depths of anguish, and yet he was essentially weak so that she could dominate him. With him she could be a heroine of romance : he was all that poor Monsieur Manson was not, and all that she had attempted to find in him. Ferdinand had had a profound effect on her life, and until she was rid of him she was not likely to be happy either with Rodat or Monsieur Manson.

That he had no objective reality is easily demonstrated: she described him as a Spanish refugee – Spain being always for her the land of romance so that a short sojourn there had endowed even prosaic Monsieur Manson with short-lived glamour : then he had been, apparently, a Frenchman who had lived in Spain long enough to learn how to make love; then he had become the son of Clarissa's 'cousin' whom she had gone to visit in the mountains; and finally she had called him a relative of her friend Madame Pons. On her way to meet him at the rendezvous, she told Rodat she knew neither the street nor the house – but in fact she had been born in a house in the rue des Hebdomadiers long before the arrival of the Bancals had made it disreputable, and it was near the centre of the town in which she had lived all her life. On top of all this she described how she had sworn on a holy book that the name of Ferdinand would never again pass her lips, and here she was telling Rodat all about him.

With whom then was the fatal rendezvous? Little Madeleine's latest version of her story was that there had been not one, but two women in the Maison Bancal that night, both beautiful : Rodat may have suspected Clarissa had gone there to meet not a man but another woman, and that woman could only have been her bosom friend Madame Pons, who was Bastide's sister. He would surely have understood, if this were the case, her desperate need to deceive him and everybody else : if the truth had even been suspected, the censorious society in which she lived would have torn her reputation to shreds, and Madame Pons would immediately have been arrested as her brother's accomplice if her presence there had been known. Clarissa too, if discovered to have been on such intimate terms with the sister of the principal accused, would have been in danger of the gallows. From this time onwards, Rodat entertained the gravest fears for her personal safety.

Two Women Pray

Next morning, as soon as he had breakfasted, Rodat went to see Talliarda who had spoken as if he knew all about Clarissa's friendship with Madame Pons which now seemed to be so fraught with peril. He found it very easy to get him to talk about Madame Pons without letting him suspect that he was more interested in her than in any of the other characters involved in the case.

'Have you not seen her?' Talliarda asked. 'Some may prefer the more statuesque beauty of Bastide's other sisters, Madame Jausion and Madame Galtier, but I hold that Madame Pons far excels them, and she has a warmer personality : she is capable of making any sacrifice for someone she loves. Surely you have heard about her? She was married at the age of fifteen to a wealthy man she detested. Soon after the wedding she became so gravely ill that her husband couldn't bear to look at her : he sent her away to a house he owned in Montpellier to die or recover as she saw fit. Away from him she gradually found strength to overcome her malady, and there, in Montpellier, she found her happiness in a liaison she did not attempt to conceal. For two years she led a life of supreme contentment. Then her husband, learning that her health, and with it her beauty, had been restored, became violently jealous : she realised that her lover's life was in danger so she broke with him and returned home to weep the passing of her youth : those years, she confided to me, were the only ones in which she had truly lived.

'She is now a fully-grown woman, and although she is accomplished in all worldly and spiritual graces and as beautiful as an angel, her husband neglects her for his political ambitions and financial speculations. She is surrounded by admirers : she chooses among them with great discretion and, being very frank in her conduct, she tells them all that her first love was the only one who really counted. None have succeeded in establishing an exclusive ascendancy over her, but they all become her adoring friends.'

Rodat listened with some amusement : Talliarda's admiration knew
no bounds. His usual tone of light sarcasm and eager gossip had completely vanished and it was easy to guess that he himself had been
one of those favoured admirers who had become an adoring friend.
Although his standards of what was admirable were not quite the same
as his own, Rodat had to admit that he had painted an attractive
picture; and that, if his account of her was to be believed, she had
shown a frankness and firmness of character that were very appealing.
He asked how she had become friendly with Clarissa, and Talliarda
continued :

'It happened because the openness rather than the immorality of her
conduct offended the other women of Rodez who lived as she did but
were more secretive about it, (or else claimed that a certain laxity was
necessary for their health). Among them all she had only one friend,
Clarissa, who was equally an object of their dislike. These two became
inseparable companions : they used to wander about the countryside
at night, so it was said, disguised as men, and indulging in all sorts of
pranks.'

'What sort of pranks ?' Rodat was rather alarmed now, for if they
were accustomed to wander about the countryside at night in disguise
it was easier to imagine they had been together in the Maison Bancal.

Talliarda hesitated, wondering perhaps if Rodat would be offended
at hearing what Clarissa had been up to – or perhaps from a feeling
he was being disloyal to Madame Pons. Then his love of a good story
overcame his discretion : 'Some of the tales about them are rather . . .
in the style of Boccaccio. I'll give you an example. They say a certain
sub-prefect from Paris was violently enamoured of Madame Pons, but
she would have nothing to do with him because, spying on him in their
nocturnal wanderings, they had overheard him swearing eternal
devotion to another lady. They decided to teach him a lesson. When at
last he secured a rendezvous, at a tavern out in the country, he found
Clarissa was there also. Not at all unwilling to include her in his
amours, he ordered supper to be served in a private room – but they
put a sleeping draught in his wine : he awoke to find himself in bed
with both of them but bound hand and foot so that he could do nothing.
When they had tormented him enough they went away, leaving him
alone in the bed. He was released in the morning by the domestic – so
of course the story quickly became public property.'

When Rodat left, he thoroughly understood at last the sort of reputation that Clarissa, through her indiscretions and her defiance of conven-
tion, had acquired in her native town : he saw that, if she was accused

CHAPTER FOUR

of complicity in the murder, everyone would think the worst of her, and he realised what a great misfortune it was that she was so closely involved with Bastide's family through this notorious friendship with Madame Pons and through her earlier association with young Bessières-Veynac, Bastide's nephew.

It was only to be expected that as soon as the news became public that she had admitted to being present in the Maison Bancal, some pressure would be brought to bear on her by the families of the accused: Rodat was not surprised, therefore, when he next called on her, to find she had received a note from Madame Pons announcing her intention of paying her a visit that evening. Being very anxious to see the lady, he determined to be present when she arrived.

Clarissa had also received several anonymous letters threatening her life : with diabolical cunning they had been written in a hand that might have been her own so that if she showed them to the authorities it would be thought she had written them herself, and yet they would lose nothing of their menacing effect. After studying them carefully and comparing them with the note that Madame Pons had sent that morning, Rodat came to the conclusion that they could have been her work : Clarissa agreed it was possible her ferocious brother had forced her to write them.

'She knows, of course, that he is the murderer,' she said, 'but in spite of this she is probably coming here this evening to implore me in the name of friendship to save his life by withdrawing my deposition.' Rodat earnestly begged her to resist all pressure of this kind, and to fearlessly tell the truth.

When he was presented to Madame Pons she made an impression on him quite different from what he had expected. There was something about her that compelled his respect in spite of all he had heard about her : he might even, in happier circumstances, have shared Talliarda's adoration. Although she had come to visit a friend who had just publicly accused her brother of the foulest murder, she showed no sign of anger or resentment. He thought he had never seen such humanity, such tenderness, expressed in a woman's face. 'I admit I was dazzled by her beauty,' he wrote,

> The grief expressed in her enchanting features made them more enchanting. . . . This night, I thought, decides Clarissa's fate : the tears of her lovely friend will cause her to forget what she owes to herself and to justice. The veil of mystery surrounding her is growing more obscure. . . . The two friends held each other in a close embrace, their emotions preventing them from speaking.

They expected him to leave them, and he did so. They must have spent that night together, for early next morning he saw them enter the cathedral : they lit candles, knelt down side by side and solemnly prayed. One would have thought these two fair women were asking to be led along the paths of truth and virtue : he had good reason to fear they were praying to the Madonna and all the saints to strengthen Clarissa to retract her evidence in the name of their friendship, and thus save Bastide's life.

That very day Clarissa, without consulting him or her father, wrote the following passionate appeal to the marquis d'Estourmel :

> Listen to me, Monsieur le Préfet, in the name of Heaven ! Listen to me and take pity on the frightful state of my conscience. In you alone I place all my hopes. If there is still time, don't pass on my deposition. I'm almost out of my mind. I have eaten nothing all day. I can't put my thoughts together. Tomorrow, if you will give me until tomorrow, I will open my heart to you, withholding nothing. Oh have pity on me. I have only been imprudent. But time presses. – I have the honour to be, etc., E. Manson.

This was followed by a declaration, dated 5th August, in which she formally denied having been in the Maison Bancal, not only on 19th March, but ever, until she was taken there by the Prefect. She said she had spent the whole night of 19th March in her own lodging in the rue Neuve and hadn't left it until nine o'clock on the morning of the 20th : 'And this I shall maintain,' she concluded, 'all through the hearing of the case, and until my dying day.'

To understand the sensation caused by the withdrawal of her deposition one would have had to be in Rodez at the time. The people who had cried out against her for saying she had been in the Maison Bancal, now cried out against her even more indignantly for saying she hadn't been. No one believed her. It was generally assumed she had been bribed or terrorised, though no one knew how. The public clung instinctively to their image of her as the mysterious veiled woman watching an atrocious murder, and they would not give it up.

When Rodat went round to reason with her and show her what she owed to herself, to her friends, to her family and to justice he found an entirely different Clarissa : she laughed aloud at his solemn remonstrances and behaved with a simple gaiety that he was convinced couldn't be sincere – it was as if she hadn't a care in the world. All his attempts to convince her of the seriousness of the affair made no effect on her at all.

They were interrupted by the arrival of her father who had been advised by the Prefect of what had happened: he had borne with fortitude the news that she was involved in the case and had treated her with less than his usual severity, but now he stormed, shouted, pleaded, threatened and cried out that his honour was involved in her deposition, and that it must never be said that the daughter of a magistrate was protecting assassins. Clarissa answered firmly that she had originally made a false declaration because she hadn't dared to admit that she had been lying to Clémendot and mocking him, but now that she understood the whole seriousness of the affair in which she had so thoughtlessly become involved she had decided to pocket her pride and confess she knew nothing at all about the murder. She had been very foolish and she was sorry for what she had done.

'Do you expect me to believe,' her father shouted, beside himself with rage, 'that you or anybody else would have indulged in such a piece of *badinage*? I'll throw myself at the feet of the king and get an order for you to be shut up for the rest of your life, for I see you mean to carry your head to the scaffold!'

'Then I shall carry it high,' she replied with some spirit but with lips trembling, 'and I shall die without remorse, and with a good conscience.'

At that he burst into tears: 'Unhappy daughter,' he sobbed, 'and what of your family? You have a father who has always shown you the path of honour. You have an adoring mother: you poignard her and leave her with hardly a breath of life on her bed of misery. You reduce your brother to impotent despair. And your son – what an inheritance you leave him!' At last, seeing that father and daughter were equally stubborn and equally emotional, Rodat persuaded him to leave, and he went out shaking his head despondently.

Alone with her once more, Rodat told her he was aware her retraction had been dictated by her devotion to Madame Pons. She admitted it, and warned him:

Do not attempt, dear Auguste, to dissuade me. I have steeled myself to resist even the prayers of my mother – what bitter tears I have caused her to shed! . . . My friend dictates to me what I must do, she thinks and acts for me. Her *sang-froid* is admirable. With indefatigable zeal she travels all day long to be with me at night. With her, close to her, I forget my troubles. I feel happy when her sweet voice says to me, 'Misfortunes overwhelm us, but your generous devotion not only renders the bonds of our friendship indissoluble but melts our two souls into one. We shall live together always – we still have so long to weep. . . . All I possess is yours, and my heart also.'

Much as he deplored what she had done, Rodat understood her and she had all his sympathy : he was too deeply aware of the sacredness of friendship to blame her for it. But then he explained that by making him her confidant she had put him in a very difficult position because he would certainly be questioned about what she had told him, about all that had passed between them, and that it would be his duty to tell the magistrates that she had described to him in great detail the murder of Monsieur Fualdès in the Maison Bancal. Clarissa, who had borne up through the stormy scene with her father, now began to cry. 'Even you condemn me !' she said. 'I am lost !' She sobbed bitterly for some minutes. When she had recovered her composure, she took up an entirely different attitude : 'Tell me what to do,' she said quietly. 'You are my counsellor. I'll say whatever you wish. But all the same,' she added defiantly, 'I was never at the Bancals.'

Next day, in order to establish once and for all whether she had been or not, he suggested taking her to the Hospice of St Anne where the children were being cared for, and confronting her with little Madeleine. She was perfectly willing to go, but assured him it would be a waste of time because Madeleine had never seen her before and wouldn't recognise her.

When they arrived at the hospice the grey-haired porter left them in the large stone vaulted hall and hobbled away to announce them. As soon as he had gone the figure of a woman appeared, or, rather, seemed to materialise from between the pillars, and stood regarding them thoughtfully : she was wearing a rough peasant skirt, a light-coloured threadbare shawl, a round straw hat perched above an elaborate coiffure, and clogs. Clarissa whispered that it must be Marianne Bancal, the nineteen-year-old daughter. She looked hollow-eyed and withdrawn from worldly things, more like a woman possessed by the muse of tragedy than the sordid young prostitute they knew her to be.

Suddenly she spoke : 'It is kind of you to come so far . . . so far. . . .' It was like someone talking in a dream. 'Kindly be seated, Madame. Kindly be seated sir. But first let me wipe the blood from the chairs. . . .' With the hem of her skirt she carefully wiped two cleanly scrubbed wooden chairs and brought them. 'You come to talk with Madeleine?' she continued. 'They all do. But I can tell you more. My father died in prison – poisoned. Did you know that ? He took the few copper coins he had with him, soaked them in urine at the bottom of his shoe. When they were covered with verdigris he drank the mixture . . . and died . . . but pray be seated, sir.'

Trying not to show any reaction to this revolting story, they thanked her and were about to sit down when the porter returned and announced that the children would be brought. He took Marianne's arm and led her away. When he came back, he muttered, 'The good God must take that girl to himself before long, or she will make a bad end.'

The children entered all in a bunch clinging round the voluminous skirts of a sister of mercy : their bare feet pattered softly on the stone paving. It was a spectacle of deplorable indigence. There were two boys and three girls, all between the ages of four and a half and nine; their clothes were of coarse cloth, frayed and torn. They looked very unhappy, except Madeleine who was entirely indifferent to her surroundings, and the youngest boy, Victor, a more graceful child than the others, with curly hair, and apparently untouched by their misery. Rodat tried to caress Alexis, aged eight, who was wearing a tall hat many sizes too big for him : he began to cry.

'Couldn't you wash his face sometimes?' he asked the sister, whereupon he ran away and hid. When he had been brought back, Rodat said, 'What is it, Alexis? Aren't you happy here?'

He answered 'No.'

'What?' asked the sister, 'Isn't the soup good here?'

Again he answered no. It was well-known, however, that this hospice took great care of the numerous sick people who came to them.

They gave the children cakes and fruit, and when they were all eagerly munching, Rodat asked Madeleine if she had really seen the murder of Monsieur Fualdès. 'Of course! Didn't it happen in our kitchen?' and she glibly repeated the stories he had already heard from Talliarda and others. 'I keep on remembering other things,' she added hopefully, but he didn't take the hint. 'Madeleine has a wicked tongue,' her younger sister remarked, but she went on quite unperturbed : 'I remember when they brought poor Monsieur Fualdès into our house there were two loaves that he himself had sent us : when they threw him onto the table it fell over and was broken and the loaves rolled on the floor and stayed there and were covered with his blood.'

'Wicked tongue!' her sister commented.

'Oh yes! Wicked! Wicked!' they all chimed in.

He turned to them and asked, 'Didn't the rest of you see anything?'

'I saw two gentlemen,' Alexis piped up. 'One was very big, with big boots. They came into our house carrying a sick man, and they put him on our table. He kicked his legs out. He was very naughty.'

'Well? What happened then?'

'They found his handkerchief . . . and there was blood. . . .'

That was all they could get out of him, but those few words, because of their ingenuousness, impressed Rodat very much.

Then he became aware with a shock that the second girl was wearing a mop cap that exactly matched Clarissa's dress. 'Did you give that child a piece of the material?' he asked. She denied it emphatically, but seemed quite put out by the coincidence. She knelt down in front of Madeleine, took her hand and said, 'Look at me carefully. You've never seen me before, have you?'

Madeleine looked at her stonily, then she smiled, 'Yes, I have.'

'Where?'

'In our kitchen.'

Clarissa, extremely disconcerted, insisted on leaving at once. Rodat should have been satisfied with this positive statement, but a small doubt assailed him: something in Madeleine's tone had conveyed to him the thought that by identifying Clarissa as the mysterious lady in her stories she was claiming a friend, or perhaps a fellow conspirator.

'That detail about the loaves was not new to me,' he remarked on the way home.

'No,' Clarissa said. 'You got it from me.' While strenuously denying she had been in the Maison Bancal she kept on saying things that implied the contrary as if she were trying to serve both God and Mammon: when she was directly questioned she denied knowing anything about the murder; the hints that she knew a great deal were let fall in her unguarded moments.

Meanwhile she was being attacked both in the local and national press for retracting her evidence. The strain began to tell on her. 'Why are they all against me?' she wrote to the Prefect :

> and by what fatal imprudence have I voluntarily thrown myself into a labyrinth from which I cannot escape without a special dispensation of Providence? Had it not been for my fatal passion for the theatre I should be living in peace, unknown almost to everybody : now I am forced to struggle against my despairing family, against my dearest friends, against the local authorities, against all the people in the district, against the whole of France that cries out for vengeance, and will surely obtain it.

It seemed now that the authorities might have to abandon the case against Bastide and Jausion because of insufficient evidence against them, but the Prefect had been quietly searching for people to whom Clarissa might also have told her story, so that he could get it at least at second hand. He found two, besides Rodat : her old nurse Victoire

Redoulez, and a certain Madame Constans whose dress shop was one of the gossip centres of the town. He analysed her alleged statements to them to see if she had let fall anything she could only have known had she in fact been present at the murder. Therefore, although Madame Pons came to her every evening to keep her firm in her resolution, Rodat began to hope she might be made to realise the futility of her denials.

She had protested all along that the murderers were as abhorrent to her as to everybody else, and that if she knew the slightest thing that would be helpful to the authorities she would tell them. She had frequent talks with the Prefect. On one occasion he said to her, 'If you were not the mysterious woman in the Maison Bancal, then who was it?' She answered that two days after the crime Rose Pierret had been remarkably well informed about it. Rose was immediately brought in, questioned by the police, and warned that she would have to give evidence at the trial: it was soon being whispered around that she too had been in the Maison Bancal – and whom could she have been meeting there, but Edward?

Rodat found her behaviour on this occasion most reprehensible, and he told her so. She explained that she was only trying to be helpful and had not for a moment considered the implications of what she was saying, but she hung her head and accepted his rebuke just as she had always done when they were children. She said she had no idea why she had mentioned Rose. Possibly it was a reaction of resentment because Edward had washed his hands of her when she was in trouble, and she may also have wanted to show him how easily he too and his beloved might become involved: or possibly it was jealousy of Rose who had taken Edward from her, or some blind impulse of that kind.

For Edward it was the last straw: in spite of his father's express wishes he sent a challenge to Clémendot as the author of all their woes. The commander of the garrison, General Wautré, intervened and prevented their meeting: he ordered Clémendot to be confined to barracks, and Edward to be banished from Rodez for the duration of the trial. He retired to the Château Perier.

All this time nothing had been heard of Didier Fualdès, the companion of Rodat's youthful studies, son of the murdered man. It was only known he had returned from Paris and was living quietly with his mother; but when he heard of Clarissa's retraction he came to her and said he was certain Bastide and Jausion were guilty; and it was only because he had been unwilling to act hastily he had been silent so long.

'I implore you, Madame,' he said with deep melancholy in his voice, 'to pity me. Not only have I been bereft of the kindest and most virtuous of fathers, but my mother, through the intensity of her grief, has been brought to the edge of the grave. I have studied every aspect of the case : there is not the smallest doubt that the men whom he looked upon as his two best friends were guilty of his murder. With cold-hearted cynicism they came to our house and with reeking hands ransacked his papers – they even sat down at table with my mother. What was the result? It is well known that my father was rich : now I find he has nothing but creditors although he recently sold the domain of Flars and got a good price for it. Therefore I shall not only demand their punishment, I shall demand reparation – not for my own profit : I scorn to sell my father's blood! but on behalf of his creditors. His journal and some important papers cannot be found – who else could have taken them? What motive other than theft could there have been for this shocking crime? It is only from the mouths of innocent children who cannot be brought into court that we know what happened that night in the Bancals' kitchen – but Divine Providence decreed there should be another witness to their foul misdeed – You, Madame! You in whom all our hopes reside. The cause of innocence rests in your hands alone. Arise and confound them! Tell us what you saw! I shall be beside you in court, and every virtuous man and woman in France will be with you in spirit!'

For two hours he went on like this, pouring out his grief and pain, and his distress that he must tolerate, for a while at least, the continued existence of these evil men who without Clarissa's intervention would escape the sword of justice. 'Let one sentence be engraved upon your heart', he cried, ' "Vengeance for the blood of Fualdès!" Then go forth and conquer in the name of all that is good and pure upon the earth!'

Clarissa expressed her sympathy, praised his sentiments, his determination to see justice done, and wished she could help him – but she still would not admit she had witnessed the crime : it may be, however, that she was shaken by his tirade, and attracted by the dramatic role he had sketched out for her as an avenging angel straight from Heaven. Rodat was prepared to accept Didier as an ally, courageous and sincere, who might in time outweigh the pernicious influence of Madame Pons.

CHAPTER FIVE

The Trial Opens

The trial of Bastide and Jausion opened in the ancient Palais de Justice at Rodez on 18th August 1817, five months after the crime had been committed. Two of Bastide's sisters, Madame Jausion and the widowed Madame Galtier, were accused of complicity because they had been present when the two men looked through the dead man's papers and, it was alleged, had helped to force open his desk. Bastide's nephew, Pierre-Josef Bessières-Veynac, was accused with them because he had been identified as one of the men present in the Bancal's kitchen : he was the younger brother of the youth who had kissed Clarissa in the garden and shattered Rodat's youthful romance.

As if to add to their shame the following characters from the lowest strata of society were accused with them; Madame Bancal with her grown-up daughter Marianne; Bousquier who had turned King's evidence, François Bax, a smuggler; Jean Baptiste Colard, a young soldier of the supply train who had served in Spain, and his mistress Anne Benoît – they had shared a back room in the Maison Bancal – and there was a weak-minded fellow called Joseph Missonier who was accused of helping to carry the body.

Because of the importance of the case, the Chancellor (*Le Garde des Sceaux*) had appointed two extra judges to hear it in addition to the five already appointed, and ordered that there should be two additional members of the jury.

Before taking their places in the courtroom, the judges, the Prefect, the principal officers of the court and the jurymen heard Mass in the Cathedral of Notre Dame, and then were escorted by a company of the National Guard to the Palais de Justice. Clarissa, watching them pass under her window, thought the Prefect looked up at her reproachfully. There was a great crowd round the door of the courtroom, and many notable people attended, including General Desperières, military commander of the district. The ladies of Rodez, who formerly had felt honoured to be in the company of Bastide's sisters, now crowded into the reserved seats to see them on trial for their lives.

When the prisoners were brought in, there was a rustle of excitement. First Bastide, Jausion, Colard, Missonier and Bax were conducted to the highest bench reserved for the accused. Bastide looked at the crowd with cold disdain, Jausion with an ingratiating smile. Then came Bousquier and the ladies : as soon as Madame Galtier saw Bastide she flung herself into his arms and clung to him, while Madame Jausion ran to her husband and embraced him long and lovingly – it was a touching scene that reduced some of the onlookers to tears. They were separated with difficulty, and the ladies were made to sit on a lower bench.

Then the barristers for the defence filed in, wearing black robes, white cravats and square black hats. When they were in their places in front of the accused, all were required to stand. A door opened at the far end of the courtroom where there was a platform railed off from the main part of the hall : through it entered the judges, the advocate-general* and the prosecutor in their red robes and round hats. The President, or presiding judge, Monsieur Grenier, took his place in the centre of the platform with three other judges on each side of him. Behind them on the wall there was a large crucifix. The advocate-general and the prosecutor seated themselves in armchairs one at each end of the judges' table and quietly compared notes with them.

Next, the barristers for the defence rose, bowed to the President and muttered the formula required of them, undertaking not to say anything that would conflict with their consciences or be lacking in respect for the laws, and that they would express themselves with decency and moderation. The barrister defending Bastide, Maître Romiguière, objected that one of the judges had already officiated at a preliminary hearing, and therefore was ineligible : his objection was overruled but the judge in question, Monsieur de Serres, stood down of his own accord and another one took his place. The jury were elected from a list supplied by the Prefect, and sworn in – eight of them were mayors of neighbouring villages. No objections were raised to any of these, but when it came to appointing the two additional ones, Bastide requested they should not be natives of Rodez : this was ignored, and his counsel did not insist.

Then Maître Merlin, representing Didier Fualdès, stood up and read an Act of Intervention, requesting the permission of the court to inter-

---

* The advocate-general was the representative of the *Ministère Publique*, a body of permanent magistrates appointed to ensure that the laws were properly administered. His duty was to present the case against the accused to the jury, and at the end he would ask for them to be acquitted if the case against them was insufficiently proved.

vene in the case to claim damages from Bastide and Jausion. He related how the father of his client had been basely assassinated after being lured into the Maison Bancal under the pretext of discussing an advantageous business deal; and the general opinion was that his two closest friends were the authors of the crime. They had been arrested and were now on the bench of the accused :

'These monsters with human faces cut his throat in the most barbarous manner, and ignoring his cries for mercy and his appeal for time to make a last confession, took pleasure in his agony, collected his blood in a bucket and fed it to a pig – an act without parallel in the annals of crime – and all this was done by men who had enjoyed his confidence and friendship. They were so deaf to every sentiment of humanity that after throwing the body into the river they went to the home of their victim, rifled his papers, and were not ashamed to sit down at the hospitable table of the widow. But Providence, that leaves nothing unpunished, decreed that the body should float and be seen on the following day. The proofs that have been collected by the magistrates leave no possible doubt of the guilt of the accused. . . .'

And therefore, he concluded, he was putting forward as a sacred duty a claim for heavy damages on behalf of the son who had been bereft of the dearest but most unfortunate of fathers, his sole support and protection. Maître Merlin sat down, introducing with a sweeping gesture his client, Didier Fualdès, who stood up and bowed. His solemn face and long high-arched nose gave him an almost comical resemblance to his late father.

'My lords,' he said, controlling his voice with difficulty, 'Gentlemen of the jury and fellow Rhutenians, citizens of Rodez, each one of you will understand my deep and natural emotion : nothing but the call of honour gives me the strength to address these few words to you. It is true I have the consolation that justice will be done here, but on the other hand I still have to endure the frightful presence of my father's murderers. Ever since the disaster I have prayed Heaven to give me courage to support my great misfortune, and to see that innocence is rewarded and crime punished. . . .' He went on to explain that the 120,000 francs he was claiming would be devoted entirely to paying off his father's creditors : he would have presented a signed statement to that effect had he not been certain that for them the word of an honest man would be sufficient.

The intervention of Didier's civil cause was allowed by the court – to the great approval of the audience : he seemed to embody the pity and resentment all felt for the martyrdom of his father. Rodat listened with a heavy heart, knowing that before the proceedings were over Clarissa would have to undergo the ordeal of being questioned before the judges, and that he would have to report everything she had said to him. At the same time he became aware that his life now had a definite purpose – to support her and encourage her to tell the truth in spite of her fears and of the influences that were being brought to bear on her.

Didier's speech was followed by the President's address to the jury : he explained that in the old days the preliminary examination of the accused had been all important; criminals were only brought before the judges to hear their sentences; but through the work of philosophers and friends of humanity, trial by jury had been established throughout the land in the reign of Louis XVI, and the system of special interrogation, which implied the use of torture, had been abolished. In another of his beneficial acts, Louis XVI had also forbidden the degrading of prisoners by stripping them of the clothing they were accustomed to wear in their everyday lives, and he had introduced other important reforms. Trial by jury had survived the storms of the Revolution and the frequent attacks by extremist groups in that unhappy time, and it had now become part of their common heritage. Experience had shown that it served the great end of preserving innocence and punishing crime. Then, during the Revolution, class privilege had been abolished : all men were now equal in the eyes of the law.

'The firmness and impartiality of juries has long been proverbial : I expect the same from you in a case of such importance. I expect you to show the rest of your compatriots, justly incensed, that the people of the district of Aveyron, the good Rhutenians, still know how to reconcile the cause of justice with the voice of conscience. The complete confidence of his Majesty and of society rests in you for the punishment of a crime such has never before sullied the records of a court of justice.'

The Clerk of the Court then read the Bill of Indictment which presented in great detail the facts which it was alleged had so far come to light. It described how Monsieur Fualdès had been seized at the corner of the rue des Hebdomadiers, gagged, and dragged into the Maison Bancal : and it repeated all the horrors that had become known through the Bancal children, and the gruesome details of the murder that had been committed while two men, who had not been traced, played hurdy-gurdies in the street outside so that the cries of the victim should not be heard :

'Meanwhile in Rose Féral's tavern nearby in the rue de Touat, a young soldier, Colard, was drinking with Bax, Bousquier and Missonier : these were the men who later carried the body to the river, led by a tall man carrying a double-barrelled shotgun who threatened to kill anyone who reported what he had seen. On the following morning at 6 a.m. the body was found floating near the Mill of Bress. At 8 a.m. at the home of the victim his desk was forced open and the following articles were abstracted : a bag of money, his journal, commercial records, a leather briefcase and several documents concerning the sale of his domain of Flars which had been delivered to him on the previous day by the purchaser, Monsieur de Seguret. On the same morning Bastide called and asked if Monsieur Fualdès was in – at a time when the whole town was echoing to the news of his murder. He proceeded to ransack the papers in the private office. While he was officiously helping one of the servants to fold a sheet, a small key was found under it which must have fallen from his pocket : it was the key to the victim's desk.

'The Maison Bancal was the scene of this frightful crime. The cane that Monsieur Fualdès had been carrying was found only a short distance from it, and the handkerchief that had served as a gag was lying in the same street. Bloodstained linen was found in the house.

'Monsieur Bancal, the father, at the time of his arrest, was wearing a bloodstained jacket. He died in prison on 16th May last, forestalling the justice of men. With his death his crime is extinguished, but the accusation still stands against his wife and his eldest daughter, Marianne : both were witnesses to the crime and also accomplices. The mother received the money in Monsieur Fualdès' pockets – three pieces of five francs, three of fifty centimes and eleven of five centimes. She wanted to take his shirt also, but the principal authors of the crime refused her.

'Marianne Bancal while in prison lamented her misfortune in happening to be at home at the time the crime was committed : her mother replied that she shouldn't have come as she had been warned what was going to happen.

'Scarcely had the murder become known than the popular voice singled out Bastide as the principal author of the crime. He owed ten thousand francs to the unhappy Fualdès who had asked him for it, and he had replied, "I shall take steps to settle the account this evening." Three hours later Fualdès was dead, lured into a trap by Bastide on the pretence of negotiating important business. Bastide was an *habitué* of the Maison Bancal : he was seen there at the moment the body was taken from it to be deposited in the river; he led the way, armed with a shotgun. When Monsieur Bancal was told in prison that Bastide had been arrested, he said, "He is one of those who killed Monsieur Fualdès."

'Bax was one of the principal authors of the crime. On the day of the murder he engaged Bousquier to carry a bale of contraband tobacco.

He left him drinking with Colard and Missonier in Rose Féral's tavern : he came back and said the bale was not yet ready. At ten p.m. he conducted him to the Maison Bancal where instead of a bale of tobacco Bousquier saw a body lying on the table. He was one of the four who carried it to the river. Before the murder he was penniless : after it he had a pocket full of *écus*. He gave Bousquier five francs.

'Colard lived in the Maison Bancal. He had three guns in his room which are now in the possession of the police. On the night of the murder he was seen in the Bancal's kitchen. He was seen later in the tavern. At ten p.m. he helped to carry the body. On the day following the crime he said, "There will be many others." Two months before this he had boasted he would shoot any man for twenty-five louis with as little thought as drinking a glass of wine. He said wealth was badly distributed, and if everybody was like him they would take it as they pleased.

'Missonier drank with the others. He made a false statement to police that he had gone home at seven and had not gone out again that evening. He was seen in the Bancal's kitchen at ten p.m. He accompanied the body to the river.

'Anne Benoît cohabited with Colard. She was in the house when the murder was committed. When interrogated she admitted that the fatal piece of cloth found in the street, with which Monsieur Fualdès had evidently been gagged, belonged to her : she blushed when it was suggested to her that she had lent it for this purpose to her pretended husband, Colard. She took an active part in the murder because at 10 p.m. she was seen in the Bancals' kitchen. She knew everyone who had taken part in it, for she was heard to say, "They would like to know who committed the murder, wouldn't they ? But they will never find out." And she also said, "If the innocent are to pay for the guilty I will willingly discharge the contents of my stomach."

'Bousquier was drinking, on the evening of 19th March, in Rose Féral's tavern with Bax and others of the accused : he helped to carry the body to the river. A piece of bloodstained canvas was found in his possession, and also a pair of shoes that appeared to be stained with blood : he seems to have been deceived by Bax into thinking he was to carry a bale of tobacco and not a body.

'Jausion was seen in the Bancal kitchen on the evening of the murder. He accompanied the body to the river. On the following morning at eight o'clock he went to the Fualdès home accompanied by his wife and his sister-in-law, Madame Galtier. With the aid of a small hatchet they broke open a drawer in the library, and wall-cupboards in the study, extracting money, letters of credit and other important documents, warning the servants, who were observing them, to say nothing about it.

'In consequence, all the above named are accused of being guilty of the murder of Monsieur Fualdès, with premeditation, on the evening of 19th March, of throwing his body into the river, and of robbery with illegal entry into the Fualdès home, either as authors or as accomplices.'

The Clerk of the Court seemed quite unmoved by the terrible indictment he had been reading, and all eyes were fixed on the men and women on the benches of the accused. There was silence for a few moments when he had finished: then the prosecutor rose to address the jury. He first drew attention to the imposing and unusual procedure that had been ordered by the Chancellor and which showed the lively interest the government took in the case, and its desire that this great crime should be followed by a great example of justice. He then proceeded to analyse the indictment, grouping and re-grouping the facts and underlining the most significant of them : and he invited the court to contemplate with wonder the workings of Divine Providence that struck the wicked with blindness : having carefully planned and committed the crime, all their ingenuity abandoned them when it was a question of covering up their traces. This frequently happens, he said, and it leads infallibly to the discovery of the criminals : they neglect the most simple precautions : they betray themselves. Finally he went to great pains to disprove the idea, so often disastrous to the exercise of justice and to the vindication of public morality, that it was necessary for the jury to have legal proofs of the guilt of the accused before bringing in a verdict of guilty, or indeed any specific proofs :

'The jury,' he assured them, 'is accountable to society for the impression it receives, for the actual sensations it experiences, when listening to the witnesses and to the speeches of the prosecution and the defence. The legality of the proof rests on the good faith, on the religious impartiality of the investigation. Therefore silence all prejudice. Seek the truth with the candour that love of virtue gives, and it will become self-evident.'

That ended the proceedings for the first day, and the court rose. Both the public and the jury had been deeply affected by the horrors that had been described to them, and by the authority of those describing them. There seemed to be nothing that the counsels for the defence could possibly say in extenuation of so terrible a crime.

On the following day, 19th August, the witnesses came in and were seated by the ushers in a reserved section of the public stands. They were talking eagerly – it looked as if all the people in the market place on a busy day, both buyers and sellers, had unexpectedly been herded into the court of law. Suddenly came the call for silence, and the judges entered. There were 240 witnesses for the prosecution and 70 for the defence : the oath was administered to them all together, then lists of their names were distributed to the lawyers on both sides. The President ordered the indictment to be read again for the benefit of the jury – though it was not likely that any of them would have forgotten it. The witnesses were conducted to another room, and the hearing began.

First a doctor and a surgeon were called : they explained how the body had been found and identified – it was clothed in grey trousers, a black waistcoat, a cravat, a blue tailcoat and a quilted overcoat. There was nothing in the pockets except a white handkerchief. They certified that death had been instantaneous, caused by a single deep wound in the throat. The next three or four witnesses related how they had seen the body floating in the river and brought it ashore. A merchant, the seventh witness, testified that on the day of the murder he had cashed securities to the amount of 1,000 francs for Monsieur Fualdès who had taken the money away in a bag. Bastide had carried the bag for him, and he had been overheard to say, in conversation with Monsieur Fualdès, that he would negotiate the sale of some more securities for him at six per cent. Witnesses Numbers eight and nine told how the cane had been found in the rue de Terral, and the handkerchief, twisted along its whole length, in the rue des Hebdomadiers.

The President asked Anne Benoît if she recognised the handkerchief ; she replied she had used it on 19th March to tie up the bundles of laundry she had delivered to various houses in the town. It was the first time any of the accused had spoken : it caused a mild shock in the courtroom. Until then they might have been strangers from beyond the pale, but the young girl's voice was pleasant and unaffected : it bridged the gap between the accused and the public. Her homely statement was much more convincing than the prosecution's suggestion that it had been used to gag Monsieur Fualdès – but of course the evidence upon which the indictment was based had not yet been heard.

The tailor Brast, Number thirteen, who lived near the Maison Bancal, now gave a long, confused, and rambling account of how he had heard shuffling in the street, and the sound of coughs and whistles and of hurdy-gurdies, and of a door closing, but he didn't know what door. He added as an afterthought that several days before the crime he had seen Bastide and Jausion coming out of the Maison Bancal. At once Maître Rodier, counsel for Jausion, jumped up and commented it was very surprising the witness hadn't made this addition to his evidence sooner, considering his written deposition had been full of insignificant details :

whereupon Didier observed it was not at all surprising the witness had hesitated for so long to mention this fact :

'I myself at first rejected with horror the idea that my father had been done to death by the friends who were accustomed to dine with him almost daily. I had to have definite proofs before I could say anything or bring myself to take action. The witness also hesitated to accuse men who were so generally respected. His reactions were the same as my own.'

Maître Romiguière, for Bastide, supported Maître Rodier's objection : he suggested the witness had been suborned to make this addition to his evidence in the interests of the civil case for damages, and that the accused would have been less bitterly attacked if they had been less rich. There were shouts of protest from the crowd. When the President could make himself heard he ruled that the offensive remark was utterly unjustified, particularly as Monsieur Didier Fualdès was unacquainted with the witness. Maître Romiguière therefore withdrew it but, turning to the public benches, he said at a later stage he would produce arguments forceful enough to put an end to their sympathy for Didier Fualdès, and to their prejudice against the accused. Didier replied with great dignity :

'In what I have already said I have left no doubt of the purity of my sentiments. I will content myself with assuring the gentleman who has just spoken that his impudence will never impose upon me, and when the time comes, because he has provoked me, I shall know how to reply to recrimination with recrimination. As for the *interests* of which he accuses me, the word is only applicable to the cupidity of those who wished to injure me : it is those interests that have brought them to where they are now.'

Although Maître Romiguière's attack on Didier was ill-timed and had only served to antagonise the public, he stands out as the most courageous and sympathetic of the barristers : he was a man of about thirty with a round face and earnest intelligent features; one could more easily have imagined him as a musician than as leading counsel for the defence in a murder trial. He always wore glasses, and although he showed no fear of the judges or of the prosecution he was, perhaps, himself too vulnerable and sensitive to represent successfully a man in as desperate a situation as Bastide.

No further witnesses were called for the time being. The President began to question the accused, starting with the widow Bancal : as an object of general execration she should have resembled one of the witches in *Macbeth*, but she was, in fact, rather a handsome peasant type of woman in whom at first glance one would have expected to find the heroic virtues of a Roman matron instead of the vices that had made her a sink of iniquity. The President asked her :

Where were you on 19th March between eight and ten in the evening? —At home.

Were you alone? —I was with my husband and some of my children.

Didn't you receive anyone else that evening? Strangers perhaps? —No, sir.

Did you know the late Monsieur Fualdès? —No, sir.

On 19th of March last, was not the late Monsieur Fualdès dragged into your house, some time after eight in the evening; was not his throat cut on the table, and did you not take a very active part in his assassination? —No. I saw nothing of the kind, and I heard nothing; and I deny that Monsieur Fualdès was assassinated in my house.

Didn't you hear a hurdy-gurdy that played very loud and for a long time in front of your house? —No, sir.

Your two youngest children have been heard many times to say that on the evening of 19th March a man was killed in your kitchen; they have even reported details that prove the sincerity of what they have said. Besides, it is not reasonable to suppose the children would have said things of that kind if there was no truth in them. —I reply those are the stories of children who don't know what they are doing. They would say anything you please for a halfpenny.

I exhort you to tell us the truth you have hidden until now ! Abandon the system of defence that can no longer be sustained. Help the cause of justice ! Cast your eyes on this Christ you have before you; look at this God who sees all, who knows all, who reads in the depths of our souls. Prove to us you have some repentance for your crime, and tell us what happened.

Madame Bancal remained calm and impassive. She kept repeating she was innocent, and that she understood nothing of what he was talking about. The President turned to Bastide, and asked :

Were you not the relation and friend of Monsieur Fualdès? He did a great deal for you, didn't he? —It was I who did a great deal for him.

Where were you on the evening of 19th March? —I left Rodez at nightfall, and I slept at my domain of Gros.

Is it not a fact that you were in the Maison Bancal, rue des

Hebdomadiers, between eight and ten that evening? —I last set foot in that house more than four years ago. It was a shop then. Everyone knows I was at home at Gros.

Were you not at Rodez during the morning of 20th March? Did you not go to the Maison Bancal and also to the home of Monsieur Fualdès? —No. I slept at my domain of Gros : I left there about seven in the morning to set my people to work at Lamorne. I was still there when the sherriff's officer came and required me to go to Rodez and present myself to the magistrate. It was then three or four o'clock in the afternoon.

You affirm, then, that you did not appear at all in Rodez on 20th March in the morning? —Yes, sir.

You are not speaking the truth, Bastide. The evidence given in the preliminary investigation, evidence that will be given in this court, shows that on the morning of that day, 20th March, people saw you coming and going in the said town, and entering the house of the late Monsieur Fualdès. —They are mistaken, sir.

Then you persist in maintaining you did not appear in Rodez on 20th March until you received the summons, and that you are innocent of the crime of which you are accused? —Yes, sir.

Rodat in spite of himself was impressed by Bastide's voice and manner of speaking though he considered it too arrogant under the circumstances. He could well understand the devotion he inspired in his sisters — but on studying him more closely and considering the enormity of his crimes, the first favourable impression left him and he decided there was something hard and deceitful in his handsome features. Though strongly built and deep chested he was certainly not tall, but Rodat was not surprised so many people thought he was : something in his presence commanded respect, something they could not put into words except by saying he was tall.

The President now questioned Jausion for a long time about his business dealings with the late Monsieur Fualdès which were too involved for all but the specialists and which held no interest for the general public. When asked why he went to the Fualdès home on the day after the crime and searched the desk, he replied it was being said Monsieur Fualdès had been assassinated for his money, and he wanted to find out for himself whether anything had been taken. He had done this, he explained, only because he was a friend and a relation. Jausion looked insignificant beside Bastide, but he was pleasant enough and lively and intelligent, the kind of man one would readily trust in any financial business.

Next to him on the bench of the accused was a very different character – Bousquier. Rodat felt at once he was a reliable witness perhaps because everything in his physical appearance was against him : he had an extraordinarily ugly profile; his nose seemed to be in the wrong place and of the wrong size and shape; his expression was humble, almost furtive, and yet he had courageously spoken out against these dangerous assassins who had threatened his life if he dared to divulge what he had seen.

He testified that while he was drinking in Rose Féral's tavern, the smuggler, Bax, had come in and asked him if he would help to carry a heavy bale of tobacco : he agreed, and after some delay was conducted to the kitchen of the Maison Bancal where there was a large package lying on the table wrapped in a blanket and tied with a stout cord : there were two wooden handles on each side to make it easier to carry. Bax now told him it was a body which they had to carry to the river. A tall man he didn't know threatened him and said he wouldn't live long if he told anyone about it. They left the Maison Bancal, the tall man leading, armed with a double-barrelled shotgun. Monsieur Bancal and Colard supported the body in front, and Bax and Bousquier himself behind. A shorter gentleman, armed also, and Missonier walked beside them. He described in detail the route they took and the place where they had thrown the body into the river. Bax told him later, he said, when he brought him the money, that the tall gentleman was Bastide.

The President told him to look at the bench of the accused and see if the tall gentleman was among them. Bousquier looked long and attentatively at Bastide while the audience waited in suspense. Then he replied, 'Yes, sir. I recognise him. When I was confronted with him at the *préfecture* I recognised him also.' The President asked if he was quite sure, did he affirm before God that he positively recognised Bastide as the man he had seen in the Maison Bancal. 'I swear it is the same man,' he said. 'I am not mistaken.'

He then proceeded to identify Jausion, Colard, Bax, Missonier, Madame Bancal and Anne Benoît as having been present immediately after the crime. There was also another woman there, he said, whom he had supposed was Marianne Bancal, but now he saw her he thought it must have been some other woman.

All the accused in turn replied that Bousquier's story was utterly false and they were innocent of the crime. The weak-minded Missonier nodded and smiled whenever he heard his name mentioned, irrespective of what was said about him, and when questioned always replied, 'I agree with what the others have said, in every respect.'

Pierre-Josef Bessières-Veynac was now brought in, the younger brother of Rodat's rival for Clarissa's hand. He was able to produce a perfect alibi: he had been dining with one of the magistrates on the evening of 9th March, far from the scene of the crime. At Police Headquarters Bousquier had identified him as one of the assassins: now confronted with him again, he said he must have been mistaken for it was not the same man. The President accepted that it was a case of mistaken identity and ordered him to be released. He had been held in prison for forty-two days.

Several witnesses were now called to support Bousquier's story. One told of having seen shadowy groups of men under the dark trees of the boulevards who must have been carrying the body to the river; and a whole series of witnesses claimed to have caught glimpses of Bastide in the unlighted streets of Rodez on the night of the murder; that his expression was so frightening they would not have liked to meet him alone on a country road; or else that he looked wild or distracted, or they had overheard someone in a tavern say Bastide was certainly capable of murder. One woman said she was positive she had seen him in the rue des Hebdomadiers because in the pitch-dark street she had suddenly caught sight of his face in the light of the chemist's window. To all of these Bastide patiently replied that they were mistaken because he had not been in Rodez on the night of the murder.

Then a *Professeur* J. Vignes was called. He stated he had met Bastide about two o'clock on 19th March on the boulevard d'Estourmel near the garden of Monsieur de Seguret: 'I was impressed by his distracted air, and I said to my colleague, "That man has the look of a scoundrel." "But," my colleague replied, "he comes from a good family." "No matter," I said, "He has an evil face." Later I was with the same colleague near the window of the jeweller Fontana. . . . Bastide passed us. I was seized with horror and felt impelled to enter the shop. "You wish to buy something?" my colleague enquired. He was far from understanding how troubled I was and that I couldn't control my reactions. . . . When I heard later that Bastide stood accused of murder, I observed to my colleague I hadn't been mistaken.'

Invited by the President to comment, Bastide said, 'I congratulate the Department on employing a *professeur* who is such a good physionomist.'

Maître Arsaud, counsel for Madame Jausion, rose and warned the jury they must beware of statements made by many of the witnesses describing their sensations: they must accept only the simple account of what they had seen or heard. He was reproved by the President, and told not to waste the time of the court with trivial objections. Maître

Arsaud's warning, however, was completely justified, and should have been supported. The hearing continued.

Monsieur Dornes said he had seen Bastide at 7 p.m. on 19th March in the widow Ginestet's auberge. Ursula Pavillon said she saw him and Monsieur Fualdès talking together in the Place de la Cité at 3 o'clock on the day of the murder: as they parted from each other, she heard Bastide say, 'Don't forget to be there at eight o'clock.' When she heard on the following day of his death, it occurred to her he had been assassinated on the way to this rendezvous arranged by Bastide.

This was a much more damaging piece of evidence, but Bastide remained quite unperturbed. He commented. 'The witness is mistaken. I didn't leave Monsieur Fualdès till after five. She must have been thinking of some other day. It's easy to confuse one day with another.'

The next witness had heard Monsieur Fualdès say to Bastide, 'What about my 10,000 francs?' and he had replied, 'Don't worry. I'll settle the account this evening.' It was the evening of the murder.

Bastide said he didn't owe any money, but Monsieur Fualdès had asked him to raise a loan for him: possibly it was this transaction they were discussing at the time.

Witness No 65 said he was in the rue d'Ambergue between nine thirty and ten on the night of 19th March. He was carrying a lantern, and by its light he saw a man who turned towards the wall and covered his face with his hands: he was wearing light-coloured trousers, a round hat and an overcoat. He had the style and appearance of Jausion. On being questioned by Maître Rodier this witness admitted this identification had only occurred to him after Jausion's arrest. Asked to comment, Jausion said by half past nine he was already at home and in bed.

The hearing of these and similar witnesses for the prosecution lasted several days. What they said didn't amount to very much, and certainly didn't justify the terms of the indictment. It was obvious the prosecution had nothing to go on except the stories of the Bancal children and the deposition of Bousquier whose disreputable background and appearance were against him.

Altogether eighteen witnesses came forward and told stories they claimed to have heard from the Bancal children: some of these witnesses were children themselves, and the ingenuous way they repeated the horrific details made a great impression on the public. Madeleine Bancal, who was evidently familiar with the story of Snow White, was reported as having said that after the murder Bastide had found her lying on the bed in the kitchen: she had pretended to be asleep, but overheard all that passed: Bastide, afraid she would talk, had ordered her parents to kill her. This they agreed to do for 400 francs. Next day her mother told her to take her father's dinner to him – he was working in a distant vineyard. When he saw her approaching, he burst into tears, embraced her, and told her to run home. The grave he had prepared for her was used to bury the pig – it had died from drinking Monsieur Fualdès' blood.

One woman, who had been caring for the children after their parents arrest, said when she used a black-handled knife to cut the bread, the youngest child had screamed, and told her it had been used to kill a man with.

At the end of this recital, Maître Romiguière rose and asked that the Bancal children should be brought into court. His request was refused. He then asked that their original statement to the police should be read aloud because there were discrepancies in the stories : for instance, sometimes they said their mother held the lantern while their father held the legs of the victim, and sometimes it was the other way round, and Madeleine had said she didn't know any of the people in the kitchen and then proceeded to identify the accused as having been there. The President ruled that it would be highly immoral to allow the children to appear, or to use their depositions, in a criminal case against their parents.

Maître Romiguière apparently still felt he had to defend his client against prejudice and resentment rather than against any factual evidence, for he rose again, and said :

'I'm told I insulted members of the public when I said earlier, perhaps with some heat, I would overcome the popular prejudice against the accused. I had no such intention. The public is always prejudiced. This cannot be avoided, and I would not think much of the people of Rodez if they weren't. When a crime such as this is committed in the heart of a city, can one prevent the inhabitants from speculating upon who committed it ? These speculations engender suspicion, and when the justices indicate those whom they suspect, does not prejudice inevitably concentrate upon these unhappy people ? So far from being reprehensible, this sort of prejudice is natural and inevitable, born from the very horror of the crime. If I had seen in it only ill will, jealousy, machiavellianism, would I have undertaken to dissipate it ?

'The essential is that the public should not pass from prejudice to judgement without having heard all the evidence and weighed with respect the opinions of those whom the law appoints to give judgement : this wise and measured conduct I dare expect from the well-known generosity of the people of Rodez. The essential is that the jury should not share these prejudices : it must be guided along the path of truth only by its own conscience, and by the worthy magistrate appointed to direct the proceedings. I am confident this appeal will not be in vain : I have been assured of the virtues of these men who hold in their hands the life and honour of my unhappy client.'

CHAPTER SIX

Clarissa tells her Story

Clarissa had been summoned to appear in court on 22nd August. To give her all the moral support possible, and because she was estranged from her father and brother, Rodat called for her that morning to escort her to the Palais de Justice. He was rather surprised to find she was dressed exactly as the Bancal children had described the mysterious woman who had witnessed the murder. She told him she had been requested to do this, either to discomfit the accused or to aid in the identification, it was not clear which. Her appearance was striking. She was wearing a light-blue woollen dress, cut low, with short sleeves, and a black apron: round her crisply-curled brown hair she had a straw bonnet with black ribbons and a black veil hanging from it. Though she was outwardly composed, he still could not make out which way the conflict between loyalty to her friend and loyalty to the laws of her country and to her family had decided itself in her mind. He left her in the witnesses' room and went to his place on the public benches.

When her name was called, there was complete silence, and the most intense interest could be felt in the hall. All eyes followed her to the witness stand. Jausion bowed and smiled to her as she approached.

As soon as she had been sworn in, the President put to her the usual formal questions for identification, and then addressed her as follows :

'Madame Manson, the public are convinced you were thrust into the Maison Bancal accidentally and in spite of yourself. They look upon you as an angel whom Providence has destined to throw light on this horrible mystery. Even if there may have been some slight indiscretion on your part, the declaration you are about to make, the immense service you are about to render society, will efface the memory of it.'

He turned to Madame Bancal and asked her, 'Do you know this woman?'

Clarissa also turned towards her, drew back her veil, and asked, 'Do you know me?'

Madame Bancal answered, 'No.'

He then asked the same question of Bastide and Jausion. Bastide replied that he only knew Madame through having met her on the road. Jausion said, 'I only know her because she has been to my house two or three times to visit my sister-in-law, Madame Pons.'

'Then why,' said Clarissa, 'had you the effrontery to greet me as I entered the courtroom?'

Jausion might have added that he managed her father's business affairs, that her allowance was paid through him, that he had been involved in the negotiations for her marriage – and a great deal else besides. However, he accepted the rebuke and said no more.

The President, imploring her to tell the truth, asked her to state what she knew of the assassination of Monsieur Fualdès. She gave one expressive look at the accused men, covered her eyes with both hands, and fell in a dead faint. The spectators rushed to her assistance, and General Despérières carried her out onto the terrace that surrounded the building. As she was coming to, she shrieked again and again, 'Take away those assassins! I can't bear the sight of them!' It was some time before she could be persuaded to return to the courtroom.

When the interrupted session was resumed, the President said to her in his most gentle voice, 'Come, Madame, try to control your imagination. You have nothing to fear. You are in the sanctuary of justice and in the presence of magistrates who will protect you. Have courage. Make known the truth. What have you to tell us? Were you present at the assassination of Monsieur Fualdès?'

She replied, with an effort at self-control, 'I have never been in the Maison Bancal.' Then, after a moment of silence, 'I believe Bastide and Jausion were.'

'How can you believe such a thing,' the President enquired, 'if you were not present?'

She told him in a low voice she had received letters threatening her with death if she gave any information, and that Madame Pons, sister of Bastide, had come to her one evening to persuade her to retract her original declaration.

'And what did you promise this Madame Pons?'

'Simply that I would retract my accusation of Bastide.'

'Why?'

'Because it was false. I had said I was in the Maison Bancal: it wasn't true. I have never been there except with the Prefect.'

The President sat back in his chair and looked at her thoughtfully: 'You assure us your first declaration was false: therefore you know nothing about Bastide and Jausion. How can you say you regard them as guilty?'

She replied bitterly, 'A man who can kill his children can kill his friend, can kill anybody.' Jausion looked at her resentfully. 'Yes,' she went on, 'I am looking at you, Jausion.'

The President asked how he had killed his children.

'The affair was hushed up,' she said, 'but the public were not deceived.'

She was referring to a story, well-known to many people in Rodez, that Jausion when a young man had had an illegitimate child by the wife of his employer. The husband had come in just after the birth of the child and it had been hidden in a cupboard where it died of suffocation. It was generally believed that Monsieur Fualdès had suppressed the evidence and saved Jausion from being tried for murder. To bring the story up now, founded only on hearsay, could not serve the authorities, for if it was true, Jausion had a motive not to kill Monsieur Fualdès but to keep him alive as his protector.

That was evidently the President's opinion, for he brought Clarissa back to the main point: 'Have you not some other grounds for believing in the guilt of the accused?'

She glanced nervously about her as if contemplating flight, then burst out, 'I have never been in the Maison Bancal! No never! I will maintain that to the foot of the scaffold.'

The President indicated the papers in front of him, and went on inexorably: 'That is not at all what you said to irreproachable witnesses whom we shall call. I mean particularly your cousin Rodat.'

She seemed relieved that he was going to be brought into it, for she said eagerly, 'I confirm in advance anything my cousin Rodat may say. He is incapable of falsehood. It is true I have been to the Prefect several times, that I have made imprudent declarations: they were false, and I have retracted them. I promised Madame Pons. Those declarations were torn from me by my fear of my father. . . .'

The President interrupted her, and told her in moving tones it was in the name of her unhappy father, torn by a thousand sorrows, in the name of justice, in the name of humanity groaning over a horrible crime, a humanity whose closest bonds had been broken by a crime that alarms the whole of society that he implored her to tell them all she knew.

'See,' he said, 'how attentively everyone is waiting. Speak, therefore, in the name of the God whose image you see above my head. Prove to us you have been brought up in the love of justice, that you know how to obey! Remember the honour of your family never sullied by cowardice or perjury.'

During this tirade, the colour had been slowly draining away from Clarissa's cheeks, and now she swayed, held on to the bar of the witness box for a moment, and fell to the ground. This time she recovered before being carried out. As she was regaining consciousness she again found herself being supported by the general: she pointed to his sword, shrieked, 'You have a knife!' and fainted again. The general removed his sword and handed it to an attendant. In a few minutes she recovered and took her place again on the witness stand.

Didier now rose and asked permission to speak. On this being granted, he said, 'It appears that Madame Manson dares not speak because she is terrified by the image of knives, and even more terrified by the presence of the assassins of my father: I beg, therefore, that the President will order a file of eight armed soldiers to be placed between her and the accused so that she will not be able to see them.'

Then, turning to Clarissa he said, 'I beg you, Madame, be reassured, and tell us the truth. It will be in the interests of the accused if they are innocent. With a word you can save them. Speak, Madame, and avenge the blood of my father.'

The President agreed to this request and asked the general to place a file of soldiers between Clarissa and the accused. This was immediately done. The prosecutor rose and told her that now she had nothing to fear, and he himself would be responsible for her personal safety. He ordered a bodyguard of armed men should be provided strong enough to protect her from all dangers wherever she went; it would be posted day and night outside her lodgings. She thanked him, and remarked it should have been provided from the day she was called upon to testify in court.

'I hope you now realise you have nothing to fear,' the President said, 'and that you will tell us what we want to know.'

She plucked up courage and suggested in a trembling voice, 'Ask Monsieur Jausion if he did not save a woman's life in the Maison Bancal.'

The President asked accordingly, and Jausion replied, 'No, sir. Although I have performed many services in my time, I am not aware I have ever saved anyone's life.'

'Oh God!' she cried, 'There was a woman in the Bancal kitchen, Bastide wanted to kill her, Jausion saved her.'

The President turned to the accused and said, 'You were in the Bancal kitchen. Which of you wished to save. . . .'

'Not Bastide! Not Bastide!' she shouted suddenly, interrupting him.

He turned to her and asked, 'Do you know the woman who was saved?'

'I wish to God I knew her,' she answered, and she began her story again as if painfully trying to recall what had happened, while the President, the prosecutor, the jury and the public hung upon her words as if she were a mysterious priestess pronouncing an oracle. They noted every nuance, every hesitation, every inflection of her voice, trying to interpret her words as she stumbled on, speaking with difficulty.

'They say this woman . . . hearing a noise in the street . . . entered the first door that stood open. It happened to be this horrible place, and Madame Bancal met her and said to her, "Quick! Quick! You are lost! Hide yourself. . . !" '

'Where did she hide?' the President asked. 'Was it not in an alcove?'

Tears now were streaming down her cheeks. 'Yes,' she sobbed, 'They say she was hidden in an alcove.'

The President continued trying to encourage her to go on, 'And wasn't this woman taken ill in the alcove?'

'I wasn't that woman!' she moaned, 'I don't know if she felt ill or not! . . . but I know Bastide wished to kill her and Jausion saved her and conducted her to the outskirts of the town.'

Again he prompted her: 'Passing through the Bancals' kitchen, didn't this woman see a body?'

'I repeat I don't know. I wasn't there.'

'How could you know so much if you weren't?'

'Because there was an oath,' she said, and stopped.

'Did they not force this woman to swear a terrible oath? This woman who was saved by Jausion?'

'They say so, yes. A sacred oath upon the body.'

'You see, Bastide,' said the President, 'You were in the Maison Bancal at the moment of the murder. It was evidently you who proposed. . . .'

Bastide firmly interrupted him: 'I have already had the honour to assure you, sir, that in spite of what Madame says, I have never had anything to do with the Maison Bancal. . . .'

Suddenly she stamped her foot and cried, 'Confess, you wretch! Why don't you confess?' A shudder passed through the audience. There was a mournful silence.

At last the President said to her, 'How can you so confidently accuse the prisoners and not admit you were there?'

'How can they deny it?' she retorted. 'So many have testified against them.'

He turned once more to Bastide : 'Is it true you wished to kill a woman in the Bancals' kitchen and that Jausion saved her ?'

'No, sir. I have already said I am innocent, and I hardly knew that woman until I saw her in the witness box.' Then clasping his hands in front of him, which was a trick he had when he wished to be particularly impressive, he added with great composure, 'I have never known what it is to tell a lie.'

The President looked at Clarissa sternly. 'You must answer me truthfully,' he said. 'Why do you shudder when you hear Bastide's voice? Why are you so troubled when we speak of Monsieur Fualdès' body and of knives?'

'Oh God!' she cried, 'Why does not someone help me and speak up for me? I cannot say I was there, but all the same, everything is true.'

The President sighed and picked up his pen. 'You may stand down,' he said.

There was silence as she left the witness stand. Then there was a murmur of excited voices as if the curtain had just gone down on the climax of a dramatic scene in a play.

Next the conceited Monsieur Clémendot was called and took the stand. He described how during a walk with Madame Manson he had discussed with her the question that was occupying all minds – who the mysterious witness to the crime could have been :

'I told her the names of several young women that had been mentioned and discussed, and that hers was among them. She didn't reject this suggestion with as much warmth as I had expected, so I believed it was well founded. I plied her with questions until she admitted she was indeed the one who had been there. It would be difficult for me to describe the emotions that assailed me on hearing her avow this. . . . She then gave me a detailed description of what she had seen and heard . . .' and Clémendot proceeded to give the same account of it that Clarissa had given to Rodat before the trial opened. She had not, he said, divulged the names of the assassins, but when he questioned her about Bastide and Jausion her embarrassment gave him the impression that she knew all the actors in that horrible scene. 'I asked her why she had not revealed this to the authorities : she answered that their families were so well connected that sooner or later she would have to pay dear for her imprudence.'

The President asked Bastide and Jausion what they had to say to the deposition they had just heard. Jausion commented that it seemed to him Monsieur Clémendot had made Madame Manson say more than she had intended, and that he only wished she would tell the truth.

Bastide got up, and with an appealing gesture also begged her to speak the truth. 'Do you fear my family?' he asked her. 'If I were guilty they would cut me off from them.'

Didier then gave a lively exhortation, trying to persuade her to tell all she knew. She replied calmly, 'I have never been in the Maison Bancal, and I shall never say I was. I would rather be led to the scaffold. I am a woman of honour. I tell this court the truth.' And then she added, 'I never said anything to Monsieur Clémendot. I swear it.'

Clémendot grew very red, puffed out his cheeks, but made no comment. Bastide said, 'What do you fear, Madame? My family will undertake. . . .'

'I'll have no undertaking with you, Bastide!' she snapped.

The President then called her old nurse, Victoire Redoulez. Rodat remembered her well from their childhood. She had once taken him with her to see *l'homme des morts*, the man who claimed to speak with the dead. Her daughter's lover had been killed by a wolf, the girl was ailing and the old nurse wished to find out what the dead wanted of her. *L'homme des morts*, a sinister old man living in a hut behind a ruined chapel, accepted her offering – a chicken and a few silver coins – and told her the lover could not escape from Purgatory and go to Heaven until the girl joined him. Three days later she was dead.

Like most peasant women she was all in black. She evidently disliked Clémendot for she kept shaking her fist at him – no doubt she considered herself part of the affronted Enjalran family. She spoke in almost incomprehensible argot. This is a translation, more or less, of what she said:

'Hearing a rumour of what had passed between Madame Manson and Monsieur Clémendot, I went at once to her and asked if what I had heard was true. She confessed she had in fact been in the Maison Bancal, but she had felt ill in the alcove and had heard and seen nothing. She told me she had come and knocked on my door later that night, but as I hadn't answered she had spent part of the night in the ruined convent of the Annonciade. She also told me she had had several interviews with Madame Pons who had begged her not to talk.'

That was all that could be got out of her. Next it was Rodat's turn. He told the President as much as he could recall of his various conversations with Clarissa, which was roughly as follows:

'Madame Manson has been on a number of occasions at my house near Olemps. We frequently discussed the crime with our friends, and the proceedings to which it gave rise. It seemed to me she was the one who usually led the conversation round to this subject. We argued a hundred

times about the facts of the case as they had been represented by public
opinion : to the best of my recollection she never said a word from which
one might deduce that the accused were innocent; nor did she positively
say she was certain of their guilt.

'One day she asked me, "If you knew all the truth about the assassins,
what would you do?" "What a question!" I exclaimed. "I should
immediately inform the authorities, of course." "But if one of the criminals
had saved your life? Could you send him to the guillotine?" '

Here Rodat hesitated. . . 'I'm sure it isn't necessary to state what I
ventured to reply.'

The President encouraged him, saying, 'Go on, sir, so that Madame
may hear again what you have already told her. Let us have your reply.
It will benefit the public also. And as for you, Madame Manson, how can
you fail to follow the counsel of your cousin? You who have so much
esteem for him and see how greatly he is respected by the court and by
the public.'

'Your question, I told her,' Rodat continued, 'is a delicate one. . . . If
I put myself in your place, if I identify myself with you, I realise your
sex has more delicacy than ours; that it is more devoted to doing good
in the world, and it has less force to suppress the voice of sentiment at
the command of the law. In this dilemma between perjury and the painful sacrifice of a sentiment that has its roots in a generous heart, I should
say to the court : One of these men saved my life. I do not feel obliged to
reveal his name : let the court decide whether I am to speak or not.'

As these sentiments were received with evident approval both by the
President and the public, he continued :

'Sometime after this conversation, it was in the first week in July,
we met again. A friend, whom I believed to be well informed, had just
given me details of Bousquier's confession, and we were wondering how
much reliance could be placed upon it. Someone had suggested Bousquier
might very well be considered as an accomplice of the assassins, and I
was maintaining that the word of an accused man might be accepted so
long as the contrary is not established, when Clarissa plucked my sleeve
and assured me his deposition was true. This worried me at the time, and
I was not altogether surprised when I learned she had confessed to the
Prefect she had in fact been a witness.'

Pressed for further details, he then gave the whole story of Clarissa's
harrowing experiences in the Maison Bancal as she had described them
to him. The President asked her whether this was a true account of what
she had told her cousin : she agreed it was, except she could not recall
having named Jausion as one of the assassins. After a few moments

reflection she added, 'But I must have, if Monsieur Rodat affirms I did.'

Finally the President asked him to give his personal opinion : was she in the Maison Bancal or not?

'I must confess,' he replied, 'at one time I doubted it; but now, like everyone else including her own family, I am convinced she saw all that happened, and that only fear of Bastide's family and the ascendancy of Madame Pons prevent her from speaking.' That was the end of his testimony.

Clarissa's ordeal was not yet over. After a short recess the President announced he had invited Moniseur le Marquis d'Estourmel, Prefect of Aveyron, to attend a hearing. Two ushers were sent to conduct him to an armchair that had been placed for him in front of the judges' bench. The Prefect, after expressing his confidence in the high principles of the jury and the integrity of the judges stated that Madame Manson had been to see him frequently and had also written him a number of letters. He had drawn up a report of everything that had passed between them, and he suggested it should be read aloud together with the most important of her letters. The advocate-general was consulted, and the prosecutor, the judges, the counsel for Didier and for the accused : all agreed. The documents were handed to the Clerk of the Court who read them aloud.

The report described all Clarissa's interviews with the Prefect : it gave the impression he had taken a tolerant and fatherly interest in her, and had been extremely patient. The letters that followed illustrated very well the confusion and conflict of her thoughts : members of the public watched her face intently as if trying to decide which of the contradictory sentiments she had so eloquently expressed represented the truth of the matter. The net result was to shroud the whole affair in even deeper mystery and to increase the interest and speculation about her.

During the reading, Clarissa felt faint and had to be helped out of the courtroom : it was noted that the passage being read at the time was from one of her letters reporting the threats of the assassins to dispose of her by knife or poison. She soon recovered, and the President asked her if she agreed the contents of the report and the letters were true and exact. She replied that Monsieur le Préfet was incapable of reporting anything that wasn't true; whereupon he withdrew. The President began to question Clarrisa again :

Who was the woman in the Maison Bancal? —I declare I was not that woman. Someone must have been using my name. . . . I did tell

Monsieur Clémendot that I was, but it was a joke. I hadn't a chance to explain. He had spread it around everywhere. He abused my confidence.

Then how is it that all you said to him accords perfectly with what you said to Monsieur Rodat? –I was only telling them both what I had heard from others.

Why did you say to Bastide, 'Confess you wretch! Why don't you confess?' –(After a long pause) Why don't you ask him and Jausion if they knew I would be called as a witness?

JAUSION : I only knew when I was given a list of the witnesses.

Why do you ask that question? Isn't it because you know everything? –I received an anonymous letter which I believed to be from Madame Pons.

Why is it, if you are not the woman, they send you anonymous letters? Well? . . . Why are you silent? –What can I say when you use my own words against me to prove I was there when I wasn't?

What oath were you forced to swear? –All I said before was a fable. Now I speak the truth.

Didier Fualdès now questioned her :

Did you sleep at home on 19th March? –Yes, I did.
At what time did you get home? –I didn't go out at all.
You told Victoire Redoulez you spent part of the night in the ruins of the Annonciade? –No, I didn't. I mean, it wasn't true.

Didier then brought on three witnesses who testified that Clarissa had told them if she spoke the truth Jausion would be lost. She countered them all by saying she had been misunderstood, that she might have said, 'If they are guilty they'll all perish,' or 'I'll never support assassins,' or something like that. 'You try to force me to make a terrible admission but I don't know whether Jausion is guilty or not, and I shall never say so.' When the witnesses insisted they were right and reaffirmed their statements, she burst out, 'It's incredible! Everyone insists I witnessed the crime, but I didn't! It's unbelievable!' and she maintained this attitude until the court rose.

As the prisoners were being led back to the cells, Jausion was heard to say : 'That woman has killed me.'

Clarissa Manson, a portrait by Sudre, a pupil of David,
drawn while she was in prison at Albi.

Monsieur Fualdès: the victim.

Madame Bancal, drawn by Sudre.

Monsieur Clémendot.

Didier Fualdès, son of the murdered
man.

Rose Pierret.

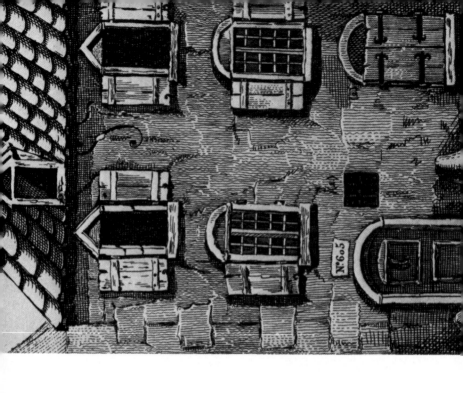

(*Above*) The Bancal children at the Hospice.

(*Right*) The Maison Bancal.

CHAPTER SEVEN

A Cloud of Witnesses

During the opening sessions of the trial Madame Pons continued to pass the nights with her friend. The rendezvous was the stone where Clarissa and Rodat had sat in the moonlight and talked without fear of being overheard, and where she had relieved her overburdened mind and heart by telling him of her terrible experiences in the Maison Bancal: they called the stone *Hay*, for that was what they always shouted when they caught sight of it. On the night following Clarissa's first appearance in the witness-box, Madame Pons joined them there. Rodat says:

> I was allowed to take part in these nocturnal discussions at which they expressed the most exalted sentiments which are the heroism and happiness of women. It was from her friend that Clarissa drew the strength to oppose all the attempts of her family to influence her, and to resist the powerful demands of justice. She upbraided Clarissa for the way she had spoken in the court, jeopardising the lives of Bastide and Jausion. 'Don't blame me,' Clarissa wailed, 'pity me! There is some power that compels me to do it, as if someone stood behind me and prompted me.' And again they wept together. And again they found money to have prayers said for them, so that Clarissa's words would be favourable to the accused; and they went to her confessor, the Abbé Brast, who urged her to tell the truth at any cost.

The influence of Madame Pons grew stronger from day to day, and at last she wrote and requested to be heard again. She was told to present herself at the Palais de Justice at 10 a.m. on 8th September.

The Bill of Indictment had been based upon the written statements of witnesses for the prosecution, but according to the law they had to repeat them verbally before the jury. As they were allowed to ramble on without interruption, this took nearly a fortnight; and as they were heard in no sort of order it was difficult sometimes to understand what it was all leading up to. Throughout this long procedure Bastide maintained an oddly detached attitude as if he were a spectator and only mildly interested in what was going on, but when he was directly addressed he answered swiftly and to the point. Even on the bench of the accused he was an imposing figure, and it was not surprising that some of his accusers, humble people, quailed and stammered in the face of his brazen denials that he had been in Rodez at the time of the crime.

When all the witnesses had been heard they were re-grouped and a special hearing was devoted to each of the accused in turn. In every case Bousquier was the principal accuser. He re-affirmed his previous testimony. The other witnesses not only re-affirmed what they had already said, they frequently improved upon it.

First there was some interesting information about Bastide's past life : Marianne Marty who had been a servant at Lamorne recalled that his aunt had once told her he had threatened his own father, and threatened a tenant also who had come to collect what was his due, and also a cowherd. Asked if Bastide had ever threatened or ill-treated her, she said no, but she had heard he had killed a man at Prades.

F. Guitard, dealer, said that about ten years ago, travelling with Bastide, they met a man to whom he gave two blows with his stick : asked why he did that, Bastide said, 'If only he had 25,000 francs !' Three years ago there was a similar incident : while they were riding together they again met a man whom Bastide struck with his stick. Asked why he ill-treated the man, Bastide replied, 'If only he had 25,000 francs !' 'I was afraid,' Guitard concluded, 'and didn't go to collect the corn I had bought from him.' It was a pointless story, but it gave an impression of how this domineering man lorded it over the country people.

Bastide's comment was, 'When a man is on the bench of the accused any fable is good enough. I leave it to the court to appreciate the value of that one.' The witness persisted and began his story all over again.

Pierre Casal, mason, had heard Monsieur Fualdès say to Bastide in a severe tone on the day of the murder, 'You didn't come after dinner as you promised.' Bastide had replied, 'I have no intention of doing you an injustice. Don't worry, I'll settle your account this evening.' This witness complained that Madame Bastide had offered his wife a sack of corn if he would withdraw his evidence, and she had replied, 'My husband is incorruptible.'

Bastide : 'It is possible Monsieur Fualdès reproached me for not coming to attend to his business. I could have replied, "You do me wrong," or "you misjudge me." My words have been twisted to suit the occasion because I am in trouble.'

Chalies, groom at the Hotel des Princes, taking the horses to the water-trough on the evening of 19th March saw three men in the rue du Terral, one of them tall.

A. Boudon said that two years ago he met Bastide's father who told him Bastide once threatened him with a pistol and demanded 1,800 francs; and on another occasion had threatened to kill him if he refused to give him money. His father had called him a bad type, capable of bringing dishonour upon the family.

Bastide: They have collected the greatest scoundrels in the district to invent all sorts of horrors about me. In fact my father loves me dearly and frequently gives me presents, and to my wife.

Françoise Lagarrigue, the widow Solonat, deposed: 'On 19th March towards ten o'clock in the evening, I left my house with Monsieur Dubocq: we went along the boulevard d'Estourmel. Opposite the cul de sac at the Bourguet's garden we heard a sound. We looked but saw nothing. In the Place d'Armes we saw a tall gentleman wearing boots, dressed in blue or green with a white waistcoat: Monsieur Dubocq shone his lantern on this man and saw he had a stick or a gun under his left arm: he looked at us with a threatening air and muttered some words we didn't catch. I thought I recognised Bastide as much by his height as by his dress. I saw him again at Mass on the following Sunday and believed that I had not been mistaken.'

Bastide denied he had been in the Place d'Armes at that time. The witness insisted she had seen him there. Bousquier was called: he said Bastide had in fact carried a gun under his left arm. Monsieur Dubocq told the same story, and added the widow Solonat had confided to him on the following day, or the day after, that she suspected the man they had seen was Bastide.

La femme Raymond said one of Bastide's servants told her he was not at Gros on the night of the crime. She was confronted by the servant in question who denied having said anything of the kind.

Bastide had remarkably beautiful eyes: he must have been well aware of this fact for he looked each witness straight in the face: some were disconcerted and hesitated or lost track of what they were saying, but most faced up to him boldly. Monsieur René de Lagoudie said that at eight o'clock or half past, Monsieur Fualdès had passed him near the Hotel des Princes: at that moment an individual or, rather, a shadow, he could not say man or woman on account of the darkness, hurried down the rue d'Ambergue.

Antoine Rozier deposed: 'On the night of 19th March about eight o'clock, I saw Monsieur Fualdès pass in front of the Hotel des Princes.

Two persons who had been waiting in the Place de la Cité followed him. Soon afterwards I heard a great deal of noise in the rue des Hebdomadiers.'

Jean Laville, beggar, testified there was a hurdy-gurdy playing in the rue des Hebdomadiers on the evening of 19th March. He heard a struggle in the street and someone banged twice on the outside of the stable door behind which he was sleeping. He heard someone being dragged along to the Maison Bancal : he heard two or three cries of which the last sounded stifled as if a man was choking. About an hour and a half later, or two hours, he heard two men pass, and then about four more walking heavily as if carrying a load. Two others followed. He added he had mentioned this on the following day to Missonier with whom he shared the stable, and he had said he also heard something.

The earlier questioning had brought to light one of Bastide's secret intrigues, or one he seems to have thought was secret but which everybody knew about, – a liaison with a young woman, Charlotte Arlabosse : she had been a servant at Gros, but he had set her up as a dressmaker at La Rochette, a village which lay between his two domains of Gros and Lamorne. As part of his alibi he had stated that on the morning of 20th March he had spoken to her on his way from Gros to Lamorne, and therefore could not have been at Rodez. When she was questioned by a man who, it transpired later, was a police agent, she had denied this, not wishing it to be known they had been together and unaware of his need for an alibi.

She now testified she had been looking out of her window at La Roquette at 6.30 on the morning of the 20th when Bastide had passed and called her to come down. They had breakfasted together in a field. She was small, fair, intelligent, with a disarming smile, obviously in love with Bastide and therefore probably prepared to say anything to help him. Although she had come up in the world, she was dressed simply as a young peasant girl with additional touches of colour and fantasy so that spring seemed to be all about her : Rodat described her as an interesting little person, and he could not but regret she had fallen into the hands of Bastide.

A. Aldebert, gardener, said he had frequently seen them together at all hours in Monsieur Fualdès' garden which was next his own : he thought she lodged in the Maison Bancal.

Marianne Bonnes deposed that some three weeks before the murder, Bastide had invited her to go with him, Charlotte and Monsieur Fualdès to the latter's garden : when she learned the meeting was to be by moonlight, she had declined. One might deduce from this that Monsieur

Fualdès had not always been the pattern of virtue he was made out to be.

Charlotte admitted she had frequently met Bastide in the garden at night, but that she didn't lodge in the Maison Bancal and had never been there. Bousquier, asked to identify her as one of those present at the murder said he didn't recognise her.

Monsieur Bruyère, who had once been an assistant-usher at the court, said that Madame Marcan de Malarme had told him a servant of Bastide's had assured her his master did not get home on the evening of 19th March until 11.30 p.m. and that he had told the servant not to unsaddle his mare as he had to leave again at three in the morning. When the servant came at three in the morning to feed the mare he found her in a lather. 'The poor animal,' he said, 'Drak* must have been riding her all night!'

This was the sort of ingenuous comment Rodat felt might lead to the solving of the mystery – supposing Bastide had in fact returned home and then ridden furiously back to Rodez to assassinate Monsieur Fualdès, and straight home again?

'What effrontery!' Bastide commented to Monsieur Bruyère's evidence, 'They presume to take upon themselves the functions of the prosecutor. Let them bring on the witness who saw me enter at 11.30 p.m. No one can be more anxious than I am to have this matter cleared up.'

Madame Giron said that some days after the event of 19th March, Bastide's servant, who had been instructed to take the grey mare to a Madame Regnes who wished to borrow her, said, 'If the poor beast could talk she would say she had worked hard enough on 19th March, and at night: she was made to go from Rodez to Gros, and from Gros to Rodez.'

'Whatever next! Bastide commented, 'Why don't you bring on the horse as a witness?' When the laugh had subsided, he added, 'I wish she could talk. She at least wouldn't betray me.'

Now came Bastide's witnesses. First Le Sieur Rudelle, Curé of Prades. He gave a favourable account of Bastide who at one time had lived in his parish. He said the report circulated soon after his arrest that he had killed a man there was entirely false: no one had been killed in the parish, and had there been, the fact would certainly have come to his notice.

The next witness was Madame Vernhes, sister of Jausion. Maître

* Drak – the local poltergeist.

Merlin objected to her being heard, on the grounds that she was related to the accused to a degree prohibited by article 322 of the *Code d'Instruction*. He raised the objection solely, he said, because it would be unfair to put her into conflict with her conscience, for she must either tell the truth and compromise Bastide, or speak for him and compromise the truth – which was reasonable enough if it was assumed Bastide was guilty, but this had yet to be proved. Maître Romiguière suggested she should be heard through the discretionary power of the President. Didier said he would consent to this because he wished to leave the accused complete freedom for their defence. Madame Vernhes, therefore, took the oath and spoke as follows :

'I was at Gros on the evening of 19th March when Bastide arrived there between seven and eight o'clock. He took off his coat, put on his bedroom-slippers and nightcap, supped and retired to bed at the usual hour. I heard him put out the candle and then talk for a long time with his wife.'

The President asked incredulously again and again if she really meant it, and if she was quite sure she was telling the truth. She insisted she was.

A priest, Le Sieur Foulquier, who said he had known Bastide for many years, since they were students together, also spoke in his favour; and all the servants and farm labourers affirmed he had been at Gros on the evening of the 19th and at Lamorne on the morning of the 20th.

The President then used his discretionary power to call several other witnesses against him. One of these, Jean-Antoine Cabrolier, saddler in the Place de la Cité, declared he had heard the door of Monsieur Fualdès' house close at about eight in the morning of 20th March, and then he had seen Monsieur Bastide pass. He knew it was Monsieur Bastide because he raised his left hand to his head and at the same time beat his hat with his right hand : he had commented to his friends, 'Monsieur Bastide is upset.' This was confirmed by Jean-Louis Lacombe, bootmaker.

Bastide commented, 'The witnesses are mistaken. I have already proved I was at La Morne at that time.'

Le Sieur Jean-Josef Dornes said he had seen Bastide in Rodez on his grey mare at seven in the evening of 19th March.

'You are quite sure,' asked the President, 'it was on the 19th and not some other day ?'

He replied he had not seen his face, but he knew him by the colour of his horse and by the way his long legs beat against its flanks. Maître Romiguière remarked it was very strange he had not thought of this before or mentioned it in his previous deposition.

Interest was now focused on the widow Bancal : the depositions concerning her were heard again. Françoise Calmals, another prisoner who had been placed in the same cell to report on her, claimed she had told her the whole story of the assassination in her kitchen — that Monsieur Fualdès had been gagged with a handkerchief, bled with a blunt knife; that she had taken a ring from his finger but had been forced to give it up, receiving six francs in exchange for it. She had also confided that if she was asked what had happened in her house, she would answer the judges they ought to know because they were there themselves.

Madame Bancal emphatically denied having said any of these things. Another witness, Marianne Febry, deposed that on 20th March she had visited Madame Bancal and found her looking sad. 'Perhaps I was sad,' Madame Bancal commented, 'because I had just heard of the death of Monsieur Fualdès.

Then Marianne Bancal was called. Her counsel, Maître Batut, a young barrister appearing for the first time at the assizes, got up and announced she was seriously ill and could not answer questions. She was carried into the courtroom on a stretcher. When asked if she agreed that the hearing should continue in her absence, she whispered 'Yes,' and was carried out again. The prosecutor, the other counsels and Didier also gave consent, and the first witness against her was called.

This was Catherine Coudère, another prisoner employed as a spy : she had been placed in the same cell as Madame Bancal and her daughter on the second night after their arrest. She said she had heard Marianne Bancal, who worked at the Hotel Glausy and usually slept there, crying and lamenting that she had gone home that evening to get some water; and her mother had replied, 'Keep your mouth shut. We'll be overheard.' When the food came, Catherine Coudère had said to her, 'If there's any left over you'd better send it to your husband.' 'He doesn't need it,' Marianne retorted. 'He's got 400 francs to spend.' 'Quiet !' her mother said. 'That's not true.'

Yet another prisoner, Marthe, illegitimate, had heard it said that Marianne Bancal lamented to her mother, 'How unfortunate I came to the house : if it becomes known, we are lost !' To which her mother had replied, 'Don't shout ! They'll hear us.'

Marianne Bon deposed that the Maison Bancal was regarded as an infamous place. In the whole quarter it was thought that only there could the murder have taken place. She had gone there on 20th March: all were mournful. She had met Marianne Bancal in the street : she looked distracted.

The widow Bancal continued to deny everything. She listened impassively to the numerous witnesses who repeated again the lurid and incriminating stories they had collected from her children, only breaking her silence to ask occasionally how much they had been paid, and commenting they would say anything you like for two sous, and would hang their father and mother for two francs. One could almost feel the shudder of horror that passed through the audience whenever she spoke : it was as if they felt they were in the presence of something evil.

The case against the handsome and arrogant Colard was considered next : it depended, like the others, almost entirely on Bousquier's denunciation, but numerous witnesses testified to his vicious character. Sometimes he did an odd job, cutting wood or working in the fields, but usually he sat in the taverns and frightened the locals by telling them what he would do to *les riches* if he got the chance, and boasting of the shotguns and the sabre he kept in his room : the prosecution claimed his shotguns had armed the assassins who accompanied the funeral cortège to the river. The witnesses who had previously testified against him were successively recalled, and all of them re-affirmed their previous depositions :

Amans Loubière, blacksmith, said that at 6.30 on the morning after the crime, Colard came into his smithy to light his pipe : he told him a body had been found : his comment was, 'I've seen nothing, and heard nothing : I was drinking with Missonier at Rose Féral's, and I went home at nine.'

Colard said he remembered nothing of this.

A juryman held up one finger like a boy at school who wants to ask a question. There was an uncomfortable pause. A juryman had the right to ask questions, but if in doing so he showed the least prejudice for or against the accused, the proceedings might have to be anulled and the trial begun again with a new jury.

Putting the best possible face upon it, the President told him to ask his question. He stood up and said, 'I find the accused's remark very singular. It seems to me only a person who knew about the assassination would have made it,' and he sat down again.

The court relaxed, the judges and the prosecutor smiled at him patronisingly, and the blacksmith continued his evidence : it was to the effect that Colard had recently repaired a shotgun in the smithy. Colard denied this.

The gardener Jolicoeur also said Colard had spoken to him about the assassination before it was generally known : he had said to Colard he regretted the death of Monsieur Fualdès, he was a good man : he had replied, 'Not particulary good, but his wife is.' And he had added, after a pause, 'There will be others. . . .'

Colard denied he knew anything about the murder, and protested he would have given his life to save Monsieur Fualdès.

The President, by virtue of his discretionary power, called Antoine Rouvellat, police spy, who had been placed in the same cell as Colard after his arrest: he reported various outrageous threats the latter had made against the magistrates and which revealed the audacity and ferocity of his nature; he had also shown a most hostile spirit towards the concierge of the prison and towards Bousquier: of the one he had said he would shoot him like a hare, and of the other one he had said he would tear out his entrails. When Rouvellat questioned him about Bousquier's revelations, he had replied, 'Anyway, if he did see me, I was not the only one he recognised.'

The concierge was called: he stated that when he separated them again he heard Colard warn Rouvellat not to repeat anything. Another prisoner, Brugière, known as Pistolet, had next been put in the cell, and he reported Colard had spoken to him in exactly the same way.

Next it was Anne Benoît's turn. Her story, on the surface, was quite plausible: she described how she supported her soldier, Colard, by working all day as a laundrymaid – she was a foundling, a *fille de l'hospice*. On the evening of 19th March, although she lived in a back room of the Maison Bancal, she had not seen or heard anything unusual. She had been busy delivering laundry to her customers. Even if there had been a disturbance, she said, Colard would not have gone down: he was not on good terms with Monsieur Bancal. She had a seductive voice and an engaging manner; she seemed more anxious to protect her lover than to clear herself.

The witnesses for the prosecution seemed in her case to be particularly vindictive: one woman, Anne Solignac, abused her for living openly with Colard, 'like the beasts of the field without the sanction of the church. Marianne Salvanhac stated: 'I asked Anne Benoît whose handkerchief it was that had been found. She replied, "It's mine." 'Then you lent it them to strangle Monsieur Fualdès with?' Anne Benoît blushed a good deal, and then said, "They'll never know who killed him." The witness added she had heard Bastide went often to the Maison Bancal, and that Anne Benoît held his hand. La femme Girou, *hôtelière*, said that on 22nd March Anne Benoît told her and Jeanne Daubusson they had bled Monsieur Fualdès and taken his blood as if he had been a pig. We asked her if she knew all about it, as she lived in the house where it took place. 'I did hear some noise and a groan from the Bancals' room,' she admitted (according to the witness), 'but no one will ever know who did it because it was the nobles for political reasons, and the police are implicated.'

Anne Benoît denied all this: she said she had never spoken to Madame Girou.

Monsieur Constans, the police commissioner who had carried out the first, unsuccessful, search of the Maison Bancal, said he remembered very well Madame Girou had reported to him these alleged remarks of Anne Benoît's at the time, but he had paid little attention to them as she was a notorious gossip and spreader of false stories. This provoked a storm of abuse from Madame Girou, and so fierce an altercation arose between her and the commissioner that they were silenced with difficulty. The Mayor of Rodez was called: he stated Madame Girou had never made any false reports to him and that he had nothing more to say about her.

Jeanne Daubusson had a slightly different account of this story. She claimed Anne Benoît had said, 'They'll find it difficult to discover who the assassins were. There were no witnesses. The crime was not committed in the Maison Bancal but outside the town, in some garden probably.' The rest of her story was the same, except she recalled Anne had said she heard someone whistle three times in the courtyard of the Maison Bancal, and some disturbance, but she wouldn't on any account have gone down as she and Colard had quarrelled with Monsieur Bancal some time before.

Anne Benoît denied she had done anything more than repeat the rumours that everyone was repeating; but when she was alone in her room that night she had heard someone whistle three times.

La Dame Anglade was the next witness. She said Anne Benoît had delivered laundry twice to her on the evening of 19th March, once at 7.30 p.m. and again at eight or a quarter past, although she had told her it could wait till the morning. When she learned she had been arrested, she realised she had come at these times only to spy on Monsieur Fualdès, for her route took her past his house.

The case of the professional smuggler Bax was now considered. Until then no one had been particularly aware of him, possibly because he had a way of sitting hour after hour completely motionless: he was like the wild animals that melt into their surroundings and become invisible. Now that attention was sharply focused upon him he appeared as a young man with straight black hair, resentful black eyes, and regular features that could have been handsome but for their sullen expression. His double-breasted coat was buttoned high up under his chin as if he wanted to show as little of himself as possible : there was still something elusive about him, as if his profession had taught him the art of deception.

First an hotelier, Martin Viola, stated that on 18th March Bax entertained a friend to dinner at his hotel on the boulevard d'Estourmel and refused to pay for it. Viola threatened to have him arrested, but let him go when he offered to leave his papers as security for the debt. Next day he returned and offered to pay for his own meal but not for his guest : Viola sent for a gendarme who confiscated his passport, but let him go. On the 20th, when Bax was arrested and charged with complicity in the murder, he said to the gendarme : 'If only you had arrested me yesterday at the hotel I wouldn't have done what I have done.'

Bax denied this, and stated what he had actually said was, 'I wouldn't have found myself in the situation in which I now am,' which wasn't the sort of phrase Bax would normally have used so probably his counsel had suggested it to him. It came out, as the hearing continued, that on the night of the crime he had had to borrow seventeen francs fifty from Bousquier : next day when he was arrested he had plenty of money on him. He admitted he didn't go home on the night of the crime and had shared a bed with Bousquier : he said it was because he had nowhere to go – but his landlady was brought on as a witness that he had a lodging but was in arrears with the rent. The impression was he was altogether a very shady character, and although perhaps not capable of planning a crime of this sort he was certainly capable of assisting in one.

The special hearing of the evidence concerning Missonier followed. Bousquier accused him not only of having helped to carry the body, but of acting as a scout before the murder, like Anne Benoît, to report to the assassins when their victim was approaching. A doctor and a surgeon gave evidence that for some time past Missonier had been in a constant state of imbecility.

Neither Colard nor Anne Benoît had called any witnesses to testify on their behalf, but quite a number were called by Bousquier whose case was considered next. First his counsel, Maître Verlac, begged to be allowed to make known to the court a fact that honoured his client : it was that yesterday the prisoners in the gaol discovered a way to get possession of the keys : they were all about to escape when Bousquier prevented them by his energy and courage. The President ordered the official record of the incident to be made available to Maître Verlac so that he might make appropriate use of it on behalf of his client.

Le Sieur Palous, Mayor of Magnac, stated Bousquier had lived for a long while in his district : he had always behaved well and his family had enjoyed a good reputation. Many inhabitants of Rodez who had employed him declared they had never had to complain of him; his faithfulness, often put to the test, had never wavered. The *curé* of Camboulazet and the *curé* of Naves, of whom Bousquier had been at various times the parishoner, also gave evidence of his good conduct and morality.

The two distinguished ladies on the bench of the accused, Mesdames Jausion and Galtier, had all along enjoyed the sympathy of the public who did not look upon them as being in any way connected with the crime except through their relationship to the principal offenders; but there were serious charges against them because they had accompanied Jausion to the Fualdès home when he went there on the morning after the murder to go through the papers of his late colleague.

Madame Jausion denied she had entered Monsieur Fualdès' office, and her sister confirmed this denial. Jausion said the servant who had accused her was an imbecile. The President asked Didier if this was so. Didier replied, 'I cannot claim this servant is endowed with superior intelligence, but it would be unjust as well as absurd to say he was lacking in common sense. I can at least assure you of this : Guillaume Destampes has two very precious qualities – unwavering fidelity, and a good heart.'

Maître Rodier maintained the witness should be disregarded because his statement that Madame Jausion had also been in the office was a late addition to his original deposition.

Didier rose again, and said : 'An explanation seems necessary here, one that will demolish the system adopted by the defence of attacking the morality of every witness dangerous to the accused. It was this servant who brought the fatal news of my father's death to me in Paris. Before I had recovered from the shock and collected my wits, he had left again for Rodez. It was only much later I had an opportunity to question him about what had really happened. When Providence had given me back enough strength to permit me to go to the assistance of my dying mother, I was besieged, as soon as I arrived in Rodez, by the visits and the touching soliticitude of almost all the inhabitants, which again prevented me from interviewing the servants.

'Among these visitors was Jausion. I must here observe to the court and to the gentlemen of the jury that this visit disturbed me profoundly although at that time I had no reason to suspect him. When he called, I was in my bed. At his approach I experienced a feeling of horror so great that I began to tremble. I sank back onto my bed of despondency and refused to see him. It was necessary, however, to learn the state of my affairs. When he had gone I got up and went to my father's precious desk : what was my surprise and grief when I found it contained only pieces of cloth and not a single paper concerning his business!

'This spoliation set me thinking about the motive for the murder, and I became convinced, as if by inspiration, that Jausion whom you see there before you, was the prime instigator of the crime! Pursued by this thought, I interrogated Guillaume, as if quite casually, about the appearance of Jausion, the accused, in my house : it was only then he told me everything. I chided him for his tardy explanation : he replied, quite naturally, that he had been told to say nothing, and that he never suspected our friends and relations could betray us. The rest you know. It was a case of, "He who does no evil suspects no evil." '

The audience were deeply moved by Didier's words which seemed to establish, in a manner not open to contradiction, the certitude of Jausion's guilt.

CHAPTER EIGHT

Murder Without Motive?

The session devoted particularly to Jausion was of less interest to the public because of the technicalities involved, but it was of great importance to the authorities: although everyone felt certain the accused were guilty, a motive for the crime had not really been established, and it was impossible to believe in a crime without a motive. The prosecution had not yet produced sufficient evidence to justify the terms of the Bill of Indictment. Didier accused Jausion of having taken certain documents from his father's desk, but he had no proof they had been there in the first place: to argue, or even to demonstrate, that Monsieur Fualdès must have possessed a journal in which to enter his business transactions did not prove that Jausion had taken it.

The President explained that the servants who had admitted him, knowing he was the intimate friend of Monsieur Fualdès, and his business associate, and because Madame Galtier was with him who was a by-word in the district for her goodness and charity, had not seen anything suspicious, at the time, in his behaviour: neither were they aware anything had been taken, for only Monsieur Fualdès had known what was in the desk. It was not, he said, until the accusing finger of the public conscience pointed him out as one of the assassins that his action in going through his friend's papers could be seen in its true light. What was he looking for? What was he so anxious to find that he had committed murder in order to gain possession of it?

The commissioners appointed to go through Jausion's papers after his arrest, and to investigate his recent dealings with Monsieur Fualdès, were called upon to report. They said they had been unable to find anything that could have provided a motive for the crime: Monsieur Fualdès at the time of his death was 43,000 francs in debt. Maître Merlin, for Didier, said another 92,000 francs should be added to this amount. The commissioners added they considered Jausion's accounts worthless as they had not been kept in the form prescribed by the law. Jausion claimed he enjoyed such a reputation for fair dealing that a simple note of his transactions was all that was necessary.

The President asked Jausion how it came about that the murdered man's estate was encumbered with such a mass of debts when it appeared from the evidence given in that court the sale of his domain of Flars should have liquidated his debts and left him with some cash in hand. Had not Jausion on several occasions been heard to say that Monsieur Fualdès was comfortably well off? Jausion justified this by saying he always tried to keep up the credit of his friend.

'But why,' asked the President, 'had he to raise these considerable loans? It is well known he lived very simply.'

Jausion remarked his son spent up to 15,000 francs a year in Paris.

Witnesses for the defence were called. Monsieur Yence, Bastide's uncle, a public notary, testified he had frequently deposited large sums with Jausion without a receipt, and they had always been faithfully returned. Monsieur Carrier testified in the same sense, and also Monsieur Raynal, farmer.

As the prosecution presumed there must have been money or securities in Monsieur Fualdès' possession that the accused wanted to get into their own hands, they tried to demonstrate this was in fact the case. They called Monsieur de Seguret, member of an influential family, who had recently purchased Flars. The President asked him if the money he had paid Monsieur Fualdès had been sufficient to pay off all the latter's debts. He answered he thought so, and that he would have been left with a considerable sum in hand – but no evidence was produced to show that Monsieur de Seguret knew what these debts amounted to.

The President then asked him what, in his opinion, were the motives for the crime. De Seguret answered he didn't see how so terrible a crime could be the result of any trivial pecuniary motive : he had heard two accusations against Bastide; the first was he wanted to liquidate a debt of 10,000 francs, but this could not be seriously considered as a motive in view of the extent of Bastide's fortune. The second accusation was that he wished to steal securities worth 26,000 francs; this was equally unrealistic considering he had already had these securities in his hands and had not stolen them, and in any case they were not negotiable and could have been recovered by the family. That there was a motive of robbery in the case of Bastide was, in his opinion, highly improbable. It was equally difficult to believe robbery was Jausion's motive. He too was a wealthy man and had had plenty of opportunities to rob Monsieur Fualdès had he wished to do so.

Pressed further by the President to suggest a reason for Jausion to have forced the desk, he answered he had puzzled for a long while over that point, and he was still completely undecided; but a colleague, Monsieur Gallibert, had hazarded a possible explanation : he thought if Jausion had been raising loans on the signature of Monsieur Fualdès, there could have been an agreement of some kind between them by which Jausion was to accept the whole liability should Monsieur Fualdès ever wish to pull out : if there was such an agreement, Jausion might have been trying to find and destroy it so the whole liability would fall upon the Fualdès estate : 'It is very far fetched, of course,' he said, 'a very doubtful supposition, but it is the only one I have heard that makes any sense at all.' Monsieur Gallibert was called, and he too stressed that his suggestion was only a tentative one, and he had no firm ideas about it. Jausion invited to comment said the whole idea was ridiculous; there had never been any agreement of that kind.

There was one very obvious objection to this theory : if it was true, Monsieur Fualdès had been indulging in business of more than doubtful morality, which to most of those present was unthinkable. It seemed, therefore, that all attempts by the authorities to suggest a motive for the crime, and to establish that something had been stolen, had come to nothing, and that, in spite of all their zeal and their imposing array of witnesses they would not be able to make good their case against the accused. The public seemed to sense this, to judge by their restiveness : they felt so strongly the men were guilty that they were impatient of these long-drawn-out attempts to find a motive : it was being said openly that if Bastide was acquitted he would be lynched, and the lives of the judges would be in danger.

Didier was not in his usual place in court during that part of the hearing devoted to Jausion's accounts, a fact noted with concern by many members of the public who feared he was unwell. On the following day he appeared, carrying one of his father's account books he had accused Jausion of stealing. He asked permission to speak, and addressed the court as follows :

'I have the honour to submit to the court the sole journal that has been found in my father's desk. It relates only to the administration of the domain of Flars, and has no other significance except to confirm the existence of another account book.

'I have learned that the accused Jausion, and his counsel, profiting by my absence, have put forward the monstrous supposition that my father, the most simple and the most virtuous of men, ran through his considerable fortune in a short space of time, and they implied that the enigma of this obvious impossibility was explained by my expenses in

Paris. I will now do a service to Maître Rodier by making this matter clear : he will no longer be able to sustain his system of allegations. The kindness of my unhappy father for his son was, like his tenderness, without bounds; but as a natural consequence of this same affection, and of his own experience, he set bounds to his liberality. I can confirm before this court that my *dissipations* that have been made so much of, have not averaged more than 3,500 francs a year. I live modestly in a bachelor apartment which is comfortable but not luxurious. It will be said, perhaps, that I frequent high society. Anyone familiar with life in Paris will understand this is an honourable way to economise, because no reciprocity is expected. To frequent the court, to attend upon ministers and princes, is not expensive except for the cost of one's clothes; and is it not known my father had an income of 12,000 francs? In view of these facts, the system adopted by the defence collapses. No doubt I have paid tribute to my youth; but I have the satisfaction of being able to descend to the depths of my conscience without finding there a single painful souvenir. My life has always been that of an honest man.'

It was thus apparent either that Didier had been lying when he said his father's desk contained nothing but pieces of cloth, or that the journal had been placed in it since : however, no questions were asked about where it had been all this time, or about where the other missing books might be. His account of his frugal life seems also to have been accepted though one of Monsieur Fualdès' unpaid bills was 1,000 francs for furniture supplied to him in Paris.

The witnesses for the prosecution who claimed they had seen Jausion in the streets of Rodez on the night of the crime were now heard again : they all confirmed what they had previously said. One at least was mistaken – he was confronted in court with the man he had really seen, a Monsieur Prevoît – but he still insisted doggedly and against all reason, as if his life depended on it, that he was certain it was Jausion. Bousquier too repeated his evidence that he had seen Jausion in the Maison Bancal and also while carrying the body to the river.

Among the witnesses for the defence were Jausion's house servants; just as in the case of Bastide, they all swore their master had come home early on the night of the crime, supped and gone to bed.

In these circumstances Maître Merlin, who was now called upon to speak for Didier, being unable to produce any definite evidence of their guilt, based his appeal to the jury on the universal prejudice against the accused. He was obviously a very experienced counsel and looked older than the judges. He got slowly to his feet, and began :

'Gentlemen of the jury, one could search the annals of crime in vain to find a record of one like this, of such unheard of cowardliness, inconceivable audacity and disregard of social and domestic duties and the ties of blood : confidences violated, friendship betrayed – all crimes united in a single crime. Is it possible our unhappy country has nourished in her breast monsters capable of conceiving and executing such a project? . . . What infamy! The imagination most inflamed by the fascination of crime, the most perverse heart, the most ferocious character, the villain most hardened by evil doing, would they have dared to conceive a torture comparable to what was inflicted on Monsieur Fualdès in order to rob him of his worldly goods? . . . O disastrous night of horrible memory for this town! Happily, blinded by their own wickedness, they did not foresee the river would give up the body; the very next day, the crime was discovered. Universal sorrow and indignation brought a profound terror to their souls that can only cease upon the scaffold! In vain the criminals who dipped their hands in the blood of this innocent victim flattered themselves their evil deed would remain for ever hidden in the womb of time : it was revealed through the lips of innocent children !

'It is particularly upon you, members of the jury, that we rely to pronounce your verdict in a wise and enlightened manner : it is particularly upon you we rely to protect our lives and property. No considerations whatever must prevent you from expressing your most intimate conviction that this outrageous crime must not go unpunished : it has deeply disturbed us, but you will be able to restore our confidence and our tranquillity by declaring the criminals guilty.

'I am sure it is not necessary for me to speak to you, gentlemen, of the unfortunate son of the victim who is also claiming your impartial justice. His fate is too much to be pitied, the blow is too terrible, his situation too painful : he inspires so much interest among you I need not describe the keen sensations felt by all our hearts when we recall the terrible situation to which this blow has reduced him. What was most dear to him in the world they have taken away from him, a father and a friend : and not content with this, the accused have attacked the purity of his intentions : it has only served to redouble our sympathy for him.'

Next he spoke for a very long time and in the greatest detail about the financial situation between Jausion and the late Monsieur Fualdès, adopting as true Monsieur de Seguret's far-fetched theory that letters of exchange must have existed and that Jausion must have abstracted them, because the commissioners had discovered that instead of Monsieur Fualdès possessing a fortune of 165,000 francs from the sale of Flars he actually owed Jausion or his associates 45,000 francs.

Commenting on the ladies, Mesdames Jausion and Galtier, he said he was persuaded Jausion himself could not escape the just punishment he merited, but he left it to the wisdom of the jury to consider the circumstances that were favourable to them, although they were accomplices in the material fact of housebreaking.

He then turned to Madame Bancal and advised her it would be in her own interest to approach the judges with the accent of grief and confess the whole truth : she might hope to extenuate her fault and perhaps find some favour with them. Her obstinacy in contesting the evidence was unfavourable to her as it was to the rest of the accused. 'Speak out !' he exhorted her, 'The favourable moment for you to speak has arrived. It has been proved the murder took place in your house. Relate all the details of the fearful tragedy of which you were a witness ! Your silence compromises everything. Give us the names of all the conspirators who took part in it !'

There was a long pause while everyone waited for her to speak : she said nothing.

'You see, gentlemen ? She persists in her silence. She denies the evidence. I abstain from all further comment.

'Now I come to Bastide-Grammont. In this trial, remarkable both for the enormity of the crime and for the quality of some of the accused, we are obliged to face the fact, however painful it is for the magistrates, for the jury and for the citizens who have come in crowds to the Palais de Justice, that Monsieur Fualdès was murdered by his close friends because they wished to seize his fortune. It would be difficult to believe this if we did not have positive proof; if by his previous conduct Bastide-Grammont had not shown us that if Nature does not usually produce monsters she has in this case made an exception that is sufficiently humiliating for the human race. . . . And to whom did he address himself to help him carry out this horrible project ? Naturally to Jausion, the man who would most profit by it. Executioners were required also. . . . Where could he find them if not in the house of prostitution and debauch he was accustomed to frequent ? At the house of this same Bancal who had already manifested hatred and the desire for vengeance against Monsieur Fualdès. Here he found Colard with his concubine, Colard who was so depraved he did not fear to say property here below was unfairly distributed, and that if everyone was like him they would help themselves to it; and that he would not scruple to shoot a man for twenty-five louis. Here he found Bax and Missonier whom it was easy to seduce by playing on their terror or their greed. . . .

'What are we to make of Bousquier's evidence against which all the accused have protested with such warmth, and tried to disprove by all possible means? They will never be able to alter its force and its truth. There is not one of the facts in Bousquier's deposition that is not in accord with all the circumstances made known by the other witnesses and with what we are able to deduce from the declarations of Madame Manson. She told Monsieur Rodat Bousquier's revelations were true. . . . You will recall her esteemed cousin, by the force of his reasoning, established that no one doubted she had been present on the night of 19th March and knew the assassins. She agreed, refraining only from naming Jausion, but finally declared if he said she had named him, she must have done so. Could anything be more frank, more instructive, more touching – and more conclusive? It is obvious Madame Manson is still suffering in her imagination, still tortured by the scene of horror that passed beside her, still oppressed by the necessity to concentrate on this deadly secret she holds in her heart, torn between the need to conceal it and the duty to declare it, at least to her close friend, Monsieur Rodat; and influenced also by the gratitude of her generous heart for the man she imagined had saved her life. In the light of the revelations of this woman to her cousin and to other witnesses, it is impossible to doubt the guilt of Bastide and Jausion. After listening to her and observing her, can one entertain the smallest doubt as to where the murder was committed or refuse to declare it was at the Bancals' that Monsieur Fualdès expired under the deadly knife? One of the executioners had the ferocity to threaten this woman : he would have taken her life if she had not sworn, even on the body, to guard for ever the horrible secret that now her heart cannot contain, and of which her imagination cannot get rid of the memory.

'Madame Bancal must be considered one of the authors of the crime, or as an accomplice. Bax, Colard and Missonier not only aided in the execution but helped to carry the body to the river. Anne Benoît participated like the others. Madame Jausion and Madame Galtier assisted in the robbery. It is not necessary for me to take up your time establishing Bastide's guilt which has become so evident in the course of the trial there remains nothing for me to add. I think I hear the voice of the unhappy Fualdès, here in this courtroom that will always remind us of his uprightness and his lifelong devotion to the public good, addressing you from the depths of the tomb and saying, "What have I done to deserve such a fate? I have upheld the law, worked for the security of your persons and your property, given an example of private and social virtue. I have been a good friend, a good parent, a good father. In spite of this I have lost my life in a crime that revolts nature and has aroused the concern of the whole of France. There are the criminals! Why do you hesitate to strike? You cannot give me back my life, but you can show some regard for my son, for my widow, for the state of my affairs !" No, gentlemen, you cannot close your hearts to so just an appeal, or fail to take into consideration the mass of evidence against the accused, which is so overwhelming that only the most brazen imposter could fail to bow his head beneath its weight.

'Hasten then, members of the jury, to pronounce your verdict. All eyes, here in your town and in the whole of France, are fixed on you. Society expects from you a verdict, frank, free and disengaged from any kind of threat or influence. You must avenge the legal profession for a crime committed upon one of its members. You must strike terror into all perverse hearts that might be contemplating similar crimes. You must maintain the honour of the good men, and the good women, who have come forward as witnesses and whom the defence have not scrupled to accuse of bearing false witness. You must restore the confidence of the people of France shaken by this crime against nature, this crime without example, this monstrous assemblage of evil, this crime for which the punishment, however severe, can never match the ferocity of its authors. I reserve the right to make a claim at a later date, for damages in the interests of the victim's creditors.'

The courtroom was very hot and very crowded. Although Maître Merlin was an able speaker and marshalled his facts in such a way that the public could easily follow his reasoning, it was a relief when he finished and they were able to relax. His speech was so effective that when he descended from his high moral judgements to his demand for damages it seemed rather an anti-climax, but of course he had to do this. His sole reason for appearing in court was to represent Didier's financial interests.

The prosecutor was the next speaker. He too marshalled all the facts and analysed all the evidence that led to the inevitable conclusion the accused were guilty. It took a very long time, and they had heard it all, much more strikingly expressed, from Maître Merlin. The jurymen had propped themselves up as comfortably as they could in various attitudes expressive of attention, eyes half-closed and scarcely moving : even the devoted and conscientious Rodat was dozing off, when suddenly he heard Clarissa mentioned. The prosecutor was saying Bastide's guilt was clearly established by Bousquier's deposition supported by innumerable witnesses, and by Madame Manson's evidence; he recalled Bastide's clumsy pretence that he wanted her to tell the truth, reminding the court he had said to her, 'You have nothing to fear from my family, they are all prepared to help you.' From this he argued she was secretly in league with the accused.

Rodat was seriously alarmed when he continued, 'Gentlemen, I leave this to your discretion. For my part I shall take against her whatever proceedings I consider necessary.' The authorities had been sympathetic and extremely patient with her, but somehow she had offended this most dangerous man : it seemed proceedings would be taken against her to force her to say what she knew without immediately contradicting herself.

It was what Rodat had feared all along, and now, by applying to be heard again she was simply putting her head into the lion's mouth. What could he do? Even if he managed to persuade her to withdraw her application, made at the instance of Madame Pons, she would certainly be sent for and questioned about what she had intended to say. He listened anxiously as the prosecutor continued, but now it was all about the accused. He had an aggressive, rasping voice that jarred on him :

'The evidence proves the widow Bancal participated in the crime, and that Bax and Colard were guilty also : they are of the outcasts of society, always ready to take part in an outrage.' Anne Benoît he called 'a girl of evil life, living in shameful concubinage.' He insisted she had been employed to spy on Monsieur Fualdès so that the assassins could seize him : she had been recognised in the Maison Bancal by Bousquier who could not possibly be mistaken as she had once been his servant. Bousquier's revelations, he said, had illuminated the horrible scene and rendered him of interest to the authorities. As for Jausion, 'How could he be innocent? . . . How could one doubt that he who had robbed the heirs of Monsieur Fualdès of their fortune had also participated in the crime? The law directs that he who benefits from a crime is necessarily its author, or an accomplice.' He concluded :

'I have now given you the grounds upon which the prosecution rests. I have retraced the outline of the trial, recapitulated the facts, the declarations of the witnesses, the replies of the accused, and everything that has a bearing on the guilt of the accused who stand before you. I believe I have fulfilled my task. Your sustained attention through our long debates will have made it apparent to you who is guilty of this great crime, and your decision will terminate this trial which is too celebrated for its horrors.'

On the following day – it was now 5th September – the courtroom was full, including the aisles, when Maître Romiguière rose to speak in defence of Bastide. There were a large number of strangers, for the trial had attracted visitors from all over the country. In spite of the unpopularity of his cause, Maître Romiguière was personally liked : his manner was direct and unaffected, his ideas clearly expressed. He spoke entirely without notes, seeming to voice his inmost thoughts as they occurred to him : this made him very entertaining to listen to. He carried out his difficult task with conscientiousness and courage, putting the case of the accused in the most favourable light, as it was his duty to do :

'Gentlemen, at daybreak on 20th March a woman discovered a body floating on the waters of the Aveyron : the news spread quickly and excited only our curiosity and idle pity. Suddenly from the banks of the Aveyron came the cry, "The body is Fualdès' !" Horror and indignation succeeded indifference when Rodez learned it had to lament one of its most respected citizens, and the general grief honoured him more, per- haps, than he had been honoured in his lifetime. This grief was intensified when we learned the particulars of his death – that he had been seized by his murderers from surroundings of absolutely security and that, not con- tent with taking his life, they had enjoyed drop by drop the blood of their victim; that they condemned him to the dreadful torture of watch- ing himself die : and that to add to the monstrosity of their crime they had carried his body to the pool that had delivered it up again, refusing to be their accomplice.

'Are you surprised, gentlemen, that these scenes still live before your eyes, and that the least vindictive imagination cannot conceive a punish- ment proportionate to the crime? But if the misfortunes of the unhappy Fualdès embitter our hearts and provoke us to vengeance, do not forget there are other men too who deserve our interest and our pity. Imagine Bastide innocent – and you owe him at least this supposition – were ever misfortunes comparable to his? Fualdès suffered for an instant and passed to his eternal rest : Bastide, for five months, has been torn by grief, humiliation and despair. He is innocent in the eyes of the law, and he is loaded with chains that already wound his limbs : for five months, in despite of all laws, civil and humane, he had been held in solitary con- finement, deprived of the consolation, the embraces, and even the sight of any members of his family. . . . No, I am wrong, gentlemen. When he was led out before you, he found on the bench of the accused two tenderly loved sisters, so very worthy to be loved, and he was permitted for a moment to mingle his tears with theirs.

'Now he stands before his judges – and what judges ! Seven magistrates specially designated by the Ministry of Justice, present themselves for our veneration and our respect. The jury, chosen from the *élite* of the citizens, is remarkable for the noble character and disinterestedness of the men who compose it. They, if anybody, should know how to place themselves above prejudice, and how to detect the work of calumny.

'In this unhappy trial, who has not been slandered? Even you, in- habitants of Rodez, have I not told you that your generous hearts have caused you to confound horror for the crime with thirst for vengeance? Can't you understand the difference between accusation and condemnation? That because a man is accused you must not assume he is guilty? I have even been told it is dangerous to say anything here in favour of the accused. My presence in your midst shows you my contempt for all suppositions of that kind.

'The accusations against Bastide are neither true nor reasonable. The stories told against him are calumnies. There is nothing in his life to indicate the slightest disposition to commit so atrocious a crime. He has been a good son, a good brother and a good citizen. Monsieur Fualdès honoured him with the most constant friendship. He is a man of ample means but of simple way of life, both industrious and active. The credit he enjoyed with the merchants and dealers in the market of Rodez does not present the picture of a man with such a thirst for gold that he would commit a crime for it : besides, he knew that Monsieur Fualdès was in financial difficulties, that his assets were more than absorbed by his debts : there was nothing to be gained by murdering his friend, even had he wished to do so. What could Bastide have stolen? The fable that he had stolen 10,000 francs rests on the sole testimony of Alboni who says Bastide told him he owed Monsieur Fualdès that amount. Bastide's simple explanation is he was talking of securities to that value which Monsieur Fualdès had entrusted to him. They were found later with Monsieur Fualdès' papers. How then was he a thief? If he had been, he could simply have kept these securities, he could have robbed Monsieur Fualdès without killing him. Surely it is obvious the prosecution are trying to prove the theft by the assassination and the assassination by the theft? It is a way of reasoning subversive of all the principles of deduction from evidence. No, he was not a thief, and the very barbarity of the crime shows he had no hand in it.

'On 19th March, Monsieur Fualdès left his home at eight o'clock in the evening without saying where he was going, unaccompanied and without a lantern, after providing himself with a bag of money. He carried nothing with him that suggested he was going to keep a business appointment. Perhaps he was engaged in one of those acts of charity for which he was well known; perhaps he was on a more self-indulgent errand . . . here let us draw a veil. But we must recognise the assassination of this unfortunate magistrate was an obscure crime committed solely to rob him of the bag of money, a crime to which Bastide was a stranger.'

Maître Romiguière proceeded to examine the testimony of those who claimed they had seen him in the streets of the town on the night the murder was committed : he pointed out they contradicted each other about where they had seen him and at what time, and about what he had been wearing: that his itinerary, if we were to believe all the witnesses, would have been an impossible one : whereas the witnesses who testified he was at home at Gros at the time the crime was committed were unanimous and there was no possibility they were mistaken :

'We have a complete picture of how he spent that day, the 19th. He got up at dawn and worked with his men in the fields at La Morne until ten : then he visited the *curé* of Saint Mayme, worked with him on the parish accounts, and dined with him although he had been invited to dine with Monsieur Fualdès. It was after four o'clock when he arrived in Rodez. He went to six agents to negotiate bills of exchange for Monsieur Fualdès, then he made a few small purchases for himself and left again for Gros at half past six. Is this the way a man spends his day who is planning a desperate crime? Nothing was further from his mind. Two workmen met him on the road to Gros, and five servants saw him arrive there at eight o'clock. He supped with his wife and his sister-in-law, and retired to bed at ten. His sister-in-law heard him talking to his wife in their room until a late hour. Twenty of his work-people testify he was again in the fields at La Morne, at dawn on the 20th and that he was there until two o'clock. The time at which he arrived at Rodez on the 19th proves Ursula Pavillon could not have heard him at three o'clock give Monsieur Fualdès a rendezvous for eight o'clock in the evening. The time he left Rodez again proves that Dornes could not have seen him at seven in the auberge of the widow Ginestet; and that those who believed they had seen him in Rodez after seven were mistaken : he was not the tall man they had seen in various parts of the town between eight and ten. Everything shows he was at Gros while his friend was being murdered at Rodez. On the following afternoon when he was at the Fualdès home, he denies having let fall the key to Monsieur Fualdès' desk while helping to make a bed : the two servants themselves, thought it was already lying in the folds of the sheet.'

Maître Romiguière turned to what he called, 'the pretended revelations' of Monsieur Bancal, Bousquier and Madame Manson. Monsieur Bancal had been reported by the witness Moisset to have said Bastide was capable of the crime – a vague insignificant supposition like all those made after his arrest. 'Why,' he demanded, 'had they let Bancal die without interrogating him at his last hour? Should the typhus that raged in the prison have stopped the minister of the law when it did not stop the minister of God who braved the contagion to carry the consolation of religion to the dying man?

Bousquier's testimony, he said, was unworthy of belief because he only accused others to excuse himself :

'Interrogated five times, he gave five different versions of what he pretended to have seen, though he was perfectly safe as all the accused had already been arrested. After his arrest he should have been kept in solitary confinement, but a police official, Calvet, perfidiously gave him access to the depositions that had already been made, notably that of Monsieur Albene upon which he based his so-called confession and his accusations : Albene had said he had seen shadows that night moving under the trees of the boulevard d'Estourmel. But in spite of having previous depositions to draw upon, Bousquier's story is unrealistic. Why should he have been sent for by the assassins when, according to his own account, they already had all the men they required? He says Bax borrowed twenty-four sous from him one hour before the murder – if Bax was in need of money he was not Bastide's agent. He identified Bessières-Veynac as one of the assassins but, when he learned he had a watertight alibi, he said he must have been mistaken and that it was Jausion he saw. Could he not have been mistaken about Bastide also?'

He gave a most unsavoury account of Bousquier's past life, with instances of convictions for swindling and theft. He pointed out he had accused Bax of being one of the murderers, and he also said he shared a bed with him after the murder : 'Ah !' he cried, 'This was not the sleep of innocence, that the President of this august court called it, but of a hardened criminal. . . . But enough of this man. Let us consider Madame Manson :

'Never in the whole course of criminal justice has there been an incident like this. Only a concourse of the most extraordinary circumstances and a woman like Madame Manson could bring it about. Some have compared her to an angel sent by Providence to confound the murderers – sublime thought no doubt, but I should have been more grateful to Providence if instead of sending a witness to the crime it had preferred not to send a victim. Others think she is merely a woman with an exalted imagination, distracted by reading romances. Perhaps she aspires to incarnate an oriental genie that has the power to intervene in the lives of others and decide their destiny. Is her mind deranged? The practical spirit she has shown in her letters to the Prefect immediately dispels this idea. Some say she has no heart, but who can doubt her sensitivity when she speaks of her son in a maternal accent worthy of the Andromache of Racine? How are we to explain her fainting fits, her broken sentences, her bizarre questions? She assumes the accused are guilty merely because they are said to be guilty.

'Who, then, is this Madame Manson who doesn't speak though all try to make her speak? Who confesses nothing, but to whom one credits the most singular confessions? Who has no secret, but from whom everyone ceaselessly demands her secret? If you submit all the evidence to critical analysis, you will find the prosecution has in fact furnished neither proofs nor any serious indications that the accused are guilty.

'Gentlemen of the jury, I am as anxious as you can be to discover and punish the murderers, but I hold firmly to the maxim of Charlemagne who declared it was better a great crime should go unpunished than that the innocent should suffer. I do not propose to enlarge upon the sorrows of Bastide's father, eighty-five years old, who waits at the edge of the grave to learn from you whether he can go with an unsullied name to his eternal rest; nor on the sorrows of the wife of my client, once a model of wifely virtue, now a model of grief and affliction. I do not place these images before your eyes, you would not be able to judge them, you would only be able to weep. . . . No, it is of you alone I shall speak, and of your future : one day those two hurdy-gurdy players who disappeared the morning after the crime will appear. What will be your terror then, if you find you have condemned the innocent to the slaughter? What will you reply to the families of the accused who, dogging your footsteps, will demand back from you the heads of their dear ones struck off by the executioner? You know the people! Their prejudice today against the accused will turn to indignation against you tomorrow.

'And you, Didier Fualdès, our principal and most dangerous adversary, you say you do not wish to be accused of giving way to odious calculation and motives of gain : willingly I consent to see in you only another Hamlet pursued by the bleeding shadow of a father who demands the blood of his murderer, but the more pure your intentions are, the more you must guard against the danger of a fatal mistake. What if you are deceived? What if you are deceiving yourself? Open your eyes and look around you! Where are the friends, the old, the true friends, of your father? Unfortunate young man, they are on the bench of the accused. Ah! when you seek to assuage your grief by the sweetness of a revenge that seems so natural and so legitimate, are you not laying yourself open to the pangs of a remorse for which there can be no remedy, a remorse of which nothing will abate the agony? When you seek to appease the shade of your father beware lest it rise in anger before you because, instead of the assassins, you have sacrificed those who would have saved him, if he could have been saved. Listen to the slow march of time, slow but inexorable. It will make the truth manifest. Join with me now in asking our judges to declare – Bastide is innocent !'

It is impossible, in the narrow confines of this chapter, to give more than an indication of this splendid speech by Maître Romiguière which lasted eight hours. The public were profoundly moved with admiration for his talents – but they remained with their conviction unaltered that the accused were guilty.

CHAPTER NINE

'You are a liar, Madame!'

On 6th and 7th September the other counsels for the defence spoke for their clients: they rested largely on the arguments put forward by the orator who had preceded them. First Maître Combarel, the elder, spoke on behalf of Madame Bancal. He addressed the court as follows:

'Now that this great affair, in which so many errors and so many passions have intermingled, has been thoroughly thrashed out, let us ask ourselves what evidence has come to light that could incriminate the widow Bancal. Is her complicity in the crime established? No, gentlemen. No eye-witness has come forward to describe the circumstances of the crime except Madame Manson whose inextricably confused stories have given us nothing definite to go on. She is the angel of the shadows who promises light only to plunge us into deeper darkness.

'Bousquier, himself one of the accused, states he did not enter the Maison Bancal until after the crime had been committed: we do not know, therefore, what role each individual played in this tragic scene. In the absence of eyewitnesses and of direct proof, is the supposed location of the crime sufficient for a precise identification of Madame Bancal as one of the accomplices? And in any case how could a weak woman in the power of her husband have done anything to avert the catastrophe? Can you condemn anyone to death on no evidence but hearsay? The statements attributed to her children should make no impression on a reasonable man. These children of tender age, without any kind of education or discernment, obsessed and tempted by promises of reward, have repeated blindly all you wished them to say: even the witnesses who collected the pretended revelations were shocked by their contradictions. One shudders at the spectacle of these members of the public, blinded by their prejudice, plying the children with insidious questions, encouraging them to strike at the lives of their own parents.'

Maître Combarel then dealt with the testimony of a woman who had been planted in her cell to spy on her, an unknown woman, arrested for theft and suspected infanticide who claimed Madame Bancal had given her all the details of the murder that took place in her kitchen :

'This is simply the height of imposture. It is neither reasonable nor possible to believe that Madame Bancal who has maintained her silence though provoked by many, should single out this one stranger to talk to about it. The conversations between Madame Bancal and her daughter alleged to have been overheard by two or three prostitutes in the prison must also be rejected as unworthy of belief : it is not from these depraved witnesses one should expect the truth : corruption can only deceive.

'Madame Bancal had nothing to gain from the crime, nor did she profit by it. If she witnessed it, this was from pure mischance. We cannot reasonably suppose she took an active part in it : the assassins did not need the assistance of this old woman. It has been constantly said her secrecy is her principal accuser, that she could clear herself by divulging all she knew — but the law says secrecy is not a crime except in plots against the government. Her silence is authorised by the law. The prosecution has proved nothing against her : until it does, she is not obliged to answer.'

He paused here. Looking round the courtroom at the unresponsive faces, he evidently realised no one was convinced by his very plausible arguments, for he added rather despondently to the jury, 'It is with regret that I feel obliged to say this : if you judge she was a voluntary accomplice in the crime, at least you cannot find that it was premeditated.'

Finally he begged for their pity because she was the widowed mother of a large family who were entirely dependent on her.

The young barrister appearing in that court for the first time, Maître Batut, then spoke very well in favour of his client, Marianne Bancal : she had not been seriously attacked in the Bill of Indictment, nor by Maître Merlin, and he had no difficulty in showing that the charges against her were groundless, and that it would be neither true nor reasonable to say she had had any knowledge of the plot.

In defending Colard, Maître Foulquier's main endeavour was to disprove Bousquier's testimony. He pointed out, following Maître Romiguière, that Bousquier accused others only to exculpate himself, that he had already served a sentence for fraud, and that he was unworthy of belief. He reminded the jury there had been contradictions in his evidence, and that two witnesses, Palayrot and Rose Féral, had stated he did not leave the latter's tavern until 8.30 p.m. By that time, Monsieur Fualdès was already dead. Certainly he was the owner of several shotguns, but there was no proof they had been used to arm the assassins on their march to the river. He begged the jury to consider that the life of a man was too precious a thing to be arbitrarily disposed of, and he recommended his unhappy client to their justice.

Anne Benoît was defended along the same lines by another young barrister, Maître Rous.

Maître Combarel junior, defender of Bax, said his reunion with four of the accused in Rose Féral's tavern on 19th March was no proof of his culpability, it was purely accidental :

'Perhaps the most damaging evidence against him is his alleged remark when he was arrested : "If you had arrested me yesterday I wouldn't have done what I have done." But there were several versions of what he was supposed to have said. What he had really meant was, "I shouldn't now be involved in this procedure. . . ." If Bax had been in the employ of Bastide, would he have been without funds and have had to borrow from Bousquier? Nothing proves, nothing indicates, the least liaison between Bax and the rest of the accused, and indeed it is hard to believe that anyone planning so shocking a murder would have entrusted his guilty secret to a man like him. . . .'

Maître Grandet, defender of Missonier, began by drawing attention to the extraordinary spectacle of the bench of the accused : the friends and relations of Monsieur Fualdès were there, including Madame Galtier who was the pattern and model of all that was most noble in womankind :

'Her accusers have done well to place before her eyes the consoling image of the crucified God whom she has so long and so devoutly served. I pay her my homage, and I wish her to hear from my own lips that I and all who understand her misfortunes have almost the same degree of sympathy for her as for the murdered Fualdès. . . .

'Beside these illustrious persons, the eye lights upon Missonier, as if Fate and sent him here to play the part of the clown to amuse the spectators and temper the horror of the action. No one could imagine him physically or morally capable of taking part in an assassination. It has been proved he was in the Féral Tavern when the murder took place. He has been accused by a single witness, Bousquier, of having assisted to carry the body to the river : beginning with the law of Moses, it has been forbidden in civilised countries to condemn a man on the evidence of single witness. *Ad unius testimonium nullus condemnabitur.*

He went into details of Bousquier's disreputable life, and the contradictions in his testimony, and continued, 'Society is the union of the common interest against individual interests. Its object is to guarantee to each his life, his liberty, his goods, against any attempt against them by an individual; but it would be a terrible abuse if the law were to become the tool of the informer. A man on the bench of the accused may serve as a guide towards the discovery of the truth, but he must never be the sole judge of another of the accused. And I ask you, gentlemen of the jury, is it not implicitly laid down in the law that you cannot condemn an accused man simply on the evidence of another accused man who cannot withdraw his evidence without exposing himself to a capital charge?'

He again reminded the jury that Missonier was in an habitual state of imbecility, and begged them not water the tomb of Fualdès with innocent blood.

Maître Arsaud, who had said little since being reproved by the President at the beginning of the trial, now spoke in defence of Madame Jausion : he evidently felt, together with all who heard him, she did not need any special pleading on her behalf, for he contented himself with paying a tribute to the memory of Monsieur Fualdès and to the virtues of Madame Galtier, her sister.

Madame Galtier herself was defended by Maître de Comeiras : he presented an eloquent picture of her life and sorrows. The proceedings, he said, questioning the correctness of her intentions in visiting the widow of Monieur Fualdès immediately after the murder, might have been dispensed with :

'Her virtues serve her as a strong shield against the accusations that have caused her to be thrown into prison and to be detained there for so many months. Do not imagine, gentlemen, that the captivity that deprived her of all communication with her family, and which prevented her for so long from embracing her children, excited in her the least complaint. Her resignation and the peace of her heart are equal to her innocence and her misfortunes. She is strong in her faith and in her hope that the God she has so long and so devoutly served will protect her in this her hour of trial.'

Maître Rodier, who had been unwell for some days, had risen from his sick bed to plead for Jausion. He tried to establish his innocence by pointing out the contradictions and the uncertainty of the accusations made against him, mentioning particularly Bousquier's tardy identification of Jausion as one of the assassins in place of Bessières-Veynac when he found the latter had an alibi too strong to be challenged. He called Clarissa's evidence 'extraordinary, unrealistic and mere romances', and he reminded the jury she had not directly accused Jausion, and had twice retracted her statements. The second part of his discourse was intended to prove Jausion had no motive to commit the crime : no evidence had been produced to justify the various theories that had been put forward,

Bastide, drawn by Sudre in prison at Albi.

Jausion, drawn by Sudre.

Bastide and Jausion

A sketch of Jausion, Bastide, Madame Bancal and Bousquier at the trial.

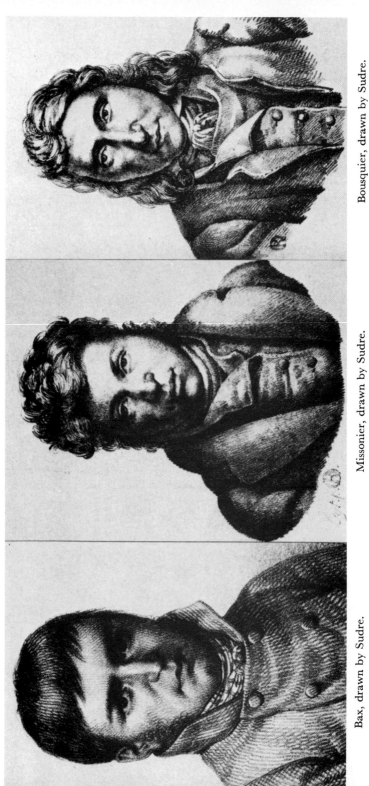

Bax, drawn by Sudre.

Missonier, drawn by Sudre.

Bousquier, drawn by Sudre.

and he gave a convincing account of his honourable dealing with Monsieur Fualdès and other clients.

Maître Verlac, a popular local barrister, defended Bousquier : He maintained his client could not be included among the authors of the murder nor among the accomplices : he it was who had disclosed to the justices all the mysteries of this horrible affair. Although the principal defender of the rest of the accused, Maître Romiguière, had tried to crush him with all the weight of his prodigious powers of oratory in order to efface by every possible means the impression Bousquier's denunciations had made upon the court, they remained unshaken. He refuted one by one all the objections that had been urged against his morality; he had been treated, he said, as if he were a reptile – but if he was indeed one it was his nature to shine in the darkness : in the midst of the confusion of shadows he had indicated the authors of the crime : his testimony had lit up the scene so that everything had been made clear.

That completed the speeches for the defence, and the session came to an end.

The next was that of 8th September at which Clarissa was to be heard again and which Rodat had awaited with the greatest anxiety : he knew it was her intention to give evidence absolutely opposed to his advice. Knowing how indiscreet she was, he feared she might involve herself more and more deeply until she could no longer extricate herself.

She was called at the very beginning of the session. When she entered the witness-box she seemed rather uncertain of herself, but she took the oath and faced the President boldly. 'Madame Manson,' he said, 'You have requested to be heard again?' He waited for her answer, and the court waited too in dead silence.

'I have been told,' she began, 'that I severely compromised the accused by the revelations I made. . . . I should be sorry to have left the wrong impression on the mind of the jury. I fainted several times, and I should be sorry if these accidents should be interpreted in a way . . . unfavourable to them.' She had said her piece quite coolly so far, it was evidently well rehearsed, but now a sort of resentment brought the old emotion into her voice as she went on, 'If only they hadn't greeted me as I came in, as if I were a friend. . . .'

'No doubt they knew you,' the President commented dryly.

'No!' she protested hastily, 'I was never at the Bancals'! Someone used my name. I wasn't there.'

The President patiently recapitulated what she had told Rodat and other witnesses before the trial opened :

'You had a rendezvous at the Maison Bancal. You found the door shut. You knocked three times: Madame Bancal opened it and said she couldn't receive you. Almost at the same time, others came to the door and knocked three times. Madame Bancal was frightened and hid you in the alcove from which you saw Bastide, Jausion and others enter, dragging Monsieur Fualdès who was gagged. They threw him onto the kitchen table; you fainted with terror. When you recovered you tried to escape into the courtyard through a small window in the alcove: the noise you made opening it drew the assassins' attention to you: they dragged you into the kitchen where Fualdès had had his throat cut. Bastide would have killed you also, but Jausion objected so he forced you with your hand on the still-warm body to take an oath to say nothing of what you had seen, on pain of death. Jausion then took you out to the ruins of the Annonciade: after warning you if you identified him you would die by dagger or by poison, he left you there.'

Clarissa objected, 'No, I didn't say that. It was only I had been told there was a woman who saw all this, and I repeated it.' The President asked her,

Madame, is it not true you went to see Madeleine Bancal recently at the hospice, to see if she would recognise you? –Yes.

Then you were in the Maison Bancal? –No, I wasn't.

The President smiled patiently as if she were a wayward child. Then he called the court usher, Glandines, and put to him the following question: 'Is it not a fact that on 2nd September, when you were taking coffee with Monsieur Constans, merchant, he repeated to you certain confessions that had been made to his wife by Madame Manson?'

'Yes, *Monsieur le Président*,' he replied, and he glibly repeated what Clarissa was supposed to have said – it was the lurid story of the murder again, as she had told it to Rodat.

But she refused to admit it. 'I couldn't possibly have said all this,' she objected. 'I wasn't there.'

Monsieur Constans was called, and he affirmed he had got the story from his wife who had got it from Madame Manson, adding that she described how she had been forced to kneel before Bastide.

CLARISSA : I have never knelt before anyone!
CONSTANS : You are a liar, Madame.

For once she was taken aback. The President waited for her answer:

Well, Madame? –I have never spoken to Madame Constans. That is, I have spoken to her very often, but I didn't say what she accuses me of saying.

Madame Constans, dressmaker, was called: to everyone's surprise she did not support her husband's statement. First she was in tears and could not speak at all. Then she said Clarissa had spoken to her just as everyone else had about the murder.

But didn't she say she had witnessed it herself? –No, sir. Once she spoke in such a way I suspected she had.

Well? What made you think so? –Once she said another woman had been there, but that she would never say who it was, even if it cost her her life. I questioned her, and because she answered only with broken sentences and fits of weeping, I came to the conclusion that she was the woman. I told all this to my husband, who shared my opinion.

After this rather inconclusive little scene, the President called Rodat and, in the most flattering terms asked him to confirm that Clarissa had described to him all she had seen in the Maison Bancal – 'Most virtuous Rodat,' he called him, and 'Worthy son of your father.' Of course he felt bound to comply, and did so. He confirmed she had in fact given him details that would indicate she had been an eyewitness of the murder. Then he took the opportunity to set his conscience at rest about another matter: ever since Maître Merlin in his speech had made such a point of his evidence that Clarissa had named Jausion to him as one of the assassins he had been asking himself whether she had in fact done so. He therefore explained now that although he had neglected nothing in trying to assure himself of the fidelity of his memory, it was still possible for him to have been mistaken in what he had heard, from whom, and when. Therefore he wished to amend his previous statement, and say he still thought she had named Jausion to him, but he was no longer prepared to swear it. The President, so far from being displeased, seemed to appreciate his anxiety to be as truthful as possible.

A juryman now indicated he wished to ask a question. Again there was the awkward pause. The question was, 'Madame Manson, you have mentioned a secret several times. What is it?'

She evidently disliked being questioned by a juryman for she answered rather testily, 'It is connected with the motives that decided me to make a false declaration to the Prefect. These motives still prevent me from speaking. Don't insist, please.'

But the juryman did insist : 'What are these motives?'

Her eyes narrowed, and she replied, 'I cannot say what they are. It is a secret I shall never tell.'

The President asked her, 'If you were not in the Maison Bancal, how do you know everything that passed there?'

'A woman told me,' she answered stubbornly, and then suddenly cried, 'What does it matter if I have to bear it all alone?'

'Name that woman!' thundered the President.

She hesitated, and then said, 'It is Rose Pierret,' and added, as if to excuse herself, 'Let her appear. I've paid long enough for others.'

Never since the unhappy trial began had Rodat been so astonished and distressed. He had hoped she would not mention Rose, and that her earlier indiscreet remark about her had been forgotten. The significance of her statement was not lost on the audience, for there was an immediate buzz of excited conversation; no doubt they were reminding each other the Bancal children at one stage had spoken of two mysterious women being present.

The prosecutor rose and said, 'Madame Manson has sworn to tell the truth. She has named Rose Pierret. We know it's a fairy tale, but let her be called and then we will press on with our own conclusions.' With this faintly ominous remark he sat down, and the President announced that while they were waiting for Rose he would take the opportunity to read to the jury a letter from Madame Manson's father. It ran as follows :

I have just learned my daughter has had the effrontery to say her deposition was extracted from her by my violence and that she has retracted it. I cannot allow myself to be thus publicly accused by one for whose existence I have the misfortune to be responsible : I therefore declare to you and to the court that in all my dealings I have been guided by those sentiments of delicacy and honour that I have tried in vain to inspire in her. As a father and a magistrate I have not ceased to impress upon her that she has a sacred duty to enlighten us about the horrible murder committed upon the person of a magistrate distinguished by his talents and his virtues, and to maintain silence about this fearful crime is to make herself the accomplice of the assassins. . . .

I consider it my duty to bring to your notice a letter I received from her on 17th August – dare she say it was dictated by my threats? I have not seen her for some days, and I am resolved never to see her again. . . .

This was the letter from Clarissa he enclosed :

I beg my father to be calm. If it is really the case that he has no sympathy for the accused, he will be satisfied. I have strong proofs he doesn't know of. I am distrustful, however, after all that has happened to me. I have decided to make a sensational revelation : the whole court will be astonished. I shall tell the whole truth. The wretches will perish ! and such. . . . Burn this letter. If they are warned, all will be lost. The defendants will take certain steps. . . .

You have cursed me. You wish for my death. You refuse to help me. I shall lose the sole support I have, because Madame Pons shared all she had with me. Never mind. You are my father, and your daughter is prepared to sacrifice everything for you. She will never lose her tenderness and her respect for you. Guard this letter well.

The President questioned her :

Do you admit you wrote this letter ? –Yes. My father is imprudent. He should have burned it.

Why do you continually offend him ? He has shown you the path of honour. –I pay for all. The prosecutor may draw his own conclusions.

When you separated from your husband, did not your father offer you an asylum under the paternal roof ? You refused, preferring to remain with Monsieur Clémendot. Did not your father go with you to the Prefect ? All you have said about him is untrue : now you must speak the truth. Would you sacrifice your honour, your child ? . . . ('And your immortal soul !' a juryman cried out.) Was it Mademoiselle Pierret who was in the Maison Bancal ? –I didn't say she was. I said she had given me all the details.

You wrote to your father, 'I have decided to make a sensational revelation.' What did you mean by those words ? –I have already said my father would have done better to burn that letter.

Rose Pierret was ushered into the witness-box. She was very shy and looked as if she had been crying. 'Bring her a chair,' the President said to the usher, and then to Rose, 'Don't be afraid. Your father is near you. When you are in a state to reply, I shall question you.' The public and the press were intrigued by this new witness, but probably no one at that time believed it was not Clarissa herself who had been in the Maison Bancal. The President began :

Do you know the accused ? –I know Jausion and Bastide. (Her voice was a mere whisper.)

After the death of Monsieur Fualdès, someone gave you details about the murder ? –No.

Have you known Madame Manson long? –Since the Fair of St Peter*.

Only since then? –Yes.

Had you never met her before? –No.

Madame Manson has stated she learned from you the details she has furnished about this affair? –I have never spoken to her about it.

When did you go to Madame Constans, the dressmaker? –I've been there often.

Was it there you confided in Madame Manson? –No. I had nothing to confide to her.

The President was evidently satisfied. He turned to Clarissa and asked her why she had waited so long before having Mademoiselle Pierret called. Ignoring his question, she stammered out hurriedly, 'I'll show that I saw her at Madame Constans' before the Fair of St Peter. . . . I didn't say she had told me she was in the Maison Bancal, but she gave me to understand. . . . I see I'm to be sacrificed for her. I thought her more generous.'

'It's because of you,' the President continued, 'I had Mademoiselle Pierret called. As she is evidently not the woman in the Maison Bancal, you must admit it was you. Reflect. You are married, you have a child, you value your honour. . . .'

'Everyone doesn't care about honour!' she interrupted bitterly. 'Why are you trembling, Rose, seeing that you don't know me?'

The President spoke to her sharply : 'Madame Manson, at present you are a witness. You could become one of the accused.'

'Yes, I know that,' she replied, 'You could have me arrested, but I wasn't there. I'm not the one, but I'm paying for her. Why doesn't someone speak up for me? Everything proves there was a woman there, but I haven't sufficient evidence. . . . I'll never denounce anyone only on suspicion . . . but I'm sure she took my name. Why didn't you arrest me three weeks ago?'

Didier now rose and said he had just been informed the widow Bancal was ready to maintain that Madame Manson was in her house : she had been overheard to mutter, 'Of course she was there. Why doesn't she say so?'

Clarissa at once protested, 'I don't care if all the accused say so, I'll never admit it, because I wasn't there. Please, *Monsieur le Président,* ask the widow Bancal if on 19th March in the evening a woman didn't come in the evening wearing a black veil that reached down to her knees.'

* 30th June.

The President asked accordingly, but she only replied with her usual phrase. 'I know nothing of all that.'

'But it was your daughter who told me !' Clarissa said angrily.

'I know nothing of all that,' the widow repeated.

'Surely,' the President remarked to Clarissa, 'I've seen you in a black veil ?'

'I didn't buy it till March,' she told him.

He looked at her doubtfully; 'Then you persist in your denial ?'

'Yes.'

Rodat sat miserably watching her entangle herself more and more, powerless to assist. She seemed to be courting disaster.

Monsieur Clémendot, who was near him in the places reserved for important witnesses, had been showing signs of indignation – he evidently felt Clarissa's latest retraction reflected on the integrity of his own deposition. As soon as there was a pause, he got up and asked to be heard. He requested Madame Manson should be asked if she had anything to add to her testimony, because if not he wished to add to his own. Clarissa answered, 'I have nothing more to say.'

Clémendot, very conscious of his own importance, strode to the witness-box and said so far he had exercised the greatest consideration and reserve towards Madame Manson in the hope she would reveal the whole truth, but now he found it necessary to disclose exactly what his relations were with this woman, so everyone would be able to understand the circumstances in which he had obtained her confidences and judge of their veracity, and only the love of truth and justice. . . .'

'Go on, then. Tell them!' she interrupted defiantly, but before he could do further damage to her reputation the President came to her rescue and assured him his evidence had not been contradicted and the details of his exact relationship with Madame Manson could add nothing to the esteem with which he was regarded by all. The advocate-general added that his honour was intact : the frank and loyal manner in which he had given his evidence would be appreciated at its true worth.

Monsieur Clémendot, mollified by these assurances, did not insist further : he returned to his place having sunk even lower in Rodat's esteem. Clarissa's honour was saved, so far as the official record was concerned, but he had made it clear to all that their relations had been intimate. Rodat's opinion was that the sole purpose of his ungentlemanly outburst was to boast in public of his conquest of this extremely interesting woman whose fame was now spreading far beyond her native Rodez.

After another long speech from Maître Merlin and some replies from the defending counsel, which were mere repetitions of what had already been said, the court rose at 4 p.m. It was announced the next session would be on the day after tomorrow, because the 9th was the date of the annual fair. Thus ended this session so ominous for Clarissa's future.

CHAPTER TEN

The Verdict and Appeal

An article in *La Quotidienne* of Paris shows how interest in this famous trial had now extended to the whole of France : it is dated 18th September 1817:

> Never has an event excited more curiosity in the capital than the trial going on at present at the Assizes of Aveyron. In the salons, in the cafés, on the promenades in public places, no one thinks of greeting a friend without asking for the news from Rodez. Only those who have something to say about the murder of Monsieur Fualdès, about Bastide, or Jausion or Madame Manson, have the right to be heard and they captivate their hearers. We are assured it is the same in the provinces. The whole of France seems to share in a drama which is followed scene by scene with sensations of fear and disquiet.

There was a curious incident at the fair of Rodez, which was not only for amusement but for the sale of mules which were exported to Spain on a considerable scale, and also for turkeys, pigs and farm produce : a pig that a woman drove to market was recognised as the one that had drunk Monsieur Fualdès' blood; she was nearly lynched and the pig was left to wander as an outcast.

When the trial was resumed after this interval, the proceedings opened with a complaint from the janitor of the Palais de Justice that Bastide had tried to bribe him to carry a letter to his wife – which was likely enough under the circumstances. Then an attempt was made to prove that on 19th March Madame Bancal had prepared a more ample dinner than usual as if she were expecting guests. When all the witnesses concerned had been heard, about a chicken having been roasted for her in the baker's oven, etc., she was asked whether she had in fact done so : she merely answered, 'No.'

The President announced that at the request of the prosecutor who was suffering from exhaustion owing to the great heat and the length of the trial, the final speech for the prosecution would be delivered by

Monsieur Castan, the advocate-general: it was rather surprising he consented, for his proper function was more that of a referee to see the law was properly administered. He had said little during the trial, and as far as the public was concerned, he seemed to be merely an additional judge, sitting with them at the same table and in identical robes. He rose to his feet and stood looking calmly round the courtroom until he had secured absolute silence. Then he methodically recapitulated the main charges and the evidence supporting them; then dealt successively, and dismissed, the various arguments Maître Romiguière and the other counsel had put forward in favour of the accused. He commented ironically:

'It seems, gentlemen, this crime that revolts, this crime that amazes – no one has committed it. There sit the eleven accused, and they are all innocent! Let us hasten, Gentlemen of the Jury, let us hasten to absolve them: hasten to break their fetters and return them to their families! Let us close the Temple of Justice, abandon these four walls and set up a funeral sign before them, warning strangers to keep away because here we cut men's throats like vile animals without the officers of justice being able to reach and punish the criminals, even when they are known to us!

'But no! Vain reasons embellished by the finest eloquence will have no effect upon the established facts: this region will not remain plunged in humiliation and mourning. Eloquence is like the lightning that streaks across the high clouds, like the thunder that shakes and astonishes; but truth is like the sweet dew, the gentle breeze, and the life-giving rays of the sun that repair the disorders of nature.

'Bastide even invokes the shade of Fualdès to attest his innocence. It is the evidence of the living Fualdès, not of the dead one, we need! Avid for blood, in a hurry to shed it, these monsters refused him even a few moments to lift his soul to God, to humble himself in His presence and offer Him the life that was about to be torn from him. Infernal spirits, they wished to add to the horrors of his torture the rage and despair by which they were themselves possessed. . . . That horror is not only shared by you, inhabitants of Rodez, but by the whole of France.

'The eloquent defender of the woman Bancal asks us to have pity on her because of her children, but even the interests of her children demand we should use the utmost severity with her. She formed their hearts to crime: we must show them the danger of the lessons and examples she has given them; they must remember all their lives it is only by detesting these deplorable examples they will avoid the fate of their parents.'

On the subject of Jausion, he said,

'A major crime has always a serious motive. Fualdès was not only assassinated, he was robbed : he was killed so that he could be pillaged with impunity. His fortune has disappeared; all his papers have disappeared; and Jausion forced his desk in which they were kept! Both reason and law indicate that was the motive for the crime. You are astonished, Jausion, one could even suspect you of dipping your hands in the blood of a friend, but I am not; I who know your thirst for gain, your eagerness for illicit profit that has made you the scourge of all those whose need forced them to borrow money from you. This usury is the foundation of your fortune. This passion for gold!

'What a useful moral lesson is presented by the bench of the accused! There you see an assemblage of individuals who would not even have known each other in the natural order of things : they are united and merged together in the same accusation. Two men of good family but one of them without principles and without manners, the other a usurer by profession and having no other god but money; next, a smuggler; then a vagabond, villainous by character and by profession; a prostitute; and finally a woman whom we can scarcely dignify by the name of woman! . . .

'I shall not attempt, Gentlemen of the Jury, to arouse your indignation to insure your severity : I have no need to. Surrounded as I am by the *élite* of this district, I have little fear that you who are the ornament and glory of society, could neglect or misunderstand your dearest interests. Horror for the crime is in your souls : I know that, because it is in mine. You know how to respect the oath that binds you. You know how to be just as well as human : you will lay aside all other considerations and listen only to your consciences. The rich and poor are equal in your sight as they are in the sight of the supreme judge of all, of whom you are the images on earth. You know the mandate you have accepted : I am confident you have no other desire than to fulfil it worthily.'

Turning to Didier, he addressed him as follows : 'Unfortunate son of an unhappy father, take heart. And to sweeten the bitterness of your regrets and assuage your grief, think sometimes of the sympathy you inspire in all worthy people. Your cause is theirs.'

Then to the audience : 'Citizens of Rodez, inhabitants of the Aveyron, leave it to your chosen representatives to wipe away the stain that this crime unpunished would leave upon your honour. Justly you feel sullied : justly you demand vengeance! You have only to wait a few hours now, and your indignation will turn to pity. Only a few hours, and your fears will cease, your agitation will be calmed : you will have obtained the satisfaction you have a right to expect. Peace and happiness will be reborn on your mournful river banks. In a few hours you will be able to say, "It is true a great crime was committed among us, but a sovereign court took notice of it and followed it up with zeal and enlightenment. A great crime, it is true, was committed among us, but the jurymen, whom we shall hold up to everlasting honour as models for their fellow citizens, have cleared our name from reproach. The Minister for Public Affairs has embraced our cause and supported it with ardour, and if the memory of this crime reaches our children, the monuments that record the crime will record also that it was solemnly atoned for and punished." '

This speech was listened to with intense interest, and the court rose, as usual, at 4 p.m.

By the following morning, 11th September, the prosecutor had recovered and was back in his place at the end of the judges' table. Maître Rodier spoke for two hours on behalf of Jausion, but he could do little to dispel the effect made by the advocate-general's speech. Maître Romiguière again defended Bastide. This time he made an impassioned attack on Clarissa that led to an extraordinary scene : he deplored her unsupported assertions, her retractions, and the innumerable variations in her evidence. He referred back to the prosecutor's speech in which he had implied there was some sort of an understanding between her and the accused, or with the families of the accused. On the contrary, he said, her half-statements, her silences, her implications and her denials had done his client the gravest injury. He begged her to reveal anything she knew.

'Do you fear the accused?' he asked her : 'they are in irons!'

'Not all of them!' Clarissa suddenly cried out from her place in the audience. 'You have not arrested all the assassins!'

There was dead silence in the courtroom : one could almost feel the shudder of apprehension that passed through the crowd as the significance of her words gradually dawned upon them.

Maître Romiguière, conscious that the effect of his speech, his final plea for Bastide's life, was ruined, was the first to react : 'Name them!' he shouted to Clarissa. 'I demand a full explanation for this statement!'

The President beckoned Clarissa, 'Approach, Madame Manson. . . .' She went up to him, not at all unwillingly. 'Name those who ought to be in irons!'

'I should gladly do so,' she replied, quite unabashed, 'but I can't. The truth cannot pass my lips.'

In vain Maître Romiguière protested her statement must either be implemented or withdrawn; she would say no more. The other barristers associated themselves with his protest. Clarissa remained stubbornly silent. The prosecutor said her conduct had been most reprehensible : it gave

rise to suspicions about her own part in the affair, and it might be necessary to proceed against her and to take measures laid down by the law
in the interests of justice.

Didier then addressed the court in these words : 'Gentlemen, here ends
the heavy task the law of nature and my sentiments of tenderness and
gratitude imposed upon me.

'Before the catastrophe that preoccupies us, it would have taken, I
dare say, a very extraordinary imagination to invent suffering equal to
mine. All that misfortune has of the most terrible, I have experienced it :
all that there is of poignancy in this world full of misery, I have felt it.
Particularly in the course of this melancholy trial my anguish has become
very cruel. At each day, at each hour, at each instant, sad and frightful
memories have come back to me like a dagger in my deep wound. How
different my situation was before my father's death ! Alas ! the charm of
that memory adds still more to the bitterness of my present afflictions. . . .
The blow that took the life of this good man precipitated me into a torrent
of misfortune.

'Shall I speak, alas, of the augmentation of my grief on seeing upon
whose heads alighted proofs of the crime ? I ask all of you who are listening to me, was there ever fate more pitiful than mine ?

'Providence did indeed reserve for me sweet consolations – this touching solicitude from all of you, this general interest, this universal regret,
these tears that mingle with mine – but they strive in vain to repair a
loss that is irreparable. Justice alone by its vengeance can calm my grief
by appeasing the bloody shade of my unhappy father. Magistrates and
jurymen, it is you who will avenge me and regenerate this city sullied by
a crime without example; it is from you that France, that the whole of
nature, demands it shall be punished and expiated. Gentlemen of the
Jury, the law has placed in your hands its sword of vengeance. Know
how to distinguish the innocent, but strike the guilty without pity !

'*Monsieur le Président*, and all you magistrates and functionaries, deign
to accept the homage of my admiration, and that of all my friends. The
love that burns in you for the triumph of justice renders you worthy indeed
of the confidence and esteem of the public. Maître Merlin, be pleased to
accept here the expression of my thanks. And you, people of Aveyron,
good and worthy Rhutenians, do you wish to lighten my cares? Accord
me, then, some of the affection you bore my unhappy father. Like him,
his unfortunate son cherishes all of you in his heart.'

Normally the speeches would have ended with Maître Romiguière's
final appeal on behalf of Bastide : it had frequently been said, however,
that because the last words the jury heard were from the counsel for the

defence they tended to be unduly influenced by them, and in consequence many malefactors escaped their well-merited punishment. It seems the authorities were determined that nothing of the kind should happen on this occasion, for the President, after asking the prosecution and the defence if they had anything more to say, began a final speech to the jury summing up the alleged facts of the case, and showing how they were related to each of the accused in turn, accompanied by moral reflections expressive of his horror of the crime and his love of virtue. He exhorted the inhabitants of Rodez to preserve the fine spirit by which they were at present animated, never allowing themselves to be swayed by hatred or vindictive passions. He asked them to maintain the admirable peace and unity that reigned among them : he asked them to continue to respond to the fatherly solicitude of the magistrates, guardians of their happiness, to join with them always to make justice triumph as they had done in the great trial that was about to be judged.

He spoke to the jury of the importance of the functions they were about to perform; they must be strangers to every passion : they must listen only to their own most intimate convictions; they must remember their fellow citizens were watching them, and the eyes of France were upon them. The fulfilment of their duty would have the greatest influence on public morality and on the respect due to the laws. Then he read aloud the list of questions – there were fifty-one of them – that he was submitting to them. At 12.30 they retired to deliberate.

The prisoners were led out of the courtroom, and the long miserable wait began. Sometimes Clarissa's eyes glittered, sometimes she was in tears and then, recollecting that all eyes were upon her, she would assume an air of cold indifference. More than ever, now she was in danger of arrest, she was the centre of interest and speculation, and nothing could have been more disturbing to her fellow citizens than her unexpected cry, 'You have not arrested them all!' or more damaging to the accused; it not only implied she knew Bastide and Jausion were guilty, but probably other members of their family as well. It was as if her imprudence had been specially ordained by Providence to confound them – but at what a cost to her family!

The jury returned at 6 p.m. When Monsieur Hérail, their foreman, was asked to read their findings aloud, he could not – he was unable to read. They were read for him by another juryman, Monsieur le Chevalier Masson-Latieule, Mayor of Saint-Felix de Lunel. They found Bastide, Jausion, Colard, the widow Bancal and Bax guilty of murder with premeditation; Anne Benoît and Missonier guilty without premeditation; Bousquier guilty of a misdemeanour. Bastide and Jausion were also found guilty of theft; Madame Jausion also as an accomplice. Only Madame Galtier and Marianne Bancal were found not guilty.

When the reading of the document containing the findings had been completed, the President ordered the accused to be brought back into the courtroom. The usher read the document again in their presence. When he had finished, the President ordered Marianne Bancal, Madame Galtier and Madame Jausion to be set at liberty if there were no further charges against them. Maître Merlin asked for the sum of 120,000 francs to be awarded to Didier Fualdès as recompense for the objects stolen, solely in the interests of his creditors. The prosecutor then rose and demanded the death penalty for Bastide, Jausion, Bax, Colard and Madame Bancal; hard labour for life for Anne Benoît and Missonier, and two years' imprisonment with a fine of 200 francs for Bousquier. The President and the judges then retired to the council chamber.

They returned at 8 p.m. The President gave sentence as follows : the death penalty for Bastide, Jausion, Colard, Bax and the widow Bancal; Anne Benoît and Missonier hard labour for life, they were also to be branded and exhibited in the stocks. He condemned Bousquier to serve a year in prison and to be fined fifty francs. Costs were awarded against the condemned men, both on behalf of the state and of Didier Fualdès. Maître Merlin demanded an additional sum of 100,000 francs damages on behalf of Didier. Maître Romiguière and Maître Rodier objected that he had never claimed damages but only compensation for objects stolen. The prosecutor suggested the problem should be referred to the civil courts for discussion, and this was agreed.

Maître Romiguière gave notice of appeal, then left immediately for Paris with Madame Pons and Madame Jausion. Didier, hearing of this, hastened after them to prevent, if possible, the appeal being allowed.

On 14th September, all the judges and officers of the court received the homage and felicitations of the Mayor of Rodez and left for Montpellier, taking with them, we are told, the regards and benedictions of the people of Aveyron.

Clarissa was arrested on a charge of bearing false witness : it was later amended to one of complicity in the murder of Monsieur Fualdès.

Didier's arrival in Paris was reported in the press, and he had to use an assumed name in order to avoid the many people who wished to express their sympathy. Bastide's two sisters took lodgings close to the Supreme Court of Appeal, Le Cour de Cassation; Maître Romiguière kept them informed of the progress of their cause. It was entrusted to an able lawyer, Maître Loiseau.

The appeal was heard on 9th October. First the report of the trial was read aloud by Councillor Leconier, and then Maître Loiseau stated the grounds for the appeal, that

(1) Each member of the jury had not been called upon individually by the President to take the oath.

(2) A number of witnesses, twenty or thirty, had not taken the oath in the correct form.

(3) One witness had not taken the oath at all.

(4) The foreman of the jury had not read the verdict as prescribed by law.

Maître Loiseau reminded the court that however strongly they might feel the necessity of inflicting punishment without undue delay for so terrible a crime, the sole questions they had to decide were those concerning the proper administration of the law : had the instructions laid down in the criminal code been scrupulously and completely observed? He maintained they had not. Although if the appeal was successful, he said, it would mean beginning the trial again that had already lasted for twenty-five days, and in the course of which 300 witnesses had been heard who would all have to be heard again, this must not be allowed in the slightest degree to influence their decision. He added that in this instance a delay in carrying out the sentences might serve the cause of justice. All France knew of the hesitations, the contradictions and retractions of one of the principal witnesses, Madame Manson. She had now been arrested, and it was possible she would at last lay aside the mysterious veil of obscurity that still surrounded her actions on the night of the crime; it was possible she would make a complete revelation of the truth. Perhaps other assassins would be unmasked; perhaps it would be found that some of those judged guilty were innocent.

Maître Giraud-Duplessis, advocate-general, then spoke. He considered at some length the various objections that had been raised, and then gave it as his opinion that the first was invalid : all the jurymen had taken the oath, and this was sufficient proof that each had been called upon individually by the President to do so. The third objection he considered invalid also because the witness who had not taken the oath had not been called by the prosecutor but by the President. The fourth objection, that the foreman of the jury couldn't read, he found invalid because it was only chance that had made him the foreman, his name being drawn first from the urn.

Maître Loiseau's third objection, however, that a number of the witnesses had not taken the oath in full, some having left out the words 'Nothing but the truth' and others the words 'without hatred and without fear' was a valid reason to declare the verdict nul and void. Even if the oath had actually been taken in full, which was no doubt the case, and it was only the careless reporting of the Clerk of the Court, they were bound to judge in accordance with the records. He concluded :

'In spite of what the counsel for the appellants has said I do not think an annulment will be to the advantage of the accused. One jury has given a verdict of guilty : it is very difficult to imagine that another jury will reverse this decision. There will be many days, many weeks, many months perhaps, during which their agony will be prolonged : they will have constantly before their eyes the fatal knife of the guillotine that threatens them. During this time they will suffer all the agonies, all the horrors of death which are a hundred times more harrowing than death itself – and why? Because the Clerk of the Court has omitted to record all the formalities of the oath prescribed by article 317 of the criminal code which almost certainly was in fact complied with. It is in my opinion a calamity both for the accused and for the public interest, but however that may be, gentlemen, the law is there, and only the law can be invoked in the Supreme Court of Appeal.'

After deliberating for an hour, the court annulled the proceedings of the court of the assizes of the Aveyron for contravention of Article 317 of the criminal code. Because it was laid down that when a retrial was ordered the case should come before a higher court, it was sent up to the assizes of Albi which came within the competence of the Royal Court of Toulouse.

CHAPTER ELEVEN

Clarissa Captive

The news of the Supreme Court of Appeal's decision was brought post haste to Rodez where the people took it as a personal affront : they felt their town was being dishonoured by the failure of the authorities to punish the crime within their own territory. The delay in executing Bastide and Jausion was looked upon as a concession to their wealth and family connections : a hostile demonstration was feared, and an attempt to prevent by force their removal to Albi. Women were still unwilling to enter the rue des Hebdomadiers after dark, and if they had to do so they hurried past the Maison Bancal with averted eyes : the general opinion was that it should be demolished. The closed and shuttered houses of the Fualdès and the Jausion families faced each other in silence across the Place de la Cité.

To counteract the prevailing gloom and indignation the authorities began to show great activity in preparing for the retrial and seeking for new evidence : this was all the more necessary because, they must have been well aware, the verdict had been secured more by moving appeals to the prejudices of the citizens and the derogatory statements of hostile witnesses than to any evidence that the accused were guilty : it still rested on the stories of the Bancal children, on Bousquier's statement of what he claimed to have seen immediately after the crime had been committed and on Clarissa's assertions and contradictions – all of which were open to objections of one kind or another. Now that the accused were no longer feared, more than eighty new witnesses were encouraged, or volunteered, to come forward and offer to testify against them. On the other side, several witnesses reported that Bessières-Veynac was actively engaged in collecting evidence to support his uncle's alibi : he was again arrested, together with Charlotte Arlabosse, Bastide's young woman from La Roquette, and Monsieur Yence the public notary, Bastide's uncle : this was the response to Clarissa's outburst in court that all the assassins had not been arrested. A Spanish family, the Saavedras, who had occupied the room above the Bancals' kitchen and who had disappeared soon after the crime, were traced to a neighbouring village : a commission was sent to question them, and important revelations were expected. When the commission returned, however, it was announced their testimony was insignificant.

One result of the Supreme Court of Appeal's decision was that Clarissa, instead of being tried separately, was included in the number of the accused to be tried at Albi. In the meantime she was lodged in the prison at Rodez that had once been the home of the Capuchin Friars : her room had a neat stone floor, a heavily-barred arched window, two chairs, a table and a bed. There was a fire in the room, and a cot had been supplied for her son Edward, Kleinking, who was with her. He was then five years old.

Crowded together in another room of the same prison were the ex-soldier Colard with his Anne Benoît, inseparable lovers – it was rumoured they were both paying court to the public executioner with a view to succeeding him in his office : La Bancal, all in black and silent, the picture of secret vice and misery : the shifty and deceitful Bax and the imbecile Missonier.

The two principal accused were held in the prison of the Cordeliers, the Grey Friars, an ancient building near the western ramparts with grass and ivy growing between the disjointed stones of the façade. The public were allowed to view them through a small barred window.

It was rumoured Rose Pierret had fled, and that she had been arrested working in a *modiste*'s shop in Toulouse : but this turned out to be a case of mistaken identity. Another girl whose name was Rose had been brought in and questioned, and released again when it was discovered she was the wrong one. The real Rose Pierret was still in Rodez with her father : as commander of the departmental police he occupied rooms in a house beside the ancient church that now served as a stable for his horses. Rose had a room on the first floor; it was very small and neat. The walls were hung with Indian tapestry of floral design; there were pictures also, in black wooden frames, and a large mirror. Her curtains were very white, and fringed. She could often be seen sitting at her casement window, looking out onto the street and dreaming. She usually wore a mop cap with ribbons, and a light brown shawl round her shoulders.

Gradually as the weeks passed by, some members of the public began to feel pity for the hopeless case of the condemned men and sympathy for their families : then came the startling news that Bastide had attempted to escape and would probably have succeeded had it not been for the vigilance of the gaoler : the wildest rumours spread about the town, and every stranger was suspected of complicity. Realising Bastide was still a formidable character, the people were again united in their detestation of his crime and in the urgent necessity to punish him.

When the representative of *Le Sténographe Parisien*, Monsieur de Latouche, went to the prison of the Cordeliers to find out what had happened, he was told Bastide had noticed there was some broken masonry high up in the wall – it was a window opening that had been only partially blocked up – and that there was a convenient staple close to it sticking out of the wall. It didn't seem at first sight to offer a possible way of escape. Bastide, who wanted always to be occupied, had obtained permission to make baskets for which Madame Bastide brought him the materials and took away the finished articles. Next he turned to making *chaudières* – contraptions for holding laundry while it was being dried in a furnace – and fishing nets. He employed some of the convicts to help him in this work. When, during the night of 3rd-4th December, they were surprised by the guards there was a thirty-foot ladder hanging from the staple, and Bastide with a pack on his back was about to ascend it. From the top of the ladder he could have got through the hole in the wall, jumped down onto the roof of another building and escaped from the town on the side where no guards had been posted. The ladder, expertly constructed, was displayed at the entrance to the prison : the villagers came from miles around to see this wonder and stood gaping at it for hours at a time.

When de Latouche looked into the semi-darkness of the vast refectory on the ground floor of the Cordeliers, he saw Bastide and Jausion with twenty-three other prisoners, convicted robbers, all in chains. Bastide too was in chains because of his escape attempt, although since his sentence had been annulled he was again technically innocent. Jausion had taken no part in the attempt : he was in chains because, the gaoler explained, Madame Jausion on a visit to the prison had managed to slip a note to him which he had immediately chewed up, but a few legible words had been recovered which revealed there was a plot to free the prisoners on their way to Albi : therefore precautions had been taken. These two were sitting apart from the others on a bench at the foot of an unmade bed, and they were being waited on by a convict who painfully dragged a ball and chain, secured to his ankle, across the uneven stone floor.

Bastide was wearing peasant costume – dust-coloured trousers, a short blue cotton jacket, a waistcoat of variegated colours, heavy shoes and a bonnet of black silk. His face was pale and he had grown a black beard. Even in these miserable conditions he gave an impression of sinister power and authority : he was an imposing figure among the emaciated wretches that surrounded him. While de Latouche watched, he ate heartily from a wooden bowl and drank several cups of wine : Jausion, in a long grey cloak that reached down to his ankles, sipped some coffee as if it disgusted him.

Rodat had free access to Clarissa in her captivity : he was known to be a friend of the Enjalran family, and he enjoyed the confidence of the authorities who counted on his influence to encourage her to disclose all she had seen. He was looked upon as her guardian. Her father even now did not quite despair of her, in spite of his letter to the President of the Court saying if she didn't speak out she was making herself the accomplice of the assassins – a letter which may have influenced the authorities to arrest her : he came to her one day and told her Monsieur Manson was claiming the custody of Kleinking : he had opposed this claim, he said, on the grounds that the child was too young to leave his mother.

Monsieur Manson, however, had insisted he must not remain in the prison, and so they had agreed between them he should be taken to the Château Perier to be cared for by his grandparents. Clarissa wept bitterly. Her father took the opportunity to try once more to get her to confess she had been in the Maison Bancal : she firmly denied it.

'Then,' said her father, 'You will end on the gallows.' At this she dried her tears and began to laugh. 'Or,' he continued, 'you'll pass the rest of your days in a state prison.'

She stopped laughing and turned pale : 'Why, if I am not guilty should I be deprived of my liberty, more dear to me than life ?'

He quickly followed up his advantage by announcing triumphantly, 'I'll confront you with someone who will force you to admit the truth !'

'No one,' she retorted, 'can make me say more than I intend to say.'

With that he sent for the gaoler and told him to go and fetch Madame Bancal.

The gaoler demurred, but as Père Enjalran was a magistrate and also President of the Provost's Court, he finally did as he was bid.

Madame Bancal was brought in : she stood before them with the same closed expressionless face that all through the trial had never varied. He questioned her :

Do you know my daughter ? –No. I saw her for the first time when she appeared at the trial.

Then why, when the President of the Court was urging her to confess she had been in your house, did you mutter, 'She was there. Why doesn't she say so.' ? –I did not. That imbecile of a gendarme misunderstood what I was saying. Nothing happened in my house that night. I don't know what you're all talking about.

But your own daughter Madeleine claims she saw her there on the evening of 19th March? –Madeleine is a little imbecile who for fifteen sous would have her mother guillotined !

Père Enjalran gave up and left in disgust, taking Kleinking with him. Clarissa sat for hours looking at the empty cot, and she refused to let it be taken away. That night she wrote on the walls of her prison :

> Whatever my fate may be
> My heart will know how to sustain it.
> Unfortunate, not guilty,
> I appeal to the future to judge me.
> They believe I was an accomplice in a terrible crime;
> Time will bring me back my honour
> And on Clarissa's tomb
> They will come to weep her misfortunes.

We now come to one of the most solemn and indispensable preliminaries of a criminal trial, the interrogations, which in France are conducted by a magistrate after a suspect has been arrested : in the old days they were, in fact, the trial. Although this had been changed and a verdict could only be given on the evidence the jury actually heard, they were still considered one of the most important means of discovering the truth. An account of Clarissa's interrogation by the examining magistrate Bertrandi appeared in the press. It went like this :

For a long time she maintained an obstinate silence, then suddenly burst out : 'Why do you insist on interrogating me? Is it not agreed I tell lies? Do you think you can make me say more than I wish to say? I am like the earth in my father's garden; if you dig down a foot you reach the granite. I may share my small secrets with you, but my great secrets . . . only the Devil knows them, and I am an angel ! The President told me so. What do you think of that?'

'Justice has not yet despaired of you,' the magistrate assured her, 'You can still confess at last what you have so long disputed. What will the people of Rodez think of you if you continue to obstruct the course of justice?'

Clarissa's contempt, however, for the public was unbounded : '*Quos potest rodere, rodit,*' she answered, '*Et quos non rodit, odit.*' [They disparage what they can, and what they can't, they hate.]

'Which proves,' countered Bertrandi, 'that the wisdom of nations enshrined in proverbs is sometimes at fault, for what could be finer than the generous support unanimously given by the people of Rodez to their magistrates in this crisis in our history?'

There was a long pause, then Clarissa asked, 'Aren't you tired of me? I'm certainly tired of you.' The interrogation continued :

Think of your situation, of your family, of your child! For all the thrones in the world I wouldn't choose to have to answer the terrible accusation that hangs over you! –That of complicity?

I have warned you. –The truth! That's what you want, isn't it? Only the truth. Nothing more than that. I'm sure the idea of complicity never entered your head.

When will you declare the truth? –At Albi.

And you will actually let yourself be taken there and accused? –Yes, I will – beside Anne Benoît and La Bancal.

Beside Bax, Missonier and Colard, those vile criminals? –All was well with Our Saviour between two robbers.

He saved one of them. You won't save anybody. –Yes, he saved one of them, and Himself . . . and where is my son? Where is he? They have taken him from me. Do they know what they are doing? In the midst of sorrows my spirit wanders. . . . My head will fall, but it is a ball that will knock down many skittles.

What does that mean? –It's perfectly obvious to me. You want me to talk? Very well. I'll dictate an important statement. [She turned to the waiting clerk.] Are you ready? Then write. . . . *'Turpe est mentire.'* [It is wicked to tell lies.] (There was a long pause.)

Well? Go on. –Was it Horace said that?

Never mind who said it. Go on with your statement. –I'm sorry. I thought you would know, being a magistrate. . . . There now, you've interrupted me and I have forgotten what I was going to say. . . .

And so it went on, hour after hour. She constantly changed the subject or poured out a stream of irrelevant details. At the end of the interrogation, the magistrate was exhausted, and he had learned precisely nothing. Clarissa was interrogated again and again, sometimes for six or seven hours at a time, but she never disclosed anything of value to the prosecution.

At this time she was desperately unhappy because Madame Pons, whom she had expected to come running as soon as she heard she was in prison, did not come, and did not even send a message. Rodat tried to explain to her Madame Pons was acting wisely – that if she had come they might both have been hopelessly compromised – but she remained inconsolable. 'I can bear witness,' he wrote, 'it was not Clarissa who abandoned Madame Pons : it was the other way round.'

One day, it was in the depths of winter, Monsieur Henri de Latouche came to the prison with a permit to interview Clarissa, 'The woman,' he said, 'who has become the astonishment of France.' He produced his credentials showing he was the special representative of *Le Sténographe Parisien*, sent to cover the trial at Albi. Much as Rodat deplored the publicity being given to the case, he could not refuse to admit him. Asking him to wait, he went and told her, at the same time warning her to say as little as possible to him, fearing, as always, her indiscretion.

Latouche followed Rodat up the broad staircase that led to the monks' old dormitory through which they had to pass to reach Clarissa's room : he was glancing eagerly from side to side, taking in everything that might be useful as background material for an article. Clarissa received him with becoming modesty. She liked him from the first; he was, indeed, an affable and cultured gentleman, carefully dressed but with an affectation of artistic disarray about his collar and large cravat. She was unpopular at the time both with the magistrates and with the people of Rodez, and she was grateful for his assurances of her growing renown in the rest of France.

'Everywhere on my journey here,' he told them, 'I found people, from the most frivolous to the most serious, were preoccupied with the mysterious Madame Manson.' Of course Rodat could see Latouche was flattering her, no doubt to get at her secret or, at least, to wheedle some exclusive information out of her.

'The little provincial housewives,' he continued, 'forgot to discuss the latest fashions to ask about the procedure of the trial and how she was implicated : some called her an actress; some an angel from Heaven! Even the English travellers, who swarm along the roads of Provence at this time of the year, enquired for the latest news about her after the price of the wines and the speed of the horses : the merchants on the exchanges neglected their business; the inexhaustible subject of every conversation was the great trial at Rodez and the secret of Madame Manson!'

Clarissa was delighted, of course, 'But what secret?' she asked. 'I have already said I have never entered the Bancals' house.'

'What a pity!' He shook his head sadly, but came back at once to his subject : 'In that case, wouldn't it have been better, in your present situation, if you had confessed also your irreparable, and to me inexplicable fault, of having dared to make charges against the accused without having seen with your own eyes the murder actually being committed? What was, for you, the evidence of Bastide's and Jausion's crime? What right had you, without personal knowledge of the murder, to say, "Confess you wretch!" and "Take away these assassins out of my sight!"?'

This plain speaking didn't worry Clarissa at all. 'It may be,' she allowed, 'that my conduct was inconceivable, but all the same I was never in that house. They don't understand the power of an exasperated imagination!' ('What on earth could she mean by that?' Rodat thought. 'It was she who exasperated everyone else!') 'Heads are cool here,' she went on. 'I should not have been born in the Aveyron, and above all I should not be judged here. What if I am condemned?'

They both hastened to assure her no one believed the charge of complicity could be made good. 'I really think,' she continued, 'for the *dénouement* of this famous tragedy I should be brought to the foot of the scaffold. Then, perhaps, the woman who really witnessed the murder, and for whom I have suffered so much, would make herself known and rescue me from the jaws of death!'

She loved to imagine these situations and perhaps unconsciously steered herself towards them without ever considering what would happen if the other woman didn't turn up at the dramatic moment, and that probably she didn't even exist. She entertained them for a while with similar unrealistic nonsense, and finally Monsieur de Latouche left without being any the wiser about her secret, or having any idea whether she was speaking the truth or not.

However, it seemed she had found a new champion, for he wrote in his bi-weekly letter to his editor:

Justice will seek in vain to extract a precise confession from this singular witness: like everyone else here she has adopted a system of constant denial and obscurity. I am very far from abandoning in her favour my duty to be impartial, but I confess there are aspects of her conduct that must excite the greatest interest. Her veil of secrecy lends her a charm, romantic if you wish, but which does not combine with any suggestion of participation in a crime. Actually so far she is not accused of anything but mystery, and who knows if her silence and her reserve have not a reason that is at least respectable, and perhaps heroic?

He described Rodat merely as 'a clerical-looking gentleman'.

Next day he called again and suggested she should write her memoirs. Rodat groaned inwardly when he heard this: he could see she was taken with the idea, and he feared that anything written in her present mood

could only complicate things still further : but for her it had one overwhelming advantage – it would be a way of reaching out to Madame
Pons who would be certain to read them. She demurred at first, but
Latouche told her it would be quite easy : all she had to do was to dictate
them to him, and he would not only write them down but edit them and
arrange for their publication. He added that she would make a handsome
profit. This was important to her : since she had quarrelled with her
father and was no longer sharing Madame Pons's purse, she had only a
meagre allowance from Monsieur Manson to live on, so she agreed to
his proposition. After that de Latouche came every day, and she poured
out her 'memoirs' to him. They were in the form of a long letter to 'the
dearest and most understanding of mothers'. There followed what Rodat
considered a lying account of her experiences, and a complete denial she
had ever been in the Maison Bancal. Three weeks later the manuscript
was ready : de Latouche sent it to Monsieur Pillet in Paris, editor and
printer of *La Gazette de France*. Rodat looked upon her memoirs as a
final proof of her fanatical friendship for Madame Pons :

> The inconsequent Clarissa hoped to bring Madame Pons to her again,
> but she did not respond to the appeal : she had too much sense not to
> feel the futility of the publicity stirred up by this lying manuscript, or
> possibly she no longer needed Clarissa, but it is certain that from this
> time she entirely neglected her.

The prefects of Aveyron and of the neighbouring province of Tarn had
concerted prudent measures for the safe transport of the prisoners from
Rodez to Albi, and had also established police posts at intervals along
the narrow mountain roads that separated the two towns. It had been
arranged Clarissa should be transferred first so that she would not have to
travel with the rest of the accused. When she was about to leave the
Capuchin Prison, now celebrated because of her, the magistrate Bertrandi
was still trying despairingly to get her to make a positive statement; she
brushed him off lightly, merely repeating if she had a secret she would
divulge it at Albi. The wife of the concierge, who adored her, dissolved
into tears when she said goodbye. De Latouche left at the same time to
report anything that might happen on the journey, for Clarissa was news.
The faithful Rodat also followed her.

It was a cold grey morning and the Angelus was ringing as they rode
out of the town with an escort of dragoons. After a few miles they came
upon a peasant woman whose cart, loaded with vegetables for the market,
was stuck in a snowdrift : Clarissa drew rein, spoke to the woman, who

was in great distress, and persuaded the dragoons to extricate the cart and help her on her way. At every farm and village the people ran out to see her pass : at one place they were so importunate that she set spurs to her horse, the escort were obliged to do the same to keep up with her, and they passed through it at a wild gallop. That night they put up at Sauveterre : on the second night they reached Pampeloune, the frontier between Aveyron and Tarn. Here she was handed over to a new escort consisting of three officers and seven gendarmes from Albi. She warmly thanked the dragoons for escorting her thus far, and with some emotion took leave of them.

Albi, once a Rhutenian provincial capital, lies in the centre of a wide and fertile valley where there is everything to delight and to inspire mankind : but it must for ever be associated with one of the most dreadful injustices in the bloodstained history of Europe, the extirpation of the 'Albigensian Heresy'. Many of the people of Albi and Languedoc had attained a level of spiritual development, of gentleness and purity of life, that has not since been achieved in the West. Their initiates, or *Perfecti* as they were called, set an example to the common people of humble devotion to their rather strange creed that was in strong contrast to the luxury and rapacity of the local priests and abbots.

They might eventually have reformed the Catholic Church; but Pope Innocent III instituted a crusade against them. An army of 200,000 men under the ferocious Simon de Montfort was sent to invade Languedoc with orders to kill or re-convert the inhabitants : when the Pope's legate was asked how they were to tell the heretics from the true Catholics, he replied, 'Kill them all! God will know his own!' Thousands were slaughtered with appalling savagery. With the aid of the Inquisition, the heresy was stamped out so effectively that nothing like it was attempted again for another 500 years.

The landscape is dominated by a tower that from a distance looks like an immense ruin but which is, in fact, the bell tower of the Church of St Cecilia : it was built, not as a memorial to the slaughtered innocents, but to celebrate the triumph of their slaughterers, a symbol, therefore, not of love and charity but of prejudice, intolerance and cruelty. It stands 400 feet high. The shining river Var hurls itself in vain against the foundations of the church below it which is constructed like a fortress.

Clarissa and her escort arrived at Albi a little after midday on 6th January, entering through the Faubourg du Pont: the houses, all of brick, had large windows and high ceilings, suggesting a warmer climate, and there were terraced gardens and views of distant hills. Numerous spectators had been waiting there since early morning to see her : some ran on ahead, some lined the street, others crowded to their windows to watch her pass : she threw back the hood of her cloak and saluted them with great affability, managing her horse with grace and skill. She asked the Captain of the Guard if he would enquire at the *poste restante* if a book had arrived for her : she had not yet received a copy of her memoirs. Next she asked where she would be lodged, and he replied, 'In the prison of St Cecilia.' She said she liked the idea, for she would be under the protection of the patron saint of harmony and music. She told the captain how glad she was to have left Rodez, and that her prison there reminded her of St Cecilia's description of Hell : 'A place *infecte* where one has no friends,' a remark that was scarcely justified, considering how well she had been treated there.

At Albi too, a cell had been converted for her use and made comfortable : except for the barred windows, it was more like a small private room than a prison. All this was widely reported, and not only in France. *La Gazette de Lausanne* wrote :

> It seems Madame Manson constantly aspires to greater and greater celebrity : we already have her *Letters*; she is publishing her memoirs. She wishes to conduct her own defence, she writes verse, she speaks Latin, she subscribes to the fund for shipwrecked mariners, she pays careful attention to her toilet, her sayings are quoted for their wit and their sentiments. Four months ago she was unknown outside the Aveyron : suddenly her fame has crossed the Alps, the Pyrenees, the Rhine and the Danube.

On 26th January a crowd gathered at first light outside the Capuchin Prison at Rodez. A troop of dragoons and two companies of grenadiers made their way through them, halted, and stood silently waiting. At 6.30 a.m. a cordon of police forced the people back to allow three farm carts to be driven up to the main entrance. The doors opened. Colard, Bax and Missonier were brought out and put into the first cart with a gendarme; Madame Bancal and Anne Benoît were put into the second with two gendarmes; Bastide and Jausion into the third. All the prisoners were loaded with chains which were secured to posts in the carts. Bastide stood up and addressed the crowd : he expressed his intense regret that the people among whom he had been born had so misjudged him.

He evidently believed, or affected to believe, the verdict of guilty pronounced against him was the direct result of the vindictiveness of his fellow townsmen, and at Albi his innocence would be established, for he concluded with a great shout, 'I shall never return to this accursed place where people are crucified!' Then he sent the gaoler for bread and wine, and he was seen to be eating and drinking heartily as he was driven away.

One company of grenadiers marched ahead to clear the road, then the carts followed, surrounded by gendarmes and by thirty-seven dragoons; the second company of grenadiers brought up the rear. Bousquier rode among the escort, disguised as a gendarme. The crowd trailed after them for a mile or two, and some on horse-back followed all the way. The weather was very fine, the roads clear of snow. They reached Pampeloune on the evening of the same day where they were joined by a strong force of gendarmes from the department of Tarn. At half-past three in the afternoon of the following day they reached Albi and were met by a vast crowd. While they were passing along the quay by the river Madame Bancal, who never altered her expression, was greeted with boos and catcalls. These prisoners too were taken to cells in the ancient Convent of St Cecilia which had been strengthened and fortified. Bousquier was lodged with the Sisters of Mercy who were given orders to refuse admittance to anyone asking to see him.

'What a great debt justice owes to the magistrates of Rodez!' de Latouche wrote in his letter to Paris, 'and particularly to the mayor and the prefect for the trouble they have taken, and their constant vigilance for more than a year! Their steadfast resistance to the solicitations of interested parties, their respect for the rights of the accused! The conscientiousness with which the magistrates have carried out all their duties will surely be recognised by the Ministry.'

Rodat could sense that Clarissa no longer regarded him as her most intimate friend and adviser, but as he was the only member of her family near her, he took lodgings in Albi and hoped to find an opportunity to save her from the worst consequences of her follies.

Didier Fualdès, it was reported, 'that interesting young man', had arrived on 11th January. The Bastide and the Jausion families had taken a house together : they seemed, de Latouche wrote, like families afflicted by a mortal contagion, more completely damned than the accused themselves. Bastide's sisters climbed the great bell tower and looked down, hoping to communicate with him by signals : their purpose was discovered and the tower was closed to the public. The arrogant Clémendot also came to Albi : Clarissa's memoirs were being widely read and he was so unpopular he had difficulty in finding anywhere to live, but he showed himself on the boulevards and behaved so pleasantly to the ladies that they soon decided Clarissa's description of him was prejudiced. He said he had not read the famous memoirs – he seemed to be the only person in

France of any consequence who had not done so, except Clarissa herself who was still waiting for her copy.

More and more journalists arrived : they complained bitterly that the authorities would release very little information about the interrogations that were known to be taking place, or even give an exact date for the opening of the trial. This secrecy was supposed to be in the interests of justice but it was felt as a great inconvenience by the numerous tourists who had flocked to the town in the hope of witnessing the proceedings. The inhabitants of Albi were a handsome race, the men well educated, the women charming, but mindful of ancient persecution they were distrustful of foreigners and rarely intermarried with the people of other towns : consequently they were of a distinctive type marked, like the mountaineers, by heavy dark eyebrows meeting in the centre. Their local officials aroused the resentment particularly of the visiting Parisians who complained they were as inhospitable and authoritarian as if they were still living in the days of the Empire. The journalists, however, succeeded in obtaining interviews with all who were even remotely concerned with the case; they kept the public informed of the latest rumours and also published details about the daily lives of the accused.

Anne Benoît and the soldier, Colard, continued to scandalise everyone by their unrestrained passion : when separated so that they could no longer see each other, they constantly shouted and listened for the other's voice : ignorant of how to write, they had no other means of communication. Anne Benoît, it was said, had lost none of her freshness, but Colard was in a furious temper most of the time. 'It is Madame Manson,' they told reporters, 'who is responsible for all our misfortunes. As she was in the Bancals' kitchen, why doesn't she tell them we were not there, that we are innocent ?'

One day Anne Benoît was in despair : Colard had been taken to another prison and put in the condemned cell, known as 'The Dungeon of Hell.' It was rumoured he had confessed everything and his testimony fitted in perfectly with that of Bousquier – but it transpired that the removal had merely been in response to the request of the painter, Monsieur Sudre, a pupil of David : he had permission to make a portrait study of each of the accused, and he found the light in the condemned cell was exactly what he wanted. When the portrait was finished, Colard was sent back to his original prison and each of the accused in turn had a spell in the condemned cell so that Monsieur Sudre might have a complete series of portraits. Another painter, Monsieur Persico, made fulllength studies of Bastide and Jausion, and exhibited them, on profitable terms, in his studio.

When Missonier was asked to choose a lawyer to represent him, he replied, 'What? Is the affair still going on? Maître Grandet at Rodez defended me very well; I don't want anybody else.' It was explained to him Maître Grandet couldn't come to Albi, so he then said, 'In that case I'll entrust myself to the cutler with whom I served as an apprentice; he won't let anyone harm me.' When Maître Grandet was told of this he cancelled his other engagements and came to Albi. It was rumoured, and not denied by the authorities, that Bax had turned King's Evidence.

The most eminent lawyer in the town, Maître Boyer, was instructed to defend Clarissa; but he excused himself, producing a medical certificate, and delegated the task to the youngest of his colleagues, Maître Tarreaux, an earnest young man, but not an eloquent speaker : Clarissa told him she would plead her own case but that he might prepare it. He at once set to work, but finding no basis of agreement between his client and himself, he too withdrew from the case.

One evening the news leaked out Clarissa had been taken to the Palais de Justice under cover of darkness to be interrogated : a crowd gathered to get a sight of her on the way back : their lights made the street as bright as day. When she appeared they rushed forward and thrust their torches in her face to see if they could detect any signs of emotion, or read in her expression whether she had made any important disclosures. The gendarmes with difficulty cleared a path for her. The official policy of not releasing any information had merely increased the excitement and mystery that surrounded her.

The mayor, who had once been Mayor of Brest and considered himself an important personage, was in sole control of the prison guards and gaolers. Soon after Clarissa's arrival he came to her and said, 'Madame, I shall neglect nothing for your comfort and welfare. You have only to command me and you shall be obeyed.'

'Splendid!' she replied. 'Now I shall put you to the test. Let me take your arm and you shall show me the sights of the town.'

Nothing could have been further from his intention than to go for a walk with his prisoner. He turned abruptly and went out, followed by her mocking laughter. From then on he treated her very strictly, and he came every day to make sure she was still in her cell. Even her lawyer and the prison doctor were not permitted to see her without witnesses. Everyone leaving the prison was rigorously searched because she had been forbidden to communicate in any way with her friends.

He soon found she had ignored his orders and sent out several notes. 'If you continue to disobey me,' he told her, 'I shall increase the rigour of your imprisonment.'

'How can you?' she retorted. 'You already have two men at the front entrance, two on the stairs, two outside my room and two inside. I don't see what else you can do unless you put them to bed with me!'

On another day he came fuming into her room without even taking off his hat, accused her of sending a letter again and demanded to know who had taken it out for her. 'I thought so gallant a gentleman,' she replied, 'wouldn't object to acting as my courier. Last time you were here I took the liberty of slipping my letter into the cuff of your coat sleeve: you took it out for me.'

Thenceforward the mayor not only had to have everybody else searched, he had to search himself every time he left the prison. A month passed before he would even allow her to be taken out for some fresh air and exercise: at last the prison doctor persuaded him to arrange for her to walk daily in the garden of *Monsieur le curé* of St Cecilia which adjoined the prison.

When this was announced in the press, people stood on the rooftops of the surrounding houses to observe her every movement, and they were astonished to see she danced and pirouetted in the garden, though accused of complicity in a murder. Sometimes she didn't appear: there was a recurrence of the haemorrhages from which she had suffered when her romance with Bessières-Veynac came to an end. She never asked for help.

Once when she was found unconscious in her cell and bathed in blood, she said, 'Why do you bring me back to life? Parted from my friends and my child, the prospect of death is the only good I have to look forward to. What should I do in the world, abandoned by all?'

On the anniversary of the murder, 19th March, Rodat was with her: she made an hysterical scene, said she could hear groans . . . blood dripping. . . . Her heart beat violently, she was pale with terror – but when the mayor called, he was eating out of her hand now, she went gaily out with him to the garden. Later that day the parishioners of St Cecilia were prevented by gendarmes from entering the church to hear Mass: the *curé* got as far as the porch, only to find the door locked and guarded. 'No one enters!' he was told, so he had to remain in the porch with only one sinner, the sentry. The explanation was that the mayor was showing Madame Manson the beauties of the interior, the windows, the choir-stalls, and particularly the Renaissance frescoes in which she had expressed an interest.

Opinion was sharply divided about Clarissa: some condemned her out of hand, others set no bounds to their admiration: these became known as Mansonites. The majority regarded her with the sympathy to which

Anne Benoît, drawn by Sudre.

Colard, drawn by Sudre.

Maître Romiguière.

Théron, the miller.

The Court Scene at Albi.

The prison at Albi.

Clarissa Manson in court.

Clarissa Manson in prison.

her misfortunes entitled her : a bookseller named Rami suggested she should write a book for him to be entitled, *The Encyclopedia of Misfortune*, for the guidance of the young. Another admirer offered to put her in charge of his lemonade factory as soon as she should be acquitted.

She refused both these offers, but she published a short work which she called, *My Plan of Defence in the Fualdès Trial, addressed to all sensitive hearts*. This left everything as confused as it was before : in it she lamented that although she denied she was in the Maison Bancal on the night of the murder, the conviction she had in fact been there was so firmly established she saw not how to dispute it. She explained that the Prefect of Aveyron, guided by the most noble sentiments of equity and justice had persuaded her to sign a confession, and she asked her readers, 'Was it true? I can't exactly say it was . . . but we shall see. Time is the great controller of our destinies, it causes revolutions, it brings about changes in people's minds as in events.'

She appealed for pity because the misfortunes that had dogged her all her life would reach their culminating point if she could not clear herself of complicity. Then she disputed the evidence of several witnesses who were heard at Rodez, that of Madame Constans in particular, but she admitted it was not impossible that she had been seen in the Maison Bancal. It hardly amounted to a plan of defence. She made one valid point – that if the stories believed about her were true, Bastide had wished to kill her : therefore she was not his accomplice.

There was a very disturbing incident about this time : Clarissa said she had noticed, while walking alone in the presbytery garden, a piece of paper folded at the bottom of a vase : she had taken it out and read on it the following words; *'You have already said too much. If you do not retract you will perish, you and your son, by dagger or by poison.'* She claimed to have been terrified. She wrote at once to the President of the Court of Albi enclosing the note and asking him to take the measures that were necessary for her safety. The President circulated copies to the accused and to the barristers concerned. The *curé*'s servant was arrested for having allowed one of the conspirators to enter the garden. The incident was obviously highly suspect because no one intending her to read the note would have left it at the bottom of a vase where she would be most unlikely to see it.

As soon as the mid-lenten fair at Rodez was over, it was held on 17th March, 120 witnesses for the prosecution were transported to Albi : 200 more came a week later. For their travel and maintenance, 60,000 francs had been advanced by the government : it was expected the whole of this sum would be recovered from the estates of Bastide and Jausion. The Bancal children were also brought to Albi and lodged in the same hospice as Bousquier. These witnesses freely gave interviews to the press, and their stories highly prejudicial to the accused were featured from day to day.

For one moment Rodat thought Clarissa was lost : Clémendot's memoirs appeared, and opinion turned strongly against her. Though her own memoirs had been eagerly subscribed for, they had been a disappointment : people weren't interested in reading she hadn't been in the Maison Bancal; they preferred Clémendot's version that she had. Her *Plan of Defence* had in part corrected this, but something she had written in it apparently offended de Latouche perhaps because it was at variance with much they had written together in her memoirs : anyway his attitude towards her abruptly changed. In his bi-weekly letter to Paris he praised Clémendot and wrote ironically of Clarissa's love of publicity. Rodat again became her closest friend and supporter : she again took his advice and resolved 'to give up her retractions and evasions and, quite simply, to divulge the truth.' When she formed this resolution, he tells us, a weight lifted from his heart, and he hastened to inform her family. Her mother replied,

> It was my hope that while she was in prison, and separated from those who were encouraging her false opinions, she would return to more just and reasonable ideas. All my hopes are founded in my God and in the true morality of the prosecutor and the President of the Court.

Clarissa told him she had received further threatening notes, but had treated them with contempt. She wrote,

> At last, my dearest Auguste, I am truly happy. Now I have determined to disclose the truth, the relief to my conscience has calmed my torments and dispelled the visions born of my distracted imagination.

Meanwhile the carpenters were busy erecting stands to accommodate 2,000 people in the courtroom of the Palais de Justice : it was as if Albi wanted to do everything on a grander scale than Rodez and to show how things really should be done. Rents were soaring together with the cost of living, and it was impossible to find lodgings. Tickets for the opening day were at a premium. The shopkeepers, however, complained that the great influx was of ladies of easy virtue and others who wished to make money off the tourists, rather than *bona fide* tourists who could afford to spend it.

CHAPTER TWELVE

Truth Veiled

The second trial opened at last on 25th March, 1818. By nine o'clock in the morning all the available seats were occupied by the most notable people of Albi, by visiting strangers and by the women most remarkable for their beauty or as leaders of fashion. The members of the press, Monsieur de Latouche prominent among them, stylishly dressed, had small inividual tables below the jury box: they included Monsieur Olivier of *La Quotidienne* and representatives of *Le Moniteur* and *Le Journal de Paris*. At ten o'clock about 300 witnesses were conducted to the places reserved for them: the public and the press were particularly interested in Rose Pierret, '*une fort jolie personne*,' whom Clarissa in her interrogations had continued to accuse of knowing more than she would admit. Clémendot also attracted attention; he was a dashing figure in his uniform. Meanwhile the court was hearing Mass in the church of St Cecilia.

A sedan chair with police escort was sent to bring Clarissa: she was booed when she left the prison. To avoid the pushing throng she told her chairmen to make their way along the steps in front of the church: in attempting to do so, one of them stumbled, Clarissa screamed, and the escort just saved the chair from rolling down into the crowd. The rest of the accused, all handcuffed, were brought from their prison in a large iron cage on wheels, the invention of the mayor and the chief of police: it was like a circus cage except they could not move about in it like wild animals for each of them was chained to an iron ring bolted to the floor.

When they were led into the courtroom all the spectators in a spontaneous movement stood up and tried to read their guilt in their faces. Bastide was the one who had suffered least from his long imprisonment: he had shaved off his beard and was perfectly calm and smiling: his complete lack of concern for the situation he was in was somehow frightening. Madame Bancal looked haggard with sunken cheeks. Jausion was pale and discouraged – it was agreed his attitude was more appropriate under the circumstances than Bastide's. Anne Benoît, wearing a hat with a low brim, surprised reporters by her pleasant appearance : Colard was brusque and indignant as usual and careless of his dress. Bax looked thoughtfully into the distance – he was separated from the rest of the accused by two gendarmes.

Finally Clarissa was brought in and given an inconspicuous place 'which could not have been of her own choosing', Monsieur de Latouche unkindly remarked. She was at the far end of the bench of the accused. His view was that Clarissa had given the true version in the memoirs they had written together : she had said her father frightened her into admitting she had been in the Maison Bancal, which was false : why should the authorities now try again to frighten her into saying so? A mistaken verdict in this case would be so dreadful to contemplate that he thought she should be left out of the case altogether. He had written a reasoned reply to her *Plan de Défense* and had it published in Paris.

Clarissa, as always, was quietly but tastefully dressed : she wore a long black veil, so her features were scarcely distinguishable. Didier Fualdès entered next with his lawyer, Maître Tajan : they were allocated seats exactly facing Bastide whose effrontery, Rodat considered, contrasted painfully with the modesty and profound grief written all over the features of that unhappy young man. Finally the barristers for the defence, again headed by Maître Romiguière representing Bastide, took their places : none of the others except Maître Grandet had appeared in the earlier trial.

At 11.30 the court entered : the President, the Chevalier de Faydel, looked surprisingly young for his high office but he had a great reputation for learning and ability. The scene was similar to that at Rodez but there was greater intensity of emotion, partly, Rodat thought, because Clarissa who seemed to be made for love was being arraigned beside the blackest criminals of the age; but probably it was because the accused, being better known than before to the audience, had become more real to them as individuals, and the prolonged uncertainty of their fate had added to the general feeling of suspense. The judges, the prosecutor and the advocate-general made a brave show in their red robes : the guards in their brilliant uniforms not only surrounded the prisoners but were stationed at various points in the courtroom ready to deal with any interruption or disturbance. This time there were only five additional judges or assessors.

The procedure was the same as in the previous trial. The Prefect of Tarn, the Baron Decazes, had filled his list of jurymen with members of the aristocracy, wanting to make sure, no doubt, that they could at least read : no objections were raised to any of them by the defence, nor to any of the judges. The Bill of Indictment, read by the Clerk of the Court, was similar to the one at Rodez except that part of it which concerned Clarissa. It went as follows :

'The trial before the Court of the Assizes at Rodez gave rise to incidents as extraordinary, perhaps, as the trial itself. A woman, Manson, née Enjalran, declared before the Prefect of Aveyron that she had been an eye-witness of the assassination of Sieur Fualdès. She made the same declaration before other witnesses. Later she denied she had ever been in the Maison Bancal where the crime was perpetrated. She persisted in this denial during the trial, but her assertions were contradicted by her expressions, her looks and her gestures. When she saw the accused she went into convulsions and fainting fits, real or simulated, and the words *'poignard'* and *'assassins'* escaped from her lips together with violent denunciations of Bastide and Jausion. For the remainder of the trial she offered variations of her testimony, contradictions, and complete and avowed contempt for the oath she had taken to speak the truth. Finally she audaciously declared the truth could not pass her lips.

'All these circumstances make it abundantly clear the woman Manson had inside knowledge of the mysteries of the crime committed on the person of the unhappy Fualdès, or at least of its consummation . . . her repeated declarations that in what she revealed she was telling only part of the truth and that she would reveal the entire truth during the trial at Albi only confirm and aggravate the indications of her guilt. . . . In consequence, Marie-Françoise-Clarisse Enjalran, wife of Antoine Manson, is accused of aiding or assisting with premeditation the authors of the assassination of Sieur Fualdès, either in aiding or facilitating it, or in consummating it.'

Clarissa endured all this very bravely, occasionally lowering her head, but it was too much for Rodat. He says :

> I saw Clarissa on the bench of the accused among the assassins, like virtue humiliated. There was noble pride on her forehead; I confess it broke my heart. Her pallor made her eyes more bright. I compared this Clarissa, wearing a mourning veil, surrounded by evil, the sword of justice suspended over her head, to the Clarissa of the walnut-grove, brilliant in her youth and grace, her cheeks like roses, her eyes burning with love, eager to learn, searching for her happiness in the future : then all was fair and gracious for her, her heart foresaw only the tears and sacrifices of love : alas ! when the gates of life are about to open can youth foresee any miseries but these ? Comparing these two periods in her life I felt cast down and afflicted : I went out to hide my tears from the insensitive crowd.

The President – the Presiding Judge – then gave a résumé of the circumstances of the assassination that had horrified the town of Rodez, and explained the rights of the citizens and the important function of the jury, 'the happy institution that is a guarantee of impartiality for everyone concerned.' Innocence, he said, would be protected : only crime would find enemies. He spoke at great length, more or less as follows :

'You have just heard the melancholy truth : Sieur Fualdès perished by the hand of an enemy. Suicide is out of the question : death by accident also. An association of evil-doers drawn from every class of society and from both sexes, has torn a citizen from our midst, a father from his son. Some of them, which is even more criminal, if the charges are made good, were in his debt and under obligation to him : they carried out their detestable project in order to keep possession of his property, which they could only do through his death. . . . Rhuthenians ! Shame and obloquy have been heaped upon you to your very walls ! It was within them the plot against Sieur Fualdès was hatched : it was within them, on 19th March, the conspirators gave him a rendezvous to settle his accounts – it was in fact a death trap !

'Eight o'clock on 19th March ! Sieur Fualdès, faithful to his promise, leaves his friends : he suspects nothing. . . . But the conspirators are at their posts . . . they await their victim. They are warned of his approach : shouts are heard, and warning whistles.

'The unfortunate Sieur Fualdès has taken scarcely a hundred paces when from all sides men rush upon him : he is seized, gagged with a large white cloth . . . stifled cries are heard. . . . He was to have had his throat cut in a stable close to where he was seized – but Providence intervened, Providence that confounds human calculations when it wishes to leave the punishment of a crime to the justice of men !

'He was dragged to a house in which, by a chain of circumstances that need not be divulged, there happened to be a woman. She witnessed the preparations and then the consummation of the murder, the crime that has alarmed society and which now demands retribution. For exalted sentimental reasons that will no longer be tolerated, she has forged chains for herself that now hold her captive. She had braved the hazards of facing a serious charge, she had held justice in contempt. Now that a closer experience of legal procedure seems to have disabused her, it is to be hoped she will make a clean breast of the truth, that she will surmount the barrier that has so far prevented her from speaking.'

He then described in dramatic terms Clarissa's experiences in the Maison Bancal, and her escape from death at the hands of the assassins. He continued,

'As soon as the murder became known, there was a general outcry which indicated to the authorities the men against whom justice had to act. Their troubled mien, their agitation, betrayed them; but although already under suspicion, they still wished to reap the fruits of their crime. They descended upon the home of the victim, not to condone with the widow but to commit all sorts of pillage, breaking into a desk, into cupboards, and removing account books, a bag of money and a brief-case. Accused! Do not your consciences silently acknowledge the facts I have proclaimed aloud? Accused! The jury, selected by ballot, are before you!'

After the President, the prosecutor, the Baron Gary, followed, analysing and developing the Bill of Indictment. Then, as at Rodez, the *Cause Civile* intervened, with Maître Tajan claiming damages on behalf of Didier Fualdès: he made practically the same speech as Maître Merlin, dilating upon the horrors of the crime. Didier wept copiously, but managed to address a few words to the jury, explaining that the motives animating him were without hatred and without weakness: they were those of unhappy filial piety claiming justice from the laws. He said:

'A unanimous and solemn verdict has already condemned the accused, but in spite of it the bleeding shade of my father still cries for vengeance. It is time, gentlemen, the public resentment should be satisfied and that an alarmed society and a desolated family should be avenged! It is time the innocent should be set free, and the guilty should mount the scaffold!'

The witnesses were now ordered to withdraw and the hearing began. The first to be called for the prosecution was Louis Lacombe, carpenter. His testimony was important to the President's thesis because he claimed to have overheard Monsieur Fualdès, on 9th March, reproaching Bastide for not having settled a debt, and that Bastide had replied, 'I can't find a halfpenny.' He also claimed to have seen him in Rodez on the morning of 19th March. Bastide maintained with assurance the witness was mistaken both in the date of his conversation with Monsieur Fualdès and its purport, and he gave his own quite different account of what had passed between them. The President questioned him:

Accused Bastide! Your explanations are unacceptable. I tell you your attitude in the conversation reported by the witness was one of a debtor to a creditor. Give me a direct answer: were you, or were you not, in debt to Monsieur Fualdès? –No, I was never his debtor. I did business with him only to help him. I have extricated him several times from embarrassing situations, and his son also.

That bears no resemblance to the truth. Sieur Fualdès's fortune was

large enough for him to be able to lend money when he wished to.
–Really? Then we're living in the age of miracles?

You persist in your statement that you were not in Rodez on the
morning of 19th March? –I do.

The President turned to the witness: 'What was he wearing when you
saw him?'

Lacombe hesitated; 'I don't remember, except that he had an old hat
on.'

'And that, of course,' Bastide commented smiling, 'proves the veracity
of the witness!'

The speeches had lasted so long that no further witnesses were called,
and the court rose at 4.30 p.m. For nearly the whole day, while they were
at their freshest and most receptive, the jury had listened to Bastide's
accusers repeating the horrible story of his alleged crime: no doubt he
considered it necessary by his sharp rejoinders to remind them they had
as yet heard nothing in his defence.

Before the court entered on the second day of the trial, the ushers
brought in the exhibits, *les pièces de conviction*, and piled them onto a
table – the victim's clothes and his cane, the cloth alleged to have been
used to gag him, Colard's shotguns alleged to have been used to arm the
assassins on their march to the river, the bloodstained blanket found in
the Maison Bancal in which, it was also alleged, the body had been
wrapped.

When Bastide and Jausion were brought in, they were wearing additional chains that secured their arms to their necks, a severity which the
authorities evidently considered necessary.* The spectators observed with
interest that Clarissa, the only one not handcuffed, had been given a more
prominent place on the bench of the accused.

As soon as the session was declared open, Maître Romiguière petitioned
to have the trial stopped on the following grounds: he said the Supreme
Court of Appeal had ordered that all those accused of the murder of
Monsieur Fualdès should be taken before the court of the assizes of Tarn
to be heard together in one single trial. This, he maintained, had not
been done; his client could not be brought to trial until the proceedings
already instituted against Bessières-Veynac, Louis Bastide, Yence and
Charlotte Arlabosse had resulted in them being set at liberty or brought
to trial. He asked for the Supreme Court Order to be read.

The prosecutor, to whom this petition was addressed, submitted it to
the President who ruled there was no reason not to proceed with the

---

* This was contrary to article 310 of the criminal code.

trial. The defence protested : there was a heated argument with the prosecutor who maintained the President had the sole right to decide the
matter. As Maître Romiguière persisted in his demand, the President
held a consultation with the other judges, and they made a declaration
in favour of the the prosecutor : the petition was rejected, and the
Supreme Court Order was not read. It seems, however, that Maître
Romiguière's objection was valid. Clarissa's counsel, Maître Esquilat,
submitted a counter-petition – that the trial should not be deferred to
some future date as she had a right to expect judgment should be pronounced as soon as possible on the question of her complicity. This was
accepted. The trial continued.

Bousquier was called upon to repeat his deposition : he related how he
had been engaged by Bax in Rose Féral's tavern to help to carry a bale
of tobacco : that he had been conducted to the Maison Bancal immediately after the murder had been committed and was therefore able to
identify the assassins. His was indeed the only solid piece of evidence : its
great importance was it confirmed the stories of the Bancal children, and
it proved to the court that Clarissa's account of her experiences there,
and not her retractions, were to be believed. The gaoler, Canitrot, of
the prison in Rodez was questioned. He explained how Bousquier had
come to make his confession :

'The accused Bousquier was conducted to my prison on 24th March.
The police asked me to keep careful watch over him. I put him in solitary
confinement : he communicated with nobody. For the first two days he
maintained a system of complete denial. Then Bastide was arrested. On
26th March Bousquier's wife, having brought food for her husband, saw
Bastide through the grille : "O the villain !" she cried, "It's on his account
my man is here !" She begged me to encourage him to declare the truth
and hide nothing, because that was the only way he could save himself.

'A very knowledgeable gentleman, Monsieur Calvet, was placed in the
cell with him. This gentleman consulting the criminal code advised him
that if he made a confession he would only be liable to two years'
imprisonment for accepting Bax's offer to carry a bale of tobacco on the
evening of the crime. Bousquier seemed very relieved and begged
Monsieur Calvet to take down his confession. Soon afterwards he asked
me to inform the examining magistrate he had very important revelations to make.

'He was immediately interrogated by the provost, but when he was
about to make his deposition he fell down in a dead faint. "What a
weight I had on my heart !" he told me afterwards, when he returned to

his cell, "but I have thrown it off. I have told all I know. Now I shall see my poor wife : the provost promised me." '

Canitrot, humble, insinuating and self-righteous, obviously enjoyed his task of setting agents disguised as fellow-prisoners in the cells to influence these wretched people and betray their confidences.

Next the provost himself was heard, le Chevalier de la Salle, Maréchal-de-Camp, Provost of the Department of the Aveyron. He was conducted ceremoniously by the ushers to the witness-box. Having taken the oath with a flourish, he informed the court, with rather a patronising air, that he knew a great deal about the trial because it was he who had carried out the first interrogation. He described it as follows :

'At the time of the unhappy event I heard Bousquier's deposition : he was one of the first to be arrested. He accused Bastide in lively terms. . . .

'Monsieur and Madame Jausion, Madame Galtier and Monsieur Yence came to see me. Madame Jausion spoke earnestly on behalf of Bastide and begged me to set him free : she said she was astonished that suspicion could rest for a moment on a man of such known probity connected with so many honourable families. We were at that time at the very beginning of the investigation; we had strong suspicions but no proofs; so I listened to these ladies extolling the sweetness and gentleness of his character. Madame Bastide gave me a detailed account of how her husband had passed the evening of 19th March : he had passed the whole of it with her, and he had gone to bed, she said, at 10 o'clock.

'Jausion too assured me Bastide was innocent, that he was quite certain of it : and he added Monsieur Fualdès, though elderly, still allowed himself certain indulgences. "Wouldn't it be possible," he suggested, "that Anne Benoît had given him a rendezvous and that Colard, with impulsive jealousy, murdered him?"

'I replied this seemed highly improbable, even admitting the possibility of a rendezvous and that Colard was capable of violence : this was a very long way from the sort of crime of which the assassins of Monsieur Fualdès were accused.

'Jausion complained that the police had not done their duty, that there were others whom they had more cause to arrest than Bastide. "What's that?" I said. "You know the real criminals? Name them! was it the Laquelhe Brothers?"* He stammered and replied, "No", but he said it in such a way it seemed to imply the opposite.

Jausion, invited to comment, couldn't recall having said this, 'but

---

* The Laquelhe brothers were supposed to be the sworn enemies of the late Monsieur Fualdès because, during the troubles, he had caused their father to be arrested and imprisoned.

because the provost affirms that I did, it must be so. Had it been anyone else, I should have disputed it."

The President asked, 'Was it not the denials of Jausion, *Monsieur le Provost*, that caused you to arrest him?'

Before he could reply, Jausion said bitterly, 'No. It was the denunciation of Didier Fualdès, my relation, my friend, to whom I have rendered so many services. He denounced his father's friend!'

This outburst was violently resented by the audience: Didier, when he could make himself heard, took advantage of the situation:

'It was as if by enchantment that I became convinced of Jausion's guilt! I had a visit from him towards the end of March – I was still in bed: I trembled, I shuddered, I hid myself under the bedclothes so as not to see him. It was Nature, it was Providence that inspired me! Even then I did not act at once. I already knew he had forced the desk, but I didn't suspect he had any malicious intentions in doing so. . . . On the following day in the street I saw approaching me a man whom I thought, mistakenly, was Jausion: immediately I felt ill. I ask you, gentlemen, how does one explain these presentiments? I informed the provost so that justice might take whatever steps it considered appropriate – can this be what the accused calls the *fearful denunciation* which so arouses his anger? On account of which this hall reverberates to his protests?'

Jausion replied he would not comment on these pretended tremblings and shudderings – his lawyer would deal with them. Then he embarked on a violent tirade against Didier: the President immediately stopped him, invited him to express himself with more moderation, and called the next witness for the prosecution. This was Monsieur Albene, the hotelier, who had been the first to report the movement of the assassins towards the river. He deposed as follows:

'Returning home late on the night of 19th March along the boulevard d'Estourmel I noticed, about fifty paces ahead and coming directly towards me, a mass of shadows. This seemed very extraordinary, and all the more so when, having gone another twenty-five paces, the shadows disappeared.

'Fearing they would do me an injury, I considered it prudent to walk in the middle of the road in case they were hiding in a ditch I knew lay on my left. While passing this ditch I experienced a feeling of terror which could not have been greater had I known then who these villains were I had taken for shadows.

'Next day when I learned of the death of Monsieur Fualdès I no longer doubted the shadows I had met were the murderers carrying the body to the river.'

This was the deposition that Maître Romiguière had stated, without contradiction, that the police agent Calvet had treacherously shown to Bousquier in the prison at Rodez to help him to make his own deposition.

Albene continued : 'My servant, to whom I told my story, commented that a young man had been following me that day : it was Bessières-Veynac who had been walking up and down.'

The President questioned him :

The officers of the gendarmes lodge with you, don't they? –*Oui, Monsieur.*

It seems a watch was being kept on your house to make sure nobody warned them. Is that all you know? –There's one other thing I'd like to mention; it concerns Madame Manson. Finding myself beside her in the courtroom at Rodez, I said to her, 'You have produced in me a very strong conviction of the guilt of the accused; if I were the judge I should have no hesitation in condemning them.' She replied, 'They are guilty. So much the worse for them. One is a tiger; the other is the Hyena of Gévaudon.'*

Clarissa, asked to comment, admitted she might have said, 'If they are guilty, so much the worse for them.'

Another witness was called, Monsieur de la Goudalie : he said he didn't know if Madame Manson had spoken of a tiger and a hyena to Monsieur Albene, but she certainly had done so to him.

CLARISSA : That is true, Monsieur.

There followed another long explanation from the self-righteous Clémendot : he added various little touches to his story, but by and large it was the same as before – how Clarissa had confessed to him she was the woman in the alcove. He concluded, 'My only regret is to see Madame Manson on the bench of the accused. If her conduct had been as frank and loyal as my own, she would not be there now.' He mentioned that, 'because he had tried to do his duty to justice,' he had lost his position as aide-de-camp to General Wautré – it was the only part of his speech that Rodat listened to with pleasure.

* This hyena, or 'Beast of Gévaudon' as it was called, terrorised the district for a number of years and was regarded by the natives with superstitious fear. When it was finally killed at the village of Les Ternes, near St Flour, in 1789, it was found to be a species of lynx. It became a legendary monster, the subject of many verses and popular songs.

Clarissa denied she had made a formal confession to Monsieur Clémendot though she may have looked embarrassed when he suggested she had been in the Maison Bancal. He had gone too far in his conjectures. Her counsel commented that what she was alleged to have said to Monsieur Clémendot did not agree with what she was alleged to have said to other witnesses. He flared up at once and retorted, 'I don't know if my deposition is in conformity with those of other witnesses, but I can assure you it is the same as what I said at Rodez; and if I have left out certain details it is solely out of regard for Madame Manson.'

Next there was a very different kind of witness, the tailor J. B. Brast: accustomed to sewing many hours a day, and day after day, this was obviously his great moment. He entered the witness-box, took the oath, settled himself securely on his legs, coughed, took a pinch of snuff, and addressed the court with so solemn an air that Clarissa laughed aloud.

He began again: 'Gentlemen, I ask for the assurance of the court that I will not be interrupted during my deposition. I am perfectly prepared to answer questions when I have finished.'

This was no doubt because Maître Rodier had taken strong exception to one of his statements at Rodez. The President gave the required assurance, Clarissa stuffed a handkerchief into her mouth, and Brast continued. He was very conscious of his importance because he lived in the rue des Hebdomadiers and was therefore a prime witness. He related that on the evening of 19th March a hurdy-gurdy was playing in the street. He and his wife heard people moving about outside, and shouts and whistles. Reflecting that during Lent joy was unseemly, they shouted to the people to be quiet, but no one took any notice. Then he recollected his door was not quite shut: he crept downstairs and found it was more open than he had left it. This added to his fears. . . .'

The tailor rambled on for a long time. At last came a surprise: he stated that the crowd he had heard outside his house was a procession with a tall man bringing up the rear. This sudden clear image after his vague talk gave the impression he had made it all up, that he had in fact seen nothing and this had been suggested to him by the testimony of other witnesses. He hadn't mentioned it at Rodez. When he had talked for half an hour the President at last told him they had heard enough. Now his wife came on and testified she had seen Bastide entering the Maison Bancal on 19th March, but she couldn't recall exactly when it was. Some time between midday and four o'clock.

Bastide commented with some amusement that communicated itself to the audience, 'Well! Here's yet another version! Why can't all the liars agree among themselves? Some say I was at the Bancals' at eight o'clock, others that I pretended to leave Rodez and they saw me on the high road. I really can't be everywhere at the same time.'

MADAME BRAST : I can't remember exactly when I saw him, but I'm sure it was before nightfall.

Louis Lacombe the carpenter was called again. This time he did something that might have caused the jury to suspect he had invented his evidence : instead of repeating that he had overheard Bastide say to Monsieur Fualdès, 'I can't find a halfpenny,' he added the words, 'Please be patient for another few days. We'll settle up on Sunday.' Of course Bastide objected vigorously that this wasn't what Lacombe had originally reported him as saying.

The prosecutor observed to the jury it wasn't important that the witness had not previously mentioned this fact : 'It happens frequently,' he assured them, 'that witnesses recollect additional details while they are giving evidence. It is not at all unusual.' The prosecutor may have been right, but it was clear that each witness was trying to make the small part he was called upon to play as important as possible.

There followed witness after witness who had nothing to say except they had heard that somebody else had said something to somebody. Bastide merely shrugged his shoulders pityingly. The audience grew impatient and chattered among themselves until a witness named Alibert took the stand with such an air of mystery that they were intrigued and fell silent to hear him.

He said : 'I was passing the prefecture on the evening of the 19th : several men had been posted along the wall. I hid in a doorway. One, who seemed to be directing them, signalled with a white handkerchief to come on. They went forward and disappeared in the blackness of the street, but I'm sure I recognised Colard among them. I met him next day, and he said to me, "Have you heard Monsieur Fualdès was killed during the night?" I don't recall what I replied, but he added in an undertone, "There will be many more." '

Colard jumped up and protested angrily, 'I said nothing of the kind! How could I have known such a thing? It's easy to see they plan between them what to say.'

'Those were your very words,' Alibert insisted, 'and they gave me food for thought.' The gardener Jolicoeur was called : he alleged Colard had made the same remark to him.

It was not until the fifth session, on 29th March, that the persistent rumours Bax had turned King's Evidence were confirmed : the President announced he had received a letter from him stating he had an important communication to make. He had sent for Bax and interrogated him four times. He now called upon him to repeat before the court what he had said.

Bax then spoke as follows, in a toneless voice : 'What I am about to reveal may perhaps count against me, but I put truth above all. I wish to hide nothing from justice. I wish to make known, so far as it lies within my power, the facts and circumstances concerning the death of Monsieur Fualdès.'

He described how he and Bousquier had been hired by a man they didn't know to carry a bale of tobacco from the Maison Bancal, but when they went to collect it they were told it was a body they were to carry : they had tried to retreat, but Bastide covered them with a shotgun and said, 'If you move, you are dead !' Then Monsieur Bancal gave him twenty francs, and they helped to carry the body to the river. He proceeded to identify Bastide, Jausion, Madame Bancal, Colard, Missonier, and a woman 'who was little and fair,' as having been in the kitchen, and also Bessières-Veynac : and two other women were there whom he didn't see properly. The details of his story corroborated the details already supplied by Bousquier and the Bancal children.

The President asked how many women there were in the kitchen. 'Three,' he replied. 'I thought at first one of them was Charlotte Arlabosse, but I have been confronted with her, and either her features have changed or I was mistaken.'

'Wasn't Anne Benoît one of the other women ?' he was asked.

He answered, 'I couldn't say. They turned their backs.'

Jausion asked to comment said, 'If you please, *Monsieur le Président*, ask the witness if he knew me before the trial.'

Bax immediately answered with sudden violence : 'I've spoken the truth ! I heard your name mentioned twice during the evening of 19th March. I recognised you perfectly. I'm not trying to save my life : I'm not afraid of death; I wish it had already ended my troubles. Only a father and a mother in their sixties whom my silence had reduced to despair caused me to undertake to reveal the whole truth.'

Bastide tried to reassure Jausion who had become very agitated; 'Be patient, everything will become clear.' Clarissa, who had been sitting with her head in her hands, abruptly straightened up and gazed at him in astonishment.

The President asked Bastide what he had to say. 'What do you expect me to say,' he answered, 'to a man who pretends he took part in a murder for twenty francs ? I should, however, like to ask him this :

When you reached the river, did you throw the body in at once, or did you go farther along the bank? –You know very well, Monsieur Bastide, you stopped the *cortège* at Petit-Champ, and Bancal threw the body into the river.

That does not answer my question. I wish to know if you threw the body in without going farther along the bank? –We threw it in when we got there. [Bax had forgotten Bousquier had said they went a hundred and fifty paces along the bank before throwing it in.]

Bastide turned to the jury: 'You see? Two liars never agree!' For once the President was at a loss what to say. One of the additional judges, Counsellor Pinaud, spoke for him:

PINAUD: Gentlemen of the jury, I should like Bax to reply to the following questions: Why, at the time of the earlier trial, when Bousquier turned King's Evidence and was condemned to only a year's imprisonment, did he suffer Bousquier to make him appear as the more criminal? Why did he let himself be condemned to death if he is innocent? A man may despise life, but he tries at least not to lose it on the scaffold.

BAX: I hoped to get out of the affair some other way: it was from humanity I didn't wish to speak.

BASTIDE: Didn't you say in prison that only you and Bousquier would be condemned?

BAX: How can you suggest that I said that, Monsieur Bastide? You are the most guilty, you who took the key to go and help yourself to everything? Could I possibly think I should be condemned without you?

[Before Bastide could reply, Jausion broke in with, 'Which way did I go when the body had been thrown in?']

BASTIDE: It's not the time to speak of that. Wait. Everything will come out all right.

PINAUD: Did your father come to see you in prison?

BAX: No, monsieur.

PINAUD: What prevented you from making the revelations at Rodez that you are making now?

BAX: I didn't want those accused with me to be condemned.

PINAUD: You give a very bad reason, because once they had been condemned there was no longer any risk of having them condemned.

Counsellor Pinaud's contemptuous rejection of Bax's pretended confession was the first serious criticism of one of the prosecutor's witnesses by someone in authority. Jausion plucked up courage to question Bax :

JAUSION : After the verdict, when I called upon you publicly to tell the whole truth, why did you not speak? I even had my request put to you by the President.

BAX : You said nothing to me.

JAUSION : (furious) I said nothing! Are two hundred witnesses enough to prove that I did?

PINAUD : The point is sufficiently important to require an explanation. Bax denies Jausion called upon him to speak the truth : there are lawyers here who were present at the trial at Rodez. We can ask them.

PROSECUTOR : It is easy to see these interpellations between the accused are part of a prearranged system of defence. Was not Bastide's counsel asked to find a defender for Anne Benoît?

ROMIGUIERE : It is difficult to imagine there could be a combined system of defence between the accused who for a year have been separated from each other : it is difficult also to believe that the prosecutor intended to say the system was combined by the counsels.

PINAUD : Only by the accused, I think he meant : and because the prosecutor has said so, he must hold the proof. I accept it as possible for the duration of the trial at Rodez, but not after the verdict : one doesn't keep to a system that condemns one to death.

PROSECUTOR : Empty words!

PINAUD : No one, I presume, wishes to prevent my request from being carried out. I have asked the President to question the members of the bar so that we may know whether Jausion put this question to Bax or not.

TAJAN (for Didier) : So that the accused may have complete latitude for their defence, we do not object to the lawyers being heard who were present at the Rodez trial.

PROSECUTOR : I oppose it!

The judges formed themselves into a tribunal. After brief deliberation they decided the lawyers should be heard. Two of them were questioned : they affirmed Jausion had indeed pleaded with Bax to declare the whole truth about what had happened. The result was Bax was still further discredited. This unusual scene of disagreement between the prosecutor and one of the judges was followed with interest by the spectators who had crowded into the courtroom because, on the previous day, the daughter of the concierge had been seen at the chemist's buying a bottle of *sels alcalis*: this had given rise to a rumour that Madame Manson would be heard. Unlike most rumours, it turned out to be correct.

Clarissa was asked by the President to relate all she knew about the murder of Monsieur Fualdès. She raised her veil: Rodat wondered anxiously if she would at last clear herself of the suspicion of complicity by telling the truth: it would resolve her inner conflict, he thought, and it would put her right with the authorities and with her parents. His anxiety was quickly relieved: she related all her terrible experiences as simply as if she were speaking only to him, as if they were sitting alone together on the stone, 'Hay', in the deserted moonlit landscape beneath the walls of Rodez. She was heard in religious silence. The audience were spellbound.

When she came to describe the actual murder, she began to look dazed; she swayed and leant forward as if she were about to lose consciousness. Some spectators in alarm cried out for the usher to go to her assistance: the usher shouted 'Victoire!' (which was the name of the concierge's daughter.) Victoire ran onto the scene with her bottle of *sels alcalis*, and Clarissa quickly recovered. De Latouche noted Bastide was watching her with an expression of mingled pity and despair. Soon, encouraged by the President, she was able to go on with her deposition. She had accused Bastide, but she still could not bring herself to name Jausion. When it came to the question of who had saved her, it was *un homme*: when it came to who had conducted her to the ruins of the Annonciade, it was *un homme*. Didier rose and said, 'Jausion, who is continually asking everyone to say he is innocent, will no doubt wish to ask Madame Manson to state whether or not she saw him in the Maison Bancal.'

Clarissa became very agitated; she glanced about her as if seeking a way of escape. Jausion was evidently troubled also. He looked at her, gave an affected laugh, and making his voice low and gentle, he said, 'Madame, I am asked to put this question to you.' She rested her head on her hands. A complete and mournful silence reigned in the courtroom for at least two minutes. Then she sighed, and murmured, 'I have nothing to say.'

There was a stir of protest among the audience who had clearly expected a denunciation of Jausion.

'Gentlemen of the jury,' Didier said, 'you no doubt observed the manner in which Jausion addressed Madame Manson.'

'Monsieur,' said Jausion, turning on him sharply, 'I am astonished at the bitterness with which you pursue me, considering all I have done for your father. You evidently seek my fortune, and my life.'

'Ah wretch!' Didier cried, 'this reproach from you, Jausion, is very cruel!' and he launched into an impassioned speech:

'Your fortune? I despise it! Keep your money: it is stained with the blood of my father. It would have been better if you had left him his life and taken everything I possess. One barrister at Rodez did me the frightful wrong of accusing me of base cupidity: it was Romiguière! But I am not here to indulge in recriminations. Romiguière, I pardon you. I have no other purpose but to avenge my father. Cupidity has never entered my soul. I have come here to fulfil the sacred duty nature has engraved upon my heart. Jausion is wrong to say I seek his destruction: I want no innocent blood: I only seek the truth. That is the light that guides me when I find that, although Bastide is inevitably given up to the scaffold that awaits him, Jausion is still playing for sympathy. But, Jausion, Providence is watching! We shall obtain justice, complete and entire!'

The audience were deeply moved by this speech: Jausion seemed overwhelmed by it. But Bastide faced Didier proudly, and said, 'I know you have abandoned me to the scaffold, but I....'

The President, holding up his hand, interrupted him: 'It is not Didier Fualdès, Jausion, who denounces you. You have denounced yourself. When you were asked if you went to the Fualdès home on the morning of 20th March, you replied you did not. When you were asked if you had taken anything from Monsieur Fualdès' desk, you said you had not. The contrary has been proved against you.'

Jausion replied: 'I beg you to remember, *Monsieur le Président*, I had just been arrested; I was ill; I was bewildered. When I learned it was my friend, Didier Fualdès, who was my accuser, who had denounced me as the murderer of his father, my spirit was troubled, I lost my head, I no longer knew what I was saying. I decided to admit nothing until I had taken legal advice.

'The facts, quite simply, are these. Nothing was further from my mind in going to the Fualdès home than robbery. I met two friends there, Monsieur Sasmayous and Monsieur Carrère, who suggested I should verify that none of Monsieur Fualdès' things was missing. I did so. I took nothing. The bag of money I was accused of taking was afterwards found in the cupboard.'

You admit now you forced the desk open? –Forced it? No, Monsieur. I lifted a board that was loose, as I had seen Monsieur Fualdès do. I used the little axe to tap it into place again.

This seemed a convincing explanation, and the audience were taking a favourable view of it; but just at that moment the prosecutor intervened and said, 'I think this is the moment to make known to the court and to the public the means that are being employed to intimidate witnesses,' and he read out the letter threatening Clarissa's life which she said she had found at the bottom of a vase in the presbytery garden. He followed it up with another letter, couched in similar terms which, he said, had been pushed into her sedan chair. 'You see?' he commented, 'the assassins of Monsieur Fualdès are still out for blood!' Then he read out Clarissa's letter to the President, putting herself and her son under his protection.

He turned to her, and said: 'Be assured, Madame. The laws will protect you. The names of the assassins who threatened you are known: they will pay for your life with their heads. Tell us all you know, in the name of that God whom you see before you, (pointing dramatically to the crucifix), and in the name of the most tender of mothers. Justice is listening. You have acquired a sad and deplorable celebrity: know how to make it honourable! Complete your deposition!'

Clarissa, however, having screwed up her courage to tell her story was suffering from the reaction, and was unwilling to say more. She murmured vaguely there were many people in the Maison Bancal, and she couldn't recognise any of them. The President questioned her:

Did you cross the kitchen? –Yes. I didn't notice anything on the table; the lamp gave only a dim light. When I left there were only a few people, speaking in low voices. I couldn't hear what they said.

How did you know there was blood in the bucket? –Because I heard groans that made me think someone's throat was being cut.

The man who took you away from the place. . . . How was he dressed? –I didn't look at him. I know nothing.

Speak, Madame! The law and the magistrates are watching over you!

It was no use. She was completely exhausted. 'I don't know any more,' she whispered. De Latouche's explanation was that in this extended drama Clarissa liked to divide the interest she contributed to it into acts and scenes, working each one up to an effective climax and adding nothing to spoil it. Rodat thought she could only face up to the assassins for a short period at a time, and then had to stop to recruit her strength, and that the dramatic form was purely incidental.

This time she recovered quickly and listened with interest to the next witness, Monsieur Jean François Blanc de Bourrine; he was asked if he knew Madame Manson and if he had discussed the death of Monsieur Fualdès with her. Yes, he said, he had discussed it with her several times during the assizes at Rodez : she had first of all denied she had been in the Maison Bancal; then she had asked him if he had heard it said that someone in her family was compromised in the affair, and he had admitted everyone thought so. Whereupon she commented, 'I do not wish to appear. I am too important a witness. My evidence would kill them.'

CLARISSA : I admit I discussed the murder of Monsieur Fualdès with the witness, but I never said my evidence would kill them : I never mentioned killing.
DE BOURRINES : Madame, you did say so. You spoke to me of the scaffold.
CLARISSA : No, Monsieur, I spoke neither of killing nor of the scaffold.
DE BOURRINES : This is not the first time Madame has retracted. I persist in my statement. May I also remind her that at the same time she said Madame Pons was counting on her.
CLARISSA : Yes, that is true.

The President urged her again and again to stop her evasions and explain everything. 'Tell the truth, Madame!' La Bancal chimed in. Clarissa gave her a withering glance and relapsed into silence.

Maître Dubernat, for Jausion, pleaded with her, 'In the name of truth, in the name of society, in the name of God, speak, speak, Madame, I beg of you!'

She only said, 'I can tell you nothing.' Bastide too pleaded with her :

BASTIDE : Yes! Tell the truth! Speak!
CLARISSA : Wretch!
BASTIDE : Enough of your monosyllables. Speak!

She made a violent movement as if she were about to leap at him. Then in her deepest voice she said vehemently, like a tragedy queen, 'Bastide! Do you recognise me?'

'No,' he said. 'I don't know you.'

Clarissa, as if beside herself, shouted, 'Monster! You do not recognise me, and you wanted to cut my throat!' At these words there were shouts and applause from all over the courtroom.

The President tried in vain to restore order; then he sent for extra guards : they came hurrying in and were distributed among the public benches where they shouted, 'Silence! Silence!' After a few minutes of pandemonium, the audience gradually became quiet again. Meanwhile Clarissa had fainted several times and been restored with *sels alkalis*. When she came to she was in a state of extreme agitation.

Didier asked permission to speak: 'Madame,' he said, 'You have told us the truth about Bastide: give it to us now about all the others. I ask this in the name of God.' She fainted again, and the President ordered a recess for half an hour.

During the recess, the accused were left on their benches. Bastide had assumed his usual calm and indifference: his eyes were fixed on a book that he held in his hands. La Bancal gazed at the public with disdain, Missonier with his usual imbecile smile. Jausion remained sunk in profound gloom.

At 12.30 the court re-entered. Clarissa stated she felt too unwell to remain, so the hearing was adjourned.

CHAPTER THIRTEEN

A Corner of the Veil Lifted

The next day's session opened with a lively protest from the barristers because the local authorities had put obstacles in their way when they tried to see the accused they represented, and even when they did succeed in gaining admittance to the prison they were never allowed to see their clients without a witness being present : this had resulted, they said, in malicious accounts of their conversations being circulated. 'Who is the magistrate,' Maître Romiguière demanded, 'who dares maintain that in order to see his client a barrister must have permission from the municipal authority or the mayor ! We recognise only judicial authority.'

The President and the rest of the judges, after deliberating, made the following announcement :

'Considering that the administrative authority is responsible for security measures in the courts and prisons; and considering that it is important the execution of Article 302 of the criminal code should not be hindered, the prosecutor is instructed to consult with the barristers to arrange for their free communication with the accused as far as is consistent with security.'

Now that Clarissa's ascendancy over the public, and Bax's revelations confirming those of Bousquier, had counteracted whatever advantages he may have hoped to derive from the change of scene to Albi, one would have imagined Bastide would be discouraged : on the contrary he was gay, charming and facetious : 'He laughs, he jokes with the witnesses as if he were there for his own pleasure,' Monsieur Olivier of *La Quotidienne* wrote,

but what he heard that day was no laughing matter : most of them affirmed that, whatever he might say, he was at Rodez on the morning of 20th March. . . . 'What coat was I wearing? What hat? What shoes? With whom were you when I passed? What did you say when you saw me?' are a few of the many questions he put to the witnesses. We don't think we should take up our readers' time with these endless debates about Monsieuer Bastide's jackets and trousers.

183

Bastide, however, succeeded in demonstrating that, although they all insisted they had seen him, it was impossible that they had done so, for they disagreed as to where and when, and about what he had been wearing.

Day after day, witnesses for the prosecution swore they had seen him in Rodez on the evening of the crime, or on the following morning; or they dug up discreditable stories about him, or alleged something compromising in his dealings with Monsieur Fualdès. Ursula Pavillon gave a description of how she had overheard him giving Monsieur Fualdès a rendezvous for eight o'clock on 19th March, and that evening she had seen two men posted in the rue d'Ambergue, two in the Place de la Cité, etc.

BASTIDE : Why didn't you make the same deposition at Rodez?
URSULA : I was young and timid. I forgot to say all I knew.
BASTIDE (laughing aloud) : The timidity of a young virgin who was wandering in the streets at ten o'clock at night with a young man!

The President called upon him to observe the proprieties his situation demanded. Another witness, Sabine Albui, was called. She told the President, 'I assure you I saw Bastide enter the Maison Bancal on the day of the fair.' Bastide sized her up for a moment, then questioned her :

It seems Mademoiselle was anxious for a trip to Albi? You wanted to see someone here, didn't you? Everyone has his role in this affair : yours is to say you have seen me in the Maison Bancal.
THE PRESIDENT : It is very unfortunate you cannot defend yourself except by calumniating two or three hundred witnesses. –But good God, Monsieur! They carry no weight at all against me. More than 250 of them are not even householders. (He turned again to Sabine).
Why did the witness not mention this at Rodez? –I didn't depose at Rodez because of timidity.
Did you mention it to anyone? –Yes, to Monsieur Anglade.
When? –Two months ago.
So you kept it to yourself for eleven months? Gentlemen! Here is a woman who kept a secret for eleven months! . . . (laughter).

Another witness, Anne Pascal, swore she had seen him three times in Rodez on the morning after the murder. He asked her,

Where do you come from? –From Pomayrols.

I hear the River Lot no longer runs through your district? –Of course it does. Why do you ask?

Just for my own satisfaction. (He chuckled to himself.) I wanted to hear a witness for the prosecution say something that was true!

Regularly, when they had made their deposition, the President asked them if any attempts had been made to bribe them. Many of them said Madame Bastide, or some other member of her family, had offered them money, or corn, or hay, to withold their evidence.

As more and more witnesses for the prosecution were heard, Bastide seemed at last to feel overpowered by the sheer weight of their numbers, for he suddenly cried out: 'Who are all these people? I've never seen them before! I know nothing about them!' Of course from the prosecutor's point of view this was an advantage, for if he didn't know them it was impossible for him to prove they were prejudiced against him. Bastide made this point too, and said he had no opportunity to call other witnesses to refute them. The prosecutor assured him, and the jury, that he had had full opportunity to call any witness he pleased.

Next the prosecutor brought a number of witnesses to show that Monsieur Fualdès had always paid whatever interest was due to his colleagues punctually, and always noted the amount in his account book – his intention, apparently, was to prove that he had had a account book, but it was proved incidentally that he had owed money all over the place.

The authorities evidently still felt the weakness of their case, particularly against Jausion which was based on the children's stories, the deposition of one of the accused who had turned King's Evidence to save his own skin, and the popular prejudice. Didier had still produced no evidence that anything had been stolen. The falsity of Bax's 'confession' had been shown up by Bastide and Counsellor Pinaud. Therefore the President again started to work on Clarissa to get her to name Jausion as one of the assassins. After giving the jury a résumé of her evidence so far, he asked her,

The man who brought you out of the alcove was the same man who conducted you to the Annonciade? –Yes, Monsieur.

You recall what he looked like? –No, I can't remember.

Is he among the accused? –That is possible, Monsieur. (The way she said this, her tone, her looks, seemed to indicate that her liberator was in fact on the benches of the accused.)

Maître Dubernat, for Jausion, now questioned her : 'Be so good as to explain yourself, Madame. Your half-confessions, your ambiguous answers, are more murderous than a direct accusation.'

Clarissa's voice was barely audible as she whispered, 'I have nothing to say.'

Jausion looked at her with desperate appeal, and implored her, 'Madame, it is not for myself but for my unhappy wife and for my children. Please speak : my life is in your hands. It depends on you, Madame! On you! You can save me, or send me to the scaffold!' She said nothing.

Again Maître Dubernat urged her, 'Deign to recall, Madame, what your generous father wrote to you : "To what remorse you will be a prey if by your reticence you compromise an innocent man, or save a guilty one!"'

She replied, with a most unhappy expression, '*Monsieur le Président*, I can neither save Jausion nor have him condemned.' She hid her face in her handkerchief, trying to escape Jausion's eyes that were fixed upon her. Bastide commented in a contemptuous voice :

These exclamations mean nothing at all. This is not a theatre. Madame Manson has sufficiently amused the public. Now it must end. What was all the drama about last time? What does she want today? . . .

THE PRESIDENT (interrupting him indignantly) : Stop, accused Bastide! Do you call the bench on which you are now seated a theatre? If it is true you wished to cut Madame's throat, do you expect her to reproach you coolly? Disillusion yourself. This is no comedy.

BASTIDE : Don't I know it! For me it's a tragedy. But my mind is at rest. I have nothing on my conscience.

Clarissa suddenly came to life, and said forcefully, 'You have nothing on your conscience?' She turned to the President : 'If Bastide proves his innocence, I'll go to the scaffold in his place!'

BASTIDE : Prove my innocence! Ah! That's not difficult. Madame Manson thinks she can intimidate us, but she's wrong. . . . Does one ever know what she means? She said one thing at Rodez and another thing here.

CLARISSA : I lied at Rodez. Here I told the truth. You know it, Bastide!

The President then asked her if she recognised anybody in the Maison Bancal.

'Only Bastide,' she replied.

'And did you see a body on the table?'

She made a gesture of horror as if she could still see it, and replied, 'No, no, I saw nothing, nothing.'

He continued to question her :

And were you made to kneel? –It's possible I was thrown down on my knees. . . . What could I do? One woman in the midst of a band of assassins? I saw everything through a haze. . . . I'm still trembling. . . .

Can you give us details of the oath you were made to swear? –No, I don't remember. I've said all I can, and I think justice should be satisfied.

Bastide smiled and said, looking towards the audience as if to share a joke with them, 'Who brought you to the Maison Bancal?' She didn't answer.

THE PRESIDENT : However painful it may be to you to answer that question, I am obliged to put it to you.

CLARISSA : I was following someone, and I had a right to! I heard a number of people coming along, so I took refuge in the first door that was open.

BASTIDE : And may one know who this someone was? Is it such a great mystery?

CLARISSA : Monsieur Bastide will kindly permit me not to answer that question. I think I have said enough.

Here the prosecutor intervened and said her silence, condemned by the laws and by the public interest, had no doubt originally been inspired by fear. Now, he thought, it was inspired by gratitude for the man whom she believe had saved her life : 'You have done enough for gratitude,' he said, 'act now for justice! Rise to the heights Providence seems to have ordained for you! You have named the man who wished to kill you : name the man who saved you! We are listening. . . .'

It was all in vain. Clarissa was again in control of her emotions. She answered coolly, 'I don't recognise him : I have already had the honour of telling you so.'

COUNSELLOR PINAUD : Madame, a last word on Jausion. You said at Rodez Bastide wished to kill you : you said Jausion saved the life of the woman they wished to kill. It is established, therefore, that you were the woman, and therefore it was Jausion who saved your life. We wish you to confirm this. If he is innocent, do not leave him under the weight of the overwhelming conclusions we must draw from your silence.

CLARISSA : I will not say, and I cannot say, anything definite on this subject.

BASTIDE : I prefer her invectives to her perfidious silences.

When it came to Rodat's turn to testify he had only to repeat the deposition he had made at Rodez, to the effect that Clarissa had indeed told him she had been present in the Maison Bancal and that she had described her experiences there in very great detail to him; and he repeated also the advice he had given her, to disclose the truth to the authorities. She had promised to do so in the following words, 'I'll tell the truth. I'll say it was Jausion who . . .' She had not completed her sentence.

Maître Tajan for Didier asked Clarissa what she had meant by 'I'll say it was Jausion who . . .'

She replied, 'I have already stated I don't recall saying this, but I must have if Monsieur Rodat says I did.

Maître Romiguière requested the President to ask Clarissa how she knew Monsieur Fualdès was prevented from making his Act of Contrition before dying. She made a gesture of horror, and replied, 'I heard this.'

The President asked, 'Who refused Monsieur Fualdès the time necessary for his Act ?'

She answered firmly, 'Bastide !' Pinaud commented that as she recalled the scene so well it was very strange she no longer recalled the assassins.

CLARISSA : Men committing a crime disguise themselves as much as they can : the furniture doesn't.

THE PRESIDENT : You have mentioned two other accomplices. Who are they ?

CLARISSA : They will be judged.

PINAUD : Were they in the Maison Bancal ?

CLARISSA : I shall not answer that question so long as I am on the bench of the accused.

BASTIDE (humorously) : But as Madame Manson was an accomplice, she has to answer like the rest of the accused.

CLARISSA : I ? The accomplice of Bastide ! . . .

BASTIDE : You can't in all conscience reproach us. (Pause). All these exclamations. . . . If she knows something, let her say so : let her say positively what she has seen.

THE PRESIDENT : What more can she say about you? Hasn't she repeated several times you wanted to cut her throat?

De Latouche noticed that Bastide raised his head with a sudden movement, and gave Clarissa a look so full of the intensity of despair that anyone else would have been shattered by it, but she took no notice. He said slowly, 'Does that prove anything?'

BASTIDE : She said the other day she didn't know me. That woman doesn't keep to the same story for two words together. All her statements contradict each other although she took the oath here, as at Rodez, to speak the truth. How can one believe what she says against me here, and not what she said for me there?

CLARISSA : I have never said anything in your favour!

BASTIDE : You said you didn't even know me.

CLARISSA (pointing an accusing finger) : I recognise you for the man who wanted to kill me!

THE PRESIDENT : You affirm that?

CLARISSA : I affirm it!

THE PRESIDENT : If she did not speak the truth at Rodez one can clearly see the conflict of her conscience. . . .

BASTIDE : Of her conscience! . . .

THE PRESIDENT : Yes, the conflict of her conscience against the desire not to break the oath she had taken not to name the assassins.

BASTIDE : We know all that. Madame Manson is an actress who longs for celebrity by never mind what path, that of virtue or of crime, it's all one to her. She accuses me, and she doesn't even know me. Look! Do you recognise me?

CLARISSA : I know you only too well.

THE PRESIDENT : Did you recognise him in the Maison Bancal?

CLARISSA : If I didn't know him by name there, I recognise him here as the man who wished to kill me. I declare he is one of the assassins of Monsieur Fualdès!

BASTIDE : Do you know, gentlemen, why she says that? She cannot forgive me for having prevented her marriage with one of my relations, and I really don't understand by what privilege she is allowed not to speak like the rest of the accused, and why she doesn't give her evidence without emotional outbursts. Why does she declaim like in

Racine, like in the comedies and tragedies?

PINAUD : Madame Manson, I do not ask you to name those on the benches of the accused : I ask you to point them out to the prosecutor.

Clarissa made no move to do so. Maître Boudet, defending Madame Bancal, asked, 'Cannot Madame Manson tell us if there were a large number of people present in the kitchen?'

CLARISSA : I have already replied to that question, and I don't see why I should answer it again.

BASTIDE : Yes, as she is so well informed! As she saw. . . . As she heard. . . . Let her say how many people were there.

CLARISSA : Neither do I consider myself obliged to answer that interpellation.

PROSECUTOR : I regard as premature the request that has been made to Madame Manson to name the accomplices who are not yet in the hands of the law. To reveal them now would only serve to warn them and to paralyse whatever action it may be necessary to take against them. Orders have already been given to seek them out, and I can only applaud Madame Manson's silence.

Bastide completely ignored this interruption and continued to bait Clarissa : the trial was becoming more and more a duel between them. There was nobody, except possibly her father, against whom she reacted with so much emotion. He asked her,

On the evening of 19th March, who saw you leave home? –Nobody.
Who saw you come in again? –Nobody.
How were you dressed? –As a man.
Who made your clothes? –I did.
What became of them? –I burned them. Are you satisfied? Have I replied sufficiently to all your questions?

Rodat was still in the witness-box apparently forgotten. Then another of the judges, Counsellor Pagan, addressed him : 'I have a question for you, Monsieur Rodat. Do you think Madame Manson's vacillations and changes of mood are the expression of an irresponsible character, or is she under some pressure from outside?'

He answered his intimate feeling was Madame Manson would reject with horror all that wasn't just or honourable : but it might be she had been led astray by false ideas about the oath that was demanded of her.

Her emotions were very active, and she would rather do noble actions than those dictated by wisdom or reason. He was told he could stand down.

The President began to question Madame Bancal: her attitude of complete denial seemed to be no longer tenable in the face of Clarissa's revelations, and no doubt the public expected her to break down and confess her part in the affair. She did nothing of the kind. He asked:

What happened in your home on the evening of the 19th March? —At 7.15 the miller brought the flour. I went to the bakery and from there to the hotel where my daughter works. I came home. I heard the children's prayers and put them to bed. I told Anne Benoît not to shut the door because my elder daughter would be coming home. I went to bed. A little later, being afraid of burglars, I got up and closed the door. Then I went back to bed.

Didn't you see anyone drag a woman in? —I have never seen Madame Manson before. I attest before God and justice that she knows nothing, that she saw nothing, and she cannot say what she doesn't know.

She added she didn't see Colard that evening because he had quarrelled with her husband. Witnesses were brought in to refute her statements: first Marianne Viala, Madame Calmals, police agent, who had been placed in the same cell to spy on her:

CALMALS: Madame Bancal told me, 'Monsieur Fualdès was a brigand: he should have avenged the death of my son. They say I stirred his blood: well, I did, and I'd have stabbed him myself if I could. I wish I'd accepted the 25 louis Bastide offered me to dispose of my daughter Madeleine: should I ever get out of prison I'll kill her with my own hands. And as for Bousquier, I'll put a stone in a handkerchief and smash his head in.'
When told Madame Manson had been arrested, she said, 'Ah! the bitch! She's as guilty as the rest: she kept watch at the door while they were bleeding Monsieur Fualdès.'
MADAME BANCAL: If I had revelations to make, I should make them to the authorities, not to that woman.
THE PRESIDENT: Justice was ignorant of these details until this witness provided them. She got them from you: otherwise, how could she have known them?
MADAME BANCAL: Do what you like, I've spoken to no one.

Clarissa didn't react at all to all this, except to gaze intently at the witness, but there were murmurs of indignation from the audience. More than twenty witnesses, eight more than at Rodez, now reported horrific versions of the murder related to them by the Bancal children, to all of which Madame Bancal listened unmoved, and then requested her children should be brought into court : 'They won't dare to repeat these stories in front of me!' she assured the President. Her counsel put this request to him formally, but it was refused on the grounds that it would be immoral to allow the children to bear witness against their mother who was on a capital charge. Maître Dubernat showed that Madeleine Bancal's and Clarissa's accounts were at variance.

The only important new witness was Théron, a young man who worked in the mill at Bress : it had already been noised abroad that he would make sensational revelations, so the audience awaited his deposition with keen anticipation. Before he was called, the President drew the attention of the jury to a large plan prominently displayed on the wall of the courtroom behind the benches of the accused : he said it had been drawn at his request to help them to understand Théron's deposition : this plan was certified by the signatures of the Prefect of the Aveyron and the Mayor of Rodez that it showed the route taken by the assassins carrying the body of Monsieur Fualdès through the streets from the Maison Bancal to the river.*

Théron entered the witness-box with perfect composure, took the oath, and spoke as follows : 'On the night of the 19th March I laid fishing lines in the Aveyron River. When I had finished and was walking along the bank to return home, I thought I heard people coming towards me along the same path. I stopped. Suddenly I saw something very frightening, so I hid behind a bush: it was a funeral *cortège*. Bastide was leading the way : I recognised him very well : he carried a shotgun under his arm, the barrel pointing to the ground. Following him came four men carrying, on two poles, a body wrapped in a blanket. Among them I recognised Colard and Bancal, they were in front. Of the two men supporting the poles behind the body, I recognised only Bax. Behind them came Jausion, whom I perfectly recognised. He too carried a gun under his arm : he had a white handkerchief round his head, hanging down over his eyes, and a round hat. From where I was hidden I watched the cortège crossing a field, rather laboriously because of the narrow winding path. In the middle of the field they stopped, and laid down their burden. Afraid they should discover me, I took off my shoes and ran away as fast as I could.'

* Copies of this plan were available to the public at two francs apiece. It was announced all profits from the sale would go to the poor.

During this recital, Jausion seemed troubled, but Bastide was quite un-moved. Several times he smiled ironically. The President questioned the witness :

Are you quite sure you recognised the accused whom you have named ? –Yes, Monsieur. Quite sure.

Since you made your declaration before the examining magistrate, has anyone tried to bribe you to suppress your evidence? –Yes, Monsieur. I was brought a letter giving me a rendezvous in a house in the rue des Hebdomadiers; but I dared not go there, and I didn't read the letter.

PROSECUTOR : Why have you delayed so long before giving this in-formation to the authorities? –When I learned Bastide had killed Monsieur Fualdès, I was afraid I would be treated in the same way.

Maître Romiguière requested the President to ask the witness if anyone had seen him laying his fishing lines in the river.

THERON : Fishing is forbidden in the Aveyron. I took very good care not to be seen.

BASTIDE : Would you kindly ask him what bait he used?

THERON : Worms of course. Why do you ask?

THE PRESIDENT : Well Bastide? What do you deduce from that?

BASTIDE : If only you will be patient, Monsieur. I want to get to the bottom of this.

ANNE BENOIT (to Théron) : It's because you are a false witness, my poor friend.

COUNCELLOR PAGAN : I should like Bax to answer this : you have heard the witness. Has he spoken the truth?

BAX : Yes, Monsieur. The *cortège* was formed as he described it.

COLARD : You might ask the witness, *Monsieur le Président,* if he recognised me.

THERON : Perfectly.

COLARD : It's not true! Of this crime my heart is clean, and my hands also! (This remark was greeted with a shout of laughter. When it had subsided, Colard turned to the audience, and said) Gentlemen, if you were in my place, you would not feel like laughing. . . . And as for you, *Monsieur le* Witness, you will render an account to God for your declaration. And you, Monsieur Fualdès, rest assured I am innocent of any design against your father. I would rather have given my own blood.

A third assessory judge now intervened, Monsieur le Conseiller Cambettes de Caumont. 'Accused Jausion,' he said, 'You must grant it is most singular that the deposition of this witness agrees with that of Bousquier and of Bax.

I am not afraid of death, but it is insulting to be accused by a witness who has never seen me.

Bastide leapt to his feet, and pointing at Théron, shouted : 'Look ! Gentlemen, look at his face ! See how his expression has altered !'

THE PRESIDENT : He is perfectly calm, and there is not a trace of anxiety on his features.
ANNE BENOIT : Colard did not carry the body. I shall maintain that always.
COLARD : Yes, Gentlemen. Listen to her. She knows ! Let her say whether I am guilty ! She is not my wife, but she hopes to be. . . . Let her tell you the truth !

Nobody, however, asked Anne Benoît's opinion. Bastide for once seemed to be floundering : he continued to ask Théron rather senseless questions :

Where was the witness born ? –At Tremouille.
In whose house ? –In that of my father, of course. (laughter)
I ask because I have been told there has been a conspiracy against me in that district since 1791.
THE PRESIDENT : I don't know whether the people of Tremouille are false witnesses, but of one thing I am quite sure : Théron speaks with great candour.

Maître Dubernat asked if the witness could be sent out. Then he requested Bax should be asked exactly where he had heard Bastide say to Jausion, 'Why do you stumble ? Are you afraid ?'
Bax replied, 'When they had passed the wall.'
Théron was brought in again and asked the same question. He replied he had clearly heard Bastide say something, but he couldn't distinguish the words. Maître Dubernat commented that this was not what he had said to the examining magistrate.
The prosecutor explained to the jury that declarations before an examining magistrate must be considered simply as information : only

those made before the jury and in the presence of the rest of the accused had any legal standing. The witness had done nothing more than develop his thought during the discussion. 'Théron,' he said, 'I am aware of the terrors that oppress you, and of the threats that menace you. Be without fear : you are under the protection of the law.'

THE PRESIDENT : I recall that at Rodez Madame Manson also received letters inviting her to a rendezvous.
CLARISSA : I never said that. . . . Oh, yes. I remember now. To go to the house of Madame Geniers.
THE PRESIDENT : Yesterday Thérèse Giraud declared Madame Geniers had offered her corn on behalf of Madame Bastide to retract her evidence. It is in her house plans are laid to subborn witnesses.

It was not until the session of 13th April that there were any more sensational developments. For several days there had been persistent rumours that the widow Bancal and Colard had revealed all to the authorities. On this day when the prisoners were brought in, Colard's attitude was unchanged, but the widow Bancal, instead of adopting her usual attitude of stony impassivity, was seen to be in floods of tears.

As soon as the court had entered, the President announced she had sent him a message to say she had an important communication to make to him : he had immediately visited her in the prison, and she had confessed all. He had exhorted her to persevere in her new resolution and informed her that her communication would be heard in court this morning.

When he had finished, an excited murmur arose from the audience. Madame Bancal dried her tears, and seemed astonished to find herself for the first time not only an object of curiosity but almost of friendly interest.

THE PRESIDENT : Speak now, *femme Bancal* : and then we shall hear the deposition of the concierge Canitrot who was the first to receive your confidences.
MADAME BANCAL : Gentlemen, this is what I have to say. If until now I have lied to the court, it was because I was afraid; but now I see clearly nothing worse can happen to me than the judgment pronounced against me at Rodez; and I entrust myself to your goodness, gentlemen, and I appeal to you for favourable treatment. On 19th March at half past eight in the evening, six people came into my house dragging by the arms and by the collar a *monsieur* whose face was

covered by a handkerchief. It was Monsieur Fualdès. There were four gentlemen. I recognised Bastide perfectly. One of the others was, I think, a Spaniard.

I asked my husband later who they were, but he was unwilling to tell me : all I could get out of him was that one of them was Bastide's nephew. Bax and Colard were among them. I heard Colard say, 'Where have they brought me to?' He tried to leave, but was prevented.

In the kitchen, Monsieur Fualdès cried, 'Eh! Messieurs, what have I done to you?' 'You have to die!' they said, 'Say your prayers.'

When I saw a crime was about to be committed, I rushed towards the door to escape; but Bastide ran after me, saying, 'I'll kill you if you attempt to leave.' So I fell into a chair. My husband dragged me to the stairs where I remained, and lost consciousness. I heard them close all the doors, and when they opened them again, all they had come to do had been done. I saw nothing of what passed in the kitchen. When I came to myself, Missonier was not yet there. Bousquier didn't come in for quite a while afterwards. As for Anne Benoît, I didn't see her at all that evening.

When everyone had gone, I said to my daughter Madeleine, 'What did they do, these gentlemen?' She said, 'They bled a *monsieur* who was very naughty.'

I asked my husband for details : he told me to mind my own business. 'But,' I said, 'you must have spilt blood in the kitchen, and we'll be lost.' 'Oh no,' he replied, 'we caught the blood in a bucket and emptied it onto a heap of refuse.'

The President questioned her :

Why have you concealed the truth for so long? —We thought we'd be freed on the road from Rodez to Albi.

Were there several women present in your kitchen? —Only one, I think.

But Bax said three? —(Again bursting into tears). It's Monsieur Bastide who is the cause of all our misfortunes! It's because of him I'm in prison, that my husband is dead, my children in the hospice.

At last Bastide spoke, and asked :

What is the woman talking about? I've never seen her before : I've never entered her house. She's out of her mind. Where has she seen me? Where has she known me? –I've known you for a very long time. I've seen you in Rodez a hundred times.

By chance, perhaps, but in your house? –In my house only once, but if I had known you were coming, the police would have been there first.

At what time did this mysterious cortège enter your house? –Well! You ought to know!

Femme Bancal, did I not make you promise to speak the truth when you were brought before the court? –You never spoke to me of the truth.

(He clasped his manacled hands in front of him.) It is the corner of a veil that rises, and then gradually everything becomes clear.

She seemed disconcerted, and didn't answer. Rodat was puzzled by Bastide's remark, and distracted by a murmur of excitement it provoked among the audience: they evidently took his words to mean he was admitting that she had told part of the truth and that the rest would soon follow – which could not possibly have been his intention.

After a pause, Madame Bancal concluded her deposition rather hurriedly as if she had learned it by heart and was afraid of forgetting it. 'When all was finished, my husband made me go up to our bedroom: he told me to wait there, and he would come and fetch me. I didn't wait, however. I went down, and through a crack in the door I saw a large package on the table. Afraid I would be discovered, I went upstairs again, and when I came down next, a few minutes later, it was gone, and there was nobody there.'

There followed a lively scene in which questions were fired at her from all sides:

THE PRESIDENT: Did you hear them propose to Monsieur Fualdès that he should sign some papers? –*Non, Monsieur*.

THE PRESIDENT: Before you went up to your room, did you see Missonier? Yes. I think he was brought in just at the time I was beginning to feel ill.

PROSECUTOR: Did your husband ever say he wanted to be avenged on Monsieur Fualdès? –*Non, Monsieur*.

THE PRESIDENT: Was your daughter Madeleine telling the truth when she described the murder to a number of witnesses? –Not entirely. I wasn't in the kitchen: I didn't see them cut his throat: I haven't even the courage to see a chicken bled.

PROSECUTOR: The bucket in which they caught the blood of the victim, did you miss it on the following day? –*Non, Monsieur.*

THE PRESIDENT: Did you see the cortège leave your house? –*Non, Monsieur.* I wasn't there.

PROSECUTOR: Did they give you any money? –*Non, Monsieur.*

THE PRESIDENT: Did you receive a ring? Didn't you ask for a shirt the colour of the rainbow? Didn't they come next day and take the ring away? –*Non, Monsieur.*

PROSECUTOR: Bax and Bousquier affirm they saw you at nine o'clock in the kitchen. . . . –I wasn't there.

THE PRESIDENT: You had gone to bed? –No.

PROSECUTOR: Your husband came back that night? –Yes. He came back a little later.

THE PRESIDENT: *Femme Bancal,* Bastide offered you a sum of money to kill your daughter? –No. But he said to her, 'If you talk you'll perish.'

MAITRE TAJAN: Did La Bancal positively recognise Jausion? –I only recognised Bastide.

BASTIDE: Oh, I'm the *bête noir,* of course!

MADAME BANCAL: It's you who are the cause of all our misfortunes. If I hadn't been afraid of you, I'd have spoken long ago. Besides, my counsel forbade me to reveal anything.

MAITRE ROMIGUIERE: I declare on behalf of my colleague who is absent that the proposition advanced by La Bancal is false. In his plea, Maître Combarel did not express any doubt that the crime had taken place, and it was only on the question of the woman's complicity he defended her.

PROSECUTOR (to Colard): What have you to reply to the *femme Bancal's* allegations? –She's a liar! Has not Anne Benoît assured you of my innocence? You may cut off my head, but I shall never admit to a thing like that. No. I was not in the Maison Bancal.

PROSECUTOR: Missonier, reply truthfully. You were in the Maison Bancal when the crime was committed: she believes you were held there by force, to prevent you from telling what you had seen.

MISSONIER: My God! How can she tell such lies? I have never set foot in her house since she went to live there.

THE PRESIDENT: You ran twice round the table, trying to escape? –(indicating the accused). –Ask these gentlemen if it's true! (His naivity provoked a laugh from the audience.)

THE PRESIDENT: Didn't they employ violence to force you into the house? –They didn't employ anything, because I wasn't there. Why don't you ask them? They'll tell you the truth all right. They'll tell you I'd gone home to bed.

COLARD : That's true. Missonier had gone to bed.

Maître Bole asked if Madame Bancal still persisted in affirming that Colard was one of the six individuals who dragged Monsieur Fualdès into her house.

She replied, 'Yes.'

The President made a determined attempt to persuade Colard to confess also :

THE PRESIDENT : *Femme Bancal* says as soon as Monsieur Fualdès was dragged into her house you went out, saying, 'Where have they brought me to?' This proves at this moment you must have repented : but you were brought back and forced to help in carrying the body. That excludes premeditation on your part; you are therefore in a favourable situation. You can save yourself. Tell us the truth.

MAITRE BOLE : Come on, Colard. Speak !

COLARD : If it was the truth I should say so, *Monsieur le Président*; but I wasn't there. I had nothing to do with it. I shall never make 'revelations' like the others. When you have cut my head off, my tongue will still proclaim my innocence.

THE PRESIDENT : If you were innocent, as you pretend, Bax, Bousquier and Théron would not have said with one accord you were among the assassins.

COLARD : They do so because I was the cause of Bax and Bousquier's arrest.

THE PRESIDENT : They would have been arrested in any case.

COLARD : No, *Monsieur le Président*. It is through me they came to be regarded as guilty; but if I had had anything on my conscience I should have gone away. I should not be here.

BASTIDE : It is natural those who committed the crime should accuse others. It is impossible that Fualdès was seized in the street on the day of the fair while there were lights in all the shops.

THE PRESIDENT : Not impossible, but I grant you it was audacious.

The next witness to be heard was the long-winded and self-satisfied concierge of the prison, Canitrot, who had obtained the widow Bancal's confession. He repeated at length what she had told him : it differed, in sum, not at all from her own version, except he maintained she had told him she recognised Jausion perfectly as one of the assassins.

That evening a courier arrived from Paris : late as it was, the assessory judges were immediately summoned to confer with the President. The subject of the despatch received was not divulged : the press rumour was that Counsellor Pinaud had been censured for questioning the integrity of the prosecutor's witnesses.

CHAPTER FOURTEEN

Witnesses Persecuted

It seemed to Rodat that the defence was becoming from day to day more powerless before the stern face of justice, but in spite of the overwhelming evidence now brought against him, Bastide continued to fight back and, what is more surprising, he continued to do so with great good humour. On the day following Madame Bancal's revelations, 14th April, when Mademoiselle Pal was being heard, the daughter of Clarissa's landlady at the time of the murder, he asked her;

Tell me, Mademoiselle, were you at the Aveyron River with Madame Manson? —Yes.

Good. But how does that accord with the oath she pretends to have taken?

CLARISSA : I did not take an oath not to look at the body of Monsieur Fualdès. The sisters Pal invited me to go to the river bank : I went with them so as not to arouse suspicion.

BASTIDE : Marvellous! Did Madame Manson faint on seeing the body?

MADEMOISELLE PAL : No, she did not.

BASTIDE : There's a time for everything, isn't there? Can you tell us, Mademoiselle, did she go out of your house during the evening of 19th March? I've a pretty good idea she stayed at home.

CLARISSA : I should like to ask Monsieur Bastide what interest I could possibly have to confess I was in the Maison Bancal on the day the murder was committed, I who am now accused of complicity in the crime.

BASTIDE : It is so that you will be innocent in spite of yourself, and to prove you were in your bed, as I was in mine. I should like to know why Madame Manson, who faints at the slightest provocation, did not faint when she saw the body of Monsieur Fualdès next morning?

MAITRE ESQUILAT (for Clarissa) : It's because she didn't see you there!

For some reason a shudder passed through the audience. Bastide jumped to his feet, 'Eh! *Monsieur l'Avocat*, don't judge so quickly. Everything will be cleared up.

ESQUILAT : The depositions are beginning to prove it !
BASTIDE (sitting down again) : All these marvellous things don't touch me. I prefer Madame Bancal's narration, which is as false as the rest, to the declamations of Madame Manson. I insist upon this basic fact : I am innocent. At the moment of the crime I was very far from Rodez, as I have proved.

There was still one witness who was expected to shed new light on the crime – the retired Spanish magistrate, Saavedra. The authorities had announced his deposition was of very little interest, but the public and the press could not be persuaded that the family occupying the room above the Bancals' kitchen had not heard, and probably seen everything. Several minor witnesses were first called to whom he or his wife were supposed to have spoken. Their testimony was rather involved : one of them, Monsieur Migoule, said a friend told him Madame Manson had told another friend that Saavedra had told her that, hearing a noise below, he had looked through a crack in the floor into the Bancals' kitchen and seen Monsieur Fualdès being murdered on the table.

There was a good deal more of this second or third-hand evidence, and then *la fille* Duclos (*fille de joie*), testified Saavedra had told her it was only too certain Monsieur Fualdès had had his throat cut in that house. She added, 'On the evening of 19th March I saw a woman giving a pig something in a bucket. I was astonished because it was not usual to feed the pig at that hour.'

Clarissa was asked if the noise that was made in dragging her violently out of the alcove was loud enough to be heard by the Spaniards on the floor above : she replied they must have heard it, and she had no doubt they had both seen and heard what happened. Finally Senora Saavedra was called, and the President questioned her about the assassination of Monsieur Fualdès. She replied through an interpreter :

On 19th March last year, at eight o'clock in the evening, I heard Madame Bancal saying her prayers and making her children say theirs. A few moments later I heard her taking one of the small ones upstairs to the top of the house : 'Why,' I said to myself, 'does this woman expose her child to the cold in the attic ?' When my little servant left,

I went to bed. I heard nothing more. I saw nothing. That is all I can tell you.

You went to bed at eight o'clock? –Yes, Monsieur.

You didn't see the sinister preparations in the Bancals' kitchen? You were not alarmed to the point of barricading your door with the furniture? –No, Monsieur. If I had been alarmed I should not have gone to bed.

That is, however, what you said to another Spaniard, Colonel Roque Lilo, who repeated your words to Madame Torquomeda. You described to him all that took place in the Bancals' kitchen. You told him you only went to bed at one o'clock so great was your fright. Your husband told *la fille* Duclos it was only too certain the crime was committed there. In the face of all these facts, to what can we attribute your denials? We are forced to the conclusion that you know everything and some other interest forces you to conceal it from justice. –I saw nothing. I heard nothing. I know nothing.

THE PROSECUTOR : It is impossible she heard nothing of the noise to which Madame Bancal, Madame Manson and Bax have testified, considering that, according to her own confession she only went to bed at eight o'clock, and that the room she occupied was only separated by open planks from the Bancal kitchen below. It is impossible the groans of the victim, heard in the street outside by witnesses, did not reach her. . . . I demand the exercise of my right to charge Madame Saavedra with bearing false witness.

The judges considered the question and decided in favour of the prosecutor : Senora Saavedra was put under arrest. Senor Saavedra was then called. In spite of the punitive measures taken against his wife, he was equally adamant in insisting nothing at all unusual had happened in the Maison Bancal on the night of 19th March : he too was handed over to the police.

The President asked Rodat to give the court any information he might have about the reliability of Senor Saavedra : he replied he really knew very little about him except, he recalled, a Madame Altier had told him he once repudiated a debt of fifty francs that the brother of another Spaniard, Canon Doitre, had lent him in the presence of witnesses. A Justice of the Peace had had to be called to make him pay it. The court listened with great respect, as they always did when he addressed them, but his testimony was really of very little value except to show that Saavedra was a difficult customer to deal with : perhaps he was the descendant, actual or spiritual, of the famous Cervantes de Saavedra and couldn't resist having a tilt at the august representatives of the law.

The next few sessions were taken up by Didier's servants and the rest of the witnesses testifying they had seen Bastide or Jausion near the scene of the crime : there were many more of them than at Rodez. Clarissa varied her dress from day to day, but she continued to wear a veil which she raised when she was called upon to speak. Jausion remained sunk in despondency : he only came to life when there was a question that concerned him personally. When his neighbour testified that on the day of the murder he had heard Jausion say to his wife as he entered their bedroom, 'Victoire, we are lost. The body has floated!' he jumped up and pointed out there was another room and two thick walls between his bedroom and his neighbour's house and he could not possibly have heard anything. The neighbour, however, stubbornly maintained he had overheard these words : Jausion sat down and his eyes filled with tears.

There followed renewed attempts to prove Bastide or Jausion had taken something from Monsieur Fualdès' desk : it was the most difficult part of the prosecutor's task. To make out his charge of robbery he had to rely heavily on the theory put forward by the two witnesses, Galibert and de Seguret, that bills of exchange existed that Jausion would have had to meet if he had not succeeded in gaining possession of them and destroying them. Jausion continued to insist that no such bills of exchange had existed.

The defence now submitted Jausion's accounts which showed the late Monsieur Fualdès was his debtor for about 80,000 francs : if these accounts were accepted, the whole theory of theft as the motive for the murder would have to be abandoned. Didier protested that it was quite impossible his father could have owed Jausion so large a sum. The prosecutor argued that the murder was carried out to make the theft possible, and the theft was the fruit of the murder.

He addressed the jury as follows : 'You are about to judge whether the charges against the accused have been made good. What does it matter to us now what books and papers Jausion has fabricated at his leisure to establish the pretended state of the accounts between himself and the victim, when all the Fualdès books, registers and journals that could have enlightened us have been seized by the authors of the theft?'

Didier then spoke, taking a similar line to that of the prosecutor : he also refused to consider the accounts : 'All my father's papers I might have drawn upon were taken from me by Jausion, and I have no longer the means to dispute his accounts. Unfortunately, as soon as the subject of these accounts comes up, my mind is a complete blank, and I am quite confused.

'At Rodez I thought I had to prove Jausion was the murderer of my father because he was the ravager of his fortune. Here in Albi it is quite different : I find I have to prove he was the ravager of his fortune because he was his murderer. There is no doubt, gentlemen, that he was. I ask all of you, is it possible so unheard of a crime was committed without a great profit to the murderers? You, Jausion, have only to prove you were not my father's murderer, and I shall accept all you care to say about the accounts. Does not the tiger leap upon its prey to drink its blood and feed upon its palpitating flesh? For this crime there must have been a motive, a motive of sordid interest.

'I leave the consideration of this question to the wisdom of the court. For my part, I have not the remotest interest in Jausion's accounts!'

While pronouncing the final words of his speech, he stalked out of the courtroom, disdaining to take part in any discussion that concerned only sordid financial problems. This grand gesture by the unhappy son of the late Monsieur Fualdès was greatly appreciated by the audience; and probably the jury too were glad of an excuse not to take too seriously the troublesome business of Jausion's accounts, which were difficult for them to understand.

The report by the commissioners appointed to study the financial question was then read : they said they had been unable to arrive at a definite conclusion because Jausion's accounts consisted of masses of loose pages with irregular notes on them. The discussion occupied the remainder of the session and continued for several days, but the position remained obscure.

It had taken three weeks to hear the witnesses for the prosecution : on 18th April came the turn of the witnesses for the defence. Strong representations must have been made behind the scenes about the prisoners being manacled because from this day there was a different routine : when they had been brought in and seated in their places a gendarme stepped forward, handed his sword to a comrade in case one of the accused should seize it, unlocked their handcuffs and removed their chains.

The witnesses for Missonier were called first : they gave various examples of his imbecility – that he had gone fishing and only thrown stones at the fish, that on Christmas Day he had lit his forge as usual and paraded up and down the street in front of it wearing his apron, and so on. The President questioned him :

It seems clear you give way to acts of folly? –Oh no, Monsieur. I got a blow on the head at Milhaud : everyone knows it makes a man stupid, but that's over now.

Listen Missonier. I think it possible you were dragged into the Maison Bancal against your will; perhaps those associated with the crime promised to give you a drink and you followed them in the hope of getting a couple of bottles of wine? –No, Monsieur. I haven't been there since Madame Bancal had it.

COUNSELLOR PAGAN : Woman Bancal, you recall having seen Missonier in your house on the evening Monsieur Fualdès was murdered?

LA BANCAL : I said so in my recent statement, and I repeat it.

MISSONIER (turning to her and speaking with the greatest cheerfulness): But Bancal! You have never said this to me. It is true I was in your place once : it's an amusing little story. . . .

THE PRESIDENT : Stop Missonier. . . .

MISSONIER : Oh, you speak, please. Monsieur. . . .

The President continued his questions :

Did you go out again after going home on the 19th March? –No, Monsieur, I went to bed.

How could you have opened your stable door when Laville the beggar was already asleep there? –Monsieur, it's quite easy. You put your left hand through it, and you open it.

You haven't got a key? –Yes, Monsieur. When the door was new there was a key.

Then the door is no longer new? –It was door before I was man : that is to say, the door is old.

How can you pretend you were never in the Maison Bancal when Bousquier, Bax and Bancal herself affirm they saw you there? You were also in the funeral cortège, you carried a little stick under your arm. All this agrees with what I have just said. –I don't carry a stick. I have never struck anyone in the street, and no mother can say I have ever laid hand on her child.

You never answer the question. Were you, or were you not in the Bancals' house? –Monsieur, if it gives you pleasure, I'll say so.

I don't wish you to say it to give me pleasure; I only ask you for the truth. –Oh well, if it's the truth you want, I wasn't there.

Now the authorities did something that was not only illegal and unjustifiable, it was stupid : it could have caused a more independent jury to react strongly against the prosecutor's methods, or even to give a verdict of not guilty. An old peasant woman, Marianne Albresbi, was called : she had been employed by Bastide as a shepherdess.

She stated in the witness-box : 'I saw Monsieur Bastide at La Morne on the Thursday at eight o'clock or eight thirty in the morning; it was on the day on which the usher came and summoned him to go to Rodez. I said at first when I was questioned, that we had spoken of the assassination before the arrival of the usher, but I was mistaken : it was on his arrival I learned about it.'

The prosecutor immediately rose and addressed the court as follows : 'This woman has just deposed that towards eight or eight thirty on 20th March she saw Bastide at La Morne, more 5,000 metres distant from Rodez; and you have heard a large number of witnesses declare they had seen him in Rodez at various times up until ten or eleven in the morning. I represented in vain to this woman the authority and number of the witnesses who had established the falsity of what she was saying. But because at that time she was in Bastide's service she evidently ceded to the empire he exercised over her and decided to uphold the alibi which he has the face even now to sustain when so many proofs combine with those that have come to light during the trial to establish that his alibi is a lie and a scandal. We therefore demand that the woman Albresbi be immediately placed under arrest, and that she be charged under article 330 of the criminal code.'

So the old woman who had the courage not to say what the prosecutor demanded of her was conducted out of the courtroom by an usher and placed in charge of a gendarme. Neither the public nor the barristers protested at the time.

The next witness to be called was Madame Vernhes, Bastide's sister-in-law. As at Rodez, the prosecutor objected to her being heard. Maître Romiguière said nothing prevented the President from using his discretionary power to let the witness be heard, and he quoted several precedents for this. The judges formed themselves into a tribunal and rejected the request; but the President, in spite of this, used his discretionary power in her favour. She thereupon took the oath and spoke as follows :

I was at the domain of Gros on Wednesday 19th March. I saw my brother-in-law Bastide arrive there at about eight o'clock in the evening. He went to his room, took off his boots, and came out again wearing his night-cap. We supped together. Bastide was very cheerful, he kept us all amused. Then we passed the evening together in front of the fire. Bastide dozed off, and we had to awaken him to tell him it was time to go to bed. He went to his room, which was next to mine, leaving the door open. He read for a while, and then put out the light and went to bed. During the night I heard him talking with his wife. Next morning I heard him calling his servants. I assure you that I speak the truth, as God hears me! Pay attention to what I have just said.

THE PRESIDENT: But Madame, are you sure you are not mistaken? It must have been another day.

MADAME VERNHES: How could I possibly be mistaken, Monsieur? Wasn't it on the following day the summons came for him?

While she was speaking, Bastide seemed to be overcome with grief – it was the first time this remarkable man had shown the slightest sign of weakness. The President continued to question her:

In the course of this trial we have heard an enormous mass of proofs that appear to leave no doubt Bastide was in Rodez that evening.

MADAME VERNHES (with great force): Monsieur, if I had to take all oaths, give all my blood, I should still proclaim that Bastide is innocent. He did not leave us.

THE PRESIDENT: A great number of witnesses, all worthy of belief, attest to the contrary.

VERNHES: They are all monsters! (There were violent protests from the witnesses who filled the front seats of the auditorium, but her voice rose above them, and she continued) 'Monsieur! Only our servants can attest the presence of my brother-in-law at Gros. Heaven did not grant that we were entertaining strangers; otherwise poor Bastide would not be on the bench of the accused. Our situation is tragic. I have given you all the details; pray consider them. Have pity on Bastide. He is innocent, as innocent as God and all the angels in Heaven! Those who accuse him are false witnesses! (This provoked such an uproar that she could no longer be heard.)

THE PRESIDENT: Control yourself, Madame! One might say the same about you. There are no false witnesses among us.

VERNHES: I'm sorry, Monsieur. I was carried away....

THE PRESIDENT: Go and sit down, Madame.

As she left the witness-box she turned to the benches of the accused, trying to see Bastide, but he had turned away and buried his face in a handkerchief. She went back to her seat, sobbing, 'My God! My God! I can't even see him. . . .'

The next witness for the defence, and a most interesting one, was Charlotte Arlabosse, who had been held in the Prison of St Cecilia, accused of complicity. She was *petite* and fair. Under different circumstances her undoubted charm and simple manner might have impressed the court, but as she was known to be Bastide's mistress she inspired a sort of horror that so fair a thing should be tainted by the touch of an assassin. It was generally assumed the perverted Bastide would have insisted upon her being present at the murder. The President questioned her:

What do you know about the trial this court is conducting? –On 20th March at half past five or six o'clock in the morning, I saw from my window that Monsieur Bastide was approaching. He called to me to come down. We went together up the hill at La Roquette, and I stayed with him for an hour and a half. He had brought our breakfast in his haversack.

Did you sleep at La Roquette on the night of 19th to 20th March? –Ah yes. I did indeed.

You were not at Rodez during the evening of 19th March? –No, Monsieur. Certainly not.

The President asked Madame Bancal if she recognised the witness, and was she in her house at the moment of the murder. Madame Bancal answered, 'I don't know her.' Charlotte stood up, took off her hat with a grace that reminded Rodat of Clarissa in her youth, and said,

CHARLOTTE : Look at me closely, Madame Bancal. Do you recognise me? Look at me closely, I beg of you. Say whether you have ever seen me at your house. Have I ever been there?

MADAME BANCAL : I don't recognise her.

THE PRESIDENT : Bax, do you recognise this girl?

BAX : No, Monsieur. This is not the Charlotte Arlabosse I was asked to identify at Rodez. This one is thinner and more lively.

THE PRESIDENT : And you, accused Manson, did you notice this girl among the people who surrounded you as you crossed the Bancals' kitchen?

CLARISSA : No, I don't recognise this girl; and what is more I don't recognise her as the Charlotte Arlabosse whom I met at Montegnac with Madame Pons. I think I can assure you this girl doesn't resemble her in the least.

The President called a number of witnesses including her father, a farm labourer, all of whom assured him she was indeed Charlotte Arlabosse. Bastide identified her also. Both the President and the prosecutor tried again and again to get her to deny she had been with Bastide early on 20th March at La Roquette, but she persisted in her statement which was of the greatest importance to establish his alibi. She was obviously deeply attached to him, and nothing would shake her.

Then several witnesses swore they had seen him riding on his grey mare away from Rodez in the early evening of 19th March. The rest of his servants testified they had seen their master at Gros that evening and on the following morning : the house servants described how they had served Bastide's supper, warmed his bed with the warming-pan, etc. The prosecutor took exception to the tone of one of these, Marianne Vernes :

PROSECUTOR : The impudence with which the witness has just imposed upon justice, in affirming the presence and sojourn of Bastide in a place where it was impossible he could have been, according to irreproachable witnesses, makes it my duty to demand that she be arrested.

BASTIDE : So much for the latitude you speak of for the defence ! Your witnesses are permitted to say what they please, but ours ! ...

The President did not order her arrest, but put her under police surveillance. The rest of the servants undeterred, continued to give their evidence in favour of Bastide. Several testified they had seen him on the way from Gros to La Morne; and the manageress at La Morne, Jeanne Janny, said he arrived there about eight o'clock on the morning of the 20th. The President suggested she had told someone that Bastide didn't go to Gros that day. She denied it. Madame Raymond was called : The President asked her,

THE PRESIDENT : Did not the woman Janny tell you Bastide did not appear at Gros on the evening of the 19th ? –Yes, Monsieur. She came into my shop, and in the course of our conversation she told me so.

Jeanne Janny protested that she had said nothing of the kind.

MAITRE ROMIGUIERE : Madame Raymond is evidently mistaken. Jeanne Janny could not have said Bastide didn't go to Gros : she was the manageress at La Morne and didn't know what happened at Gros.

Madame Raymond, however, continued vociferously to insist she was telling the truth, until Bastide pulled her up short :

BASTIDE : Have you not lost a child by a terrible death ?
MADAME RAYMOND : That is so.
BASTIDE : The hand of God is upon you, Madame.
PROSECUTOR : I demand the President use his power to assure to the witnesses the protection to which they are entitled, and that the outrages committed against them by the accused be rigorously suppressed. As for what the woman named Janny has just deposed, her declaration is in contradiction with other elements of the procedure, and with what she herself has said, as you have just heard, to an irreproachable witness. Your patience, *Monsieur le Président*, in this and in preceding sessions, has been excessive in view of the mass of perjuries and lies so scandalous and so deliberate.

We have tried to remove from Bastide the opportunity to say we have hindered or interrupted the defence. What his witnesses, almost all domestic servants, have repeated here is a lesson that has been dictated to them. We have had the patience to listen to them, and we have not invoked against all those complaisant witnesses the rigour of the law. But the perseverance of the woman Janny in her lying merits neither indulgence nor pity. We demand an order, *Monsieur le Président*, that she shall immediately be put under arrest and charged in accordance with article 330 of the criminal code.

The President ordered Jeanne Janny also to be put under police surveillance, leaving the question of her arrest to be decided later.

MAITRE ROMIGUIERE : The prosecutor pretends the deposition of Madame Raymond is more worthy of belief than that of Jeanne Janny; but he must prove that. It is true one of them is a witness for the Ministry, but the law authorises the accused to furnish his witnesses as well, and it does not permit them to be decried without reason. I must point out that several circumstances justify Jeanne Janny : look at her features, her bearing, her firmness, her mature age, her reputation : all prove she is worthy of your trust.

The prosecutor pretends also that because he hasn't had all the witnesses for the defence arrested, this proves his desire not to compromise the defence : I reply that he has already done so from the moment he put the old peasant woman, Marianne Albresbi, under surveillance. I ask the court to give a ruling whether the prosecutor's demand is justified or not.

PROSECUTOR : The request formulated by the defender of the accused Bastide does not come within the jurisdiction of the court but within that of the President, to whom I addressed myself, comformable to article 830 of the criminal code. The discretionary power invested in him gives him all the means to discover the truth, and to put in the hands of the law all those accused of betraying or violating the sanctity of their oath.

ROMIGUIERE : I do not contest the right claimed by the prosecutor : it belongs also to the accused under article 1330 of the criminal code. But as we are discussing this article I say, first, it would be too dangerous for anyone accused to see the Ministry exercising this right to proceed against witnesses called to establish an alibi, especially before all of them have been heard. Who has the right to judge between the witnesses who say they saw Bastide at Rodez, and those who say they saw him at the same moment at La Morne? It belongs neither to the prosecutor nor to me : this right belongs solely to you, gentlemen of the jury. No one shall take this right from you, or I shall be obliged to require the arrest of the witnesses for the prosecution. I think that after the verdict the Ministry may . . .

THE PRESIDENT : Do you presume to regulate the procedure of the public ministry and censure its acts?

ROMIGUIERE : The duties of my own ministration and the interests of my client order me to censure any act that prejudices it and which does not conform to the law. You have the power to order the arrest of a witness accused of false witness : you have not the power to put one under surveillance. This last has only the effect of intimidating the witnesses.

THE PRESIDENT : Speak more calmly, Maître Romiguière : you have adopted a tone of censure and vehemence that is disrespectful in the extreme. I must remind you of your duty, which is to express yourself with decency and moderation. If I have left in suspense the rigorous measures that the grave doubts with regard to the witness Jeanne Janny have provoked, it is precisely to leave full latitude to the defence and to protect all interests. She is in opposition to numerous witnesses, and particularly to Madame Raymond, an irreproachable witness.

He ordered a recession for half an hour. When the court reassembled,

Maître Romiguière asked whether Jeanne Janny had been placed under surveillance.

THE PRESIDENT : Orders have been issued that she is not to be permitted to leave Albi.

ROMIGUIERE : I demand a ruling from the court.

THE PRESIDENT : You evidently did not hear what I said. I have ordered, by virtue of the powers conferred upon me, that the woman Jeanne Janny be under surveillance so that she shall not leave Albi : we shall decide her fate definitely at the end of the trial.

ROMIGUIERE : I demand a ruling from the court.

The judges formed themselves into a tribunal. When they had deliberated, the President announced their decision :

The court agrees the President has the exclusive right to act on the conclusions of the prosecutor, and that they are not obliged to issue a ruling on the insistence of Maître Romiguière.

When all the witnesses for the defence had been heard – it had taken about a day and a half – the President explained to the jury that to conform with the law it was necessary now to conduct a special hearing for each of the accused. Although the witnesses had been heard already, he could not neglect any of the prescribed formalities, and he had therefore ordered them to be called again.

First all those whose testimony concerned Madame Bancal were assembled in the front seats of the auditorium and asked individually if they persisted in their depositions and whether they had anything to add. Then they vacated their seats, and those concerned with each of the accused in turn were brought in and questioned in the same manner. No doubt this procedure was intended to give the accused another opportunity to justify themselves, but actually it was of very little use to them : all the witnesses confirmed the depositions they had made before. The accused, when the evidence was favourable to them, said it was true : when it was unfavourable, as most of it was, they said it was untrue – and nobody believed them.

In the meantime, several more witnesses for the prosecution had arrived. The most important of these was a woman named Bache : she testified that Jeanne Janny, then in the service of the *curé* of Thioullières, had spoken to her on the way home from church about her service with

Bastide, saying how unfortunate she had been ever to enter his house as it had got her involved in a very bad business.

> MADEMOISELLE BACHE : I said to her she had only to tell the truth and she had nothing to fear. She replied, 'But I followed Madame Bastide's advice : she told all the servants they must affirm they had seen her husband at La Morne at eight o'clock on the morning of 20th March. I made my deposition accordingly, and now I cannot retract.' 'But listen,' I told her, 'You had better tell the truth than go on lying, it would be the wisest course for you to take.'

Her evidence was obviously a fabrication because, when the servants were first questioned and unanimously established Bastide's alibi, Madame Bastide had had neither the time nor the opportunity to influence them. Again it looked as if the prosecution were overstating their case and that the jury might be provoked into a reaction against them. Bastide commented :

> BASTIDE : I should very much like to know whether Mademoiselle Bache said all this in the presence of *Monsieur le Curé*. His statement would be at least as reliable as hers, and I think it would be as appropriate to hear a statement from him as from the mass of witnesses dragged from I don't know where.

Jeanne Janny was recalled, and Mademoiselle Bache's deposition was repeated to her, She said,

> JANNY : *Ma pauvre amie*, I have never spoken of this to you, neither could I have done so, because I told the truth when I asserted I had seen Monsieur Bastide at La Morne on 20th March at eight o'clock in the morning. As I hope for salvation, I swear that Madame Bastide did not influence me to make this declaration.

Mademoiselle Bache, however, stuck to her story.

> THE PRESIDENT : It is clear the girl Jeanne Janny richly deserved the measures the prosecutor wished to institute against her. I could have ordered her arrest without being accused of undue severity.
> BASTIDE : You are wasting your time, *Monsieur le Président*. Neither your locks nor your dungeons will prevent the truth from breaking out.

THE PRESIDENT : You are forgetting the respect due to this court. You are to adopt an attitude more appropriate to your situation.

BASTIDE : I insist the *curé* of Thioullières be heard.

Next Monsieur Blanc de Bourrine was called – he had already supplied information to the court. He deposed that the femme Albresbi, Bastide's old shepherdess, had confessed to him that her deposition, for which she had been put under arrest, had been dictated by Bastide himself; and also that it had been agreed among the servants they would all say they had seen him at La Morne on the morning of 20th March : she was now prepared to tell the truth.

BASTIDE : I was, on 20th March, at La Morne, having dinner with my servants. They will all confirm this. In the country the servants dine at eight o'clock. Monsieur de Bourrine knows this well.

DE BOURINNE : I have nothing to depose about that. All I have to say, and I declare it positively, is that the *femme* Albresbi confessed to me she was intimidated first by Bastide and then by the measures the prosecutor took against her.

The old shepherdess was brought in again. Although she could hardly speak for fear, she still maintained Bastide was at La Morne on the morning of 20th March and that she had seen him there. Asked what time it was, she didn't know : immediately after dinner she had left to take the sheep to the fields.

DE BOURINNE : In March the sheep are not taken to the fields until about ten o'clock when the white frost has melted. This remark will clear up any doubt in the minds of the court.

The prosecutor accepted her ignorance of the time as being destructive of her original deposition : he declared that as she had admitted her error, (which she had not), he would drop the charges against her. He continued,

The audacity with which Bastide maintains, and makes his valets and his servants maintain, an alibi already destroyed by fifty witnesses is not the least of the scandals against society produced by this horrible affair.

BASTIDE : I didn't mention an alibi : I merely wished to prove an evident fact. It is that on 20th March I was at eight o'clock in the morning among my servants.

PROSECUTOR : More than fifty witnesses certify you were in Rodez.
BASTIDE : Monsieur, all these witnesses have mistaken the day or the
hour. When I was arrested, my servants, although surrounded by
gendarmes, deposed of one accord that I was with them.

The assessory judge Counsellor Pinaud, who had demonstrated the
falsity of the reasons Bax gave for his 'confession', evidently felt Clarissa
had not disclosed all she knew. Much to her annoyance, he began to
question her : she gave him impatient and even disrespectful answers :

PINAUD : Madame Manson, you see we are searching for the truth.
You have declared during the trial, or in the interrogations preceding
it, that the individual who saved you in the Maison Bancal could have
been Bessières-Veynac; or we could identify him with the accused
Jausion. Be so good as to state categorically which of them it was?
–*Monsieur le Counseiller*, I have no statement to make. I will not
give you another one.
Then you will allow suspicion to rest on Bessières-Veynac? –That
suspicion I shall justify at the proper time and place.

The counsellor repeated his question in several different forms, calling
on her to name the individual she had recognised in the Maison Bancal :
was he on the bench of the accused, or wasn't he? 'To explain myself
more clearly,' he said, 'I ask you if you recognised in the Maison Bancal
any individuals besides those who are here before your eyes?'
Clarissa, who now seemed perfectly exasperated, replied spitefully :
'To sum it all up, what is it you are asking me, *Monsieur le Counseiller*?
Is it whether the individual who threw me into the alcove was the one
who afterwards saved me? No, *Monsieur le Counseiller*, they were not
the same.' The counsellor continued patiently to question her :

Did you recognise anyone in the Maison Bancal besides Bastide
and Jausion? –Perhaps.
Would you kindly explain that remark? –No, *Monsieur le
Counseiller*.
You told Monsieur Clémendot at Rodez you were thrust into the
alcove by Madame Bancal; you confirmed this to the Prefect of
Aveyron; you said the same to Madame Constans, adding that she said
to you, 'Quick! Quick! Hide yourself. . . .' –But have you heard
Madame Constans' deposition?

That's not the question at the moment. I am asking you if the individual who saved you was the same as the one who thrust you into the alcove? Was it Madame Bancal as you said at Rodez? –It was neither the woman Bancal nor the one who threw me into the alcove. I shall name him at the proper time and place.

Why did you say at Rodez they were the same? –I had my reasons. I shall not divulge them.

Madame, no reasons can justify you in concealing from justice what I ask you. Were they the same? –It is possible. I have to inform you, *Monsieur le Counseiller*, that I am incapable of following such a long-drawn-out discussion on the same subject : but my reply to you is they were not the same.

To explain Clarissa's rudeness on this occasion we have to recall that she was on the bench of the accused on trial for her life, and she knew she was safe so long as the authorities needed her evidence for the forthcoming trial of Yence, Charlotte and Bessières-Veynac, who had been arrested at her instigation. Therefore when the counsellor attempted to get more positive denunciations from her that she was reserving for the new trial, she rejected his questions in a sort of panic. The President took over the interrogation :

You were seized in the corridor. Why did they take you into the room? They would have done better to turn you out into the street. Your explanation seems very extraordinary to me. –Why should they do that? I might have warned the authorities.

The crime had not yet been committed. You could not have told them anything. –I might have run into the rest of the gang who were bringing Monsieur Fualdès.

But it is probable that whoever put you into the alcove was not an accomplice? –I believe he was.

She added she couldn't give any more details, except that she thought Madame Bancal also wished to save her : she heard her saying, 'You mustn't kill anyone in my house!' and she heard Bastide shouting, 'We must kill her!'

That terminated the hearing of the witnesses. The time had now come for the rival orators to enter the arena. First Didier was called upon. He had lost nothing of his ascendancy over the public : he was listened to in religious silence. He began with a eulogy of his father whose virtues and enlightened mind, he said, had graced for twenty-five years the highest offices in the district; but when he was about to enjoy the fruits of his labours in honourable retirement, he had been infamously betrayed and barbarously slaughtered by those whom he most trusted; he fell a victim to their base cupidity. They had refused him the mercy of a quick death, gloating drop by drop over his blood to prolong his agony. . . . 'Lower your eyes !' he suddenly cried to those sitting on the bench of the accused, 'The victim was my father !'

In order to make all the circumstances clear to this audience so far removed from the scene of the crime, Didier now explained that the assassins had forced his father to sign promissory notes before killing him; then they had thrown his body into the river expecting it to sink and only be recovered when it had reached a state of decomposition that would conceal the fact that he had been murdered. In the meantime they would have cashed all the promissory notes, and his father would have gone down in the records as a bankrupt suicide : but, as if in a mute appeal for justice, the rays of the morning sun had disclosed the body floating peacefully on the waters. . . .

'From the very first instant public opinion singled out Bastide and Jausion, enveloped them with its thousand arms, and denounced them as the instigators of the crime: in spite of their intrigues and most cowardly machinations, it has never let them go. In this too, who can fail to recognise the influence of divine solicitude? . . . Meanwhile Bastide, the atrocious Bastide, his hands still smoking with the blood of his victim, was seated at the table of the grief-stricken widow : he dried the tears that he had caused to flow : he dared to inflict on her his horrible caresses, his fearful consolations, while the *agent de change*, his partner in crime, more greedy without being less barbarous, taking advantage of the helplessness of this unhappy woman, was breaking open the precious desk to rob me of the sad inheritance that might have been mine. I ask you all, is not this the height of audacity and wickedness? . . . the conviction of his guilt that suddenly overcame me could not have been more powerful. Who else could possibly have benefited from the total disappearance of my father's fortune and of his papers except the perfidious Jausion who wished to get possession of his bills of exchange : how else could I explain his enormous debts? Thereafter I no longer had any doubt that the motive for the crime was greed. The public had already formed this opinion, and the authorities shared it without reserve. I joined with them to bring the truth to light, in spite of the unjust reproaches of Bastide's and of Jausion's families. Ah! what courage filial piety inspires in a man !

'After the murderers had been convicted at the assizes at Rodez I protested with all my might against the Minister's order for the case to be retried before a higher court, believing that a crime should be punished where it was committed, and fearing that at a distance from the tragic scene the crime would lose its horrible aspect, and that the proofs so indefatigably collected by the examining magistrates would no longer carry any weight. Need I mention the allegations that the jury had been influenced by local prejudice and sanguinary fury? I am quite sure the calm and impartial attitude of the good and wise Rhutenians abundantly refutes this odious imputation. . . .

'Such, gentlemen, were the frightful preliminaries of this immense trial. I lack the courage to say more. For too long my heart has been tormented, and I sense that the subject is beyond my powers : I confide the rest to the worthy talents of Maître Tajan.'

Maître Tajan's speech, however, had to be deferred because of new developments.

CHAPTER FIFTEEN

Bastide's Defence

On the following day, 23rd April, the President dealt first with a report from the Mayor of Albi that threatening language had been heard in the town, directed against Théron. The incident, he said, was being investigated, and in the meantime he assured the witnesses from Rodez, who might be in fear of similar threats, that the authorities appreciated their loyalty and would watch over them.

The prosecutor then rose and asked the President to have a letter read out he had received from Bax, which contained new revelations. The usher was instructed to do so, and he was about to begin when a note was handed to the prosecutor: he read it and spoke as follows:

'I have just been informed that one of the counsels for the defence has sworn at Bax and accused him of lying. I can only observe that this barrister has forgotten the dignity of his profession that imposes upon him the obligation to respect the truth, and not to hinder it from being known. He must confine his relations with the accused to that particular individual whose defence he has undertaken.'

Maître Bole, the defender of Colard, thereupon rose and said:

'I find myself under the necessity of justifying myself because the prosecutor's remarks are directed at me. Before this session opened, I visited Colard and appealed to him as I have many times before, to speak the truth and I would be responsible for his safety. He protested his innocence with such force and with an accent so true that I was quite certain he was not imposing upon me. I then turned to Bax and told him in a voice loud enough for everyone to hear, "If he is innocent, you are a scoundrel!"'

PROSECUTOR: The barrister, whom I had the discretion not to name, has just aggravated his fault. I hope, out of respect for the honourable robes he wears, he will show himself more worthy of them in future, and not again bring upon himself the censure he has merited.

MAITRE BOLE: I do not agree that my words deserve censure. I there-

fore repeat them : Bax! If Colard is innocent, you are a scoundrel!
The guillotine is too good for you!

PROSECUTOR : *Monsieur le Président*! I beg you to remind Maître
Bole of the provision of the law that orders barristers to express themselves with decency and moderation.

THE PRESIDENT : You must contain yourself, Maître Bole, and recall
the promise you made at the beginning of the trial : you are losing all
sense of what is becoming to your profession.

MAITRE BOLE : I ask the court to give a ruling on the censure pronounced by the prosecutor.

THE PRESIDENT : Your conduct merits censure; and your remarks force
me to remind you of your duties that you should never have lost sight
of. You have given way to expressions lacking in respect, and if I
attribute them solely to an excess of zeal on behalf of your client
instead of rigorously applying the rules and having you called to the
bar to hear the judgement passed against you of being struck off the
role of barristers, which the indulgence of the court would like to spare
you because of the honourable profession you exercise, and because it
might prejudice the defence of your client.

MAITRE BOLE : I appeal to the public.

From the public, however, there was no response. The usher proceeded
to read Bax's letter aloud. It was addressed to the President, and it contained a long confession in the form of answers to an interrogation conducted by the chief usher, Alexis-Etienne Loubière. It was a development
of his earlier confession. This time it contained a good deal of new
material – details and incidents that had appeared so far only in the
stories of the Bancal children : he named all the assassins who had been
in the Maison Bancal, including Yence, Louis Bastide and Bessières-
Veynac. He mentioned Jausion had a brief-case of blue or red morocco.

A graphic description followed of how Monsieur Fualdès before his
death had been forced to sign a number of documents, twelve or fifteen
of them – this fact was of great importance to the prosecution to support
Didier's assertion that his father had been forced by the assassins to sign
promissory notes or bills of exchange before being killed. Everything was
confirmed in this new 'revelation' – Bastide's refusal to allow Monsieur
Fualdès time to say a prayer before dying, Madame Bancal catching
the blood in a bucket; and also the finding of Clarissa in an alcove : he
described his own efforts to protect her from Bastide's fury, and her being
forced to swear an oath of secrecy with her hand on the body – he even
mentioned that her finger was cut. He said he recognised her as the

daughter of Monsieur Enjalran although she was disguised in men's clothes. He added that Monsieur Yence had offered him 12,000 francs to join them in other robberies, starting with a raid on the house of one of the witnesses who was then in court – Monsieur de France.

When he was asked why he had delayed so long before making these important disclosures: he replied, as he had before, 'It's never too late to tell the truth.'

The audience had been gazing with horror at Bastide through the recital of these devastating accusations, but he listened to them all with complete composure, even when the most dreadful details about the death of Monsieur Fualdès were being described – but Clarissa seemed completely overcome. The President asked Bax if everything in the deposition was true that had been read out: he protested that it was, adding, 'I don't wish to save my life at the expense of my companions.' He was then asked to repeat the whole deposition because he had, according to the law, to present everything verbally to the jury. When he had done so, the President began to question Clarissa:

You have just heard the evidence the accused Bax has given. Do you recall any details that may have escaped you before? Is it true Bax tried to help you? –I have had the honour to tell you that two men objected to Bastide's proposal to cut my throat: I thought the second was Bancal, but it could have been Bax.

Is it quite certain you were made to take the oath? –Yes, Monsieur.

You didn't recognise Bax? –*Non, Monsieur*. Bastide and the body of Monsieur Fualdès are all I remember.

You contest nothing in Bax's deposition? –*Non, Monsieur*. He was in a better plight than I was to see and hear everything. He was not in my horrible situation.

Jausion now requested the President to ask Bax if he recognised him.

BAX: Aren't you well enough known in Rodez?

JAUSION: Do you remember, gentlemen? At another session he declared he didn't know me until he saw me on the bench of the accused! You're a knave, Bax! More cruel than those who murdered Monsieur Fualdès. You have no doubt a motive for saying all this, for I've never done you any harm. Why do you thrust a poignard into my body?

BAX: Monsieur Jausion, I have told the truth. You must know it was not for vengeance Monsieur Fualdès was killed, but for his property.

THE PRESIDENT: Bax, you must answer the question. Why did you

declare you only recognised Jausion when you saw him on the bench
of the accused?

BAX : It's true that's what I said : but I hadn't told the whole truth
then.

THE PRESIDENT : Let Bousquier be called.

BASTIDE : *Monsieur le Président,* I request that all those who have
made 'revelations' be sent out : Madame Manson, La Bancal and
Bax. (He laughed). If they hear Bousquier, they'll simply repeat what
he says. You know very well they're like a lot of sheep that jump one
after the other.

Maître Romiguière advised him it was only necessary Bax should be sent
out. This was done. Romiguière then questioned Bousquier, trying to
prove that his earlier deposition did not agree with Bax's revelations :
there certainly were differences, but perhaps not important enough to
discredit either of them. Maître Dubernat claimed Bax was merely repeating the evidence of Monsieur de France when he was repeating the
stories told him by the Bancal children.

THE PRESIDENT : There is in Bax's declaration a fact of great importance : that Jausion had a brief-case with a yellow lock.

ROMIGUIERE : He had heard Monsieur Didier Fualdès say his father's
brief-case was missing : he simply placed it in Jausion's hands.

The President then questioned Clarissa :

Clarissa Manson, didn't you have a cut finger? Do you recall how
it happened? –I think Bastide had a knife in his hand; he could have
hurt me during the struggle.

Didn't it happen while you were taking the oath on a knife? –I
didn't take the oath on a knife.

In one of your interrogations, you said you did? –Yes, Monsieur,
but that was at Rodez.

A juryman, Monsieur le Chevalier Ginesti, held up his hand and requested permission to speak. He asked Bax :

GINESTI : How were the bills of exchange placed before Monsieur
Fualdès? For him to sign in the margin, or at the foot?

BAX : In the margin.

This very intelligent question, and the answer completely disposed of Didier's assertion that his father had been made by the assassins to sign bills of exchange or promissory notes – that is, if Bax was to be believed – for they would have been signed at the foot.

For Clarissa, Bax's revelations were very important: it was the first time any eye-witness, except Madeleine Bancal, had confirmed the details of her story and that she had in fact been in the Maison Bancal: but there was another aspect that was, perhaps, less pleasing to her – she would no longer be the only important witness for the prosecution against the other members of Bastide's family who were awaiting trial: Bax too had denounced all of them, except Charlotte Arlabosse, and his testimony would be required as well as hers. That was the end of the discussion provoked by Bax's second confession. The audience now settled down to hear the rest of the orators.

Maître Tajan began his speech by pointing out that Bastide and Jausion had first been judged and condemned by the supreme and terrible tribunal of public opinion: they had been singled out by their indignant fellow citizens as the authors of the crime. . . .

'All doubts have been set at rest by the number and weight of the proofs the authorities have succeeded in bringing against them, and by the testimony of one witness in particular – Clarissa Manson. Uncertain of her role, she hesitated for a long time between silence and her duty. Strongly influenced by her terrors, and because a cruel chance had placed her under an obligation, she worked out a system of answering the questions put to her that could satisfy neither her conscience nor society. . . . But, gentlemen, her situation has not lowered her in the eyes of my client. Clarissa Manson the accused has not caused him to forget Clarissa Manson the witness: her present humiliation can never make us forget her services. . . . We have lived through so many of her pitiful and disturbing scenes, and experienced with her such profound emotions that there is no need for me to describe them. Only allow me to compare the impression made upon all our hearts by her first involuntary disclosures with the direct accusations she now levels at Bastide and Jausion, and we cannot fail to realise they are profoundly true. First she admitted her presence in the alcove, then she admitted having heard sounds of a struggle and groans, and finally that she had heard blood dripping. At last we come to the great scenes in which she let all her indignation burst out that she had suppressed for too long. Will you ever forget those scenes? Do they not still ring in your ears, those exclamations Bastide himself provoked? He dared to ask her for the truth: she replied with a cry of astonishment and with the terrible accusation, "Wretch! You would have cut my throat !" It was the end for Bastide.

'The witness Albene testified during the assizes at Rodez that Madame Manson said to him, "One is a tiger : the other is a hyena." It is impossible to add to the force of these expressions. And then, in a conversation Monsieur Rodat has reported to us, she no longer hesitated to mention Jausion. So far from contesting this, she declared "Because Monsieur Rodat says so, it must be true." '

He touched briefly on the principal charges against the rest of the accused and concluded :

'My task is ended, gentlemen. The proofs have spoken. Everything has been discovered; all doubts have vanished. Plaintive cries called you to the banks of the Aveyron. There you have seen the victim. You know those who betrayed him, those who struck the blows, those who received his blood, counted his palpitations, played with his agony and hastened his last breath. The shadows could not hide so many horrors. The Maison Bancal still echoes to the groans of the unhappy man, and to the blasphemies of his executioners. . . . The veil that hid these mysteries, the veil they considered impenetrable, has been rent aside. . . . They have attempted every kind of threat and seduction to corrupt the faithful witnesses; but these vile means redounded upon their own heads and increased the conviction of their guilt. Courageous voices have revealed everything; and this woman, whom these perverted men ordered to keep silent, has ceded at last to the inspiration of justice, and hurried them to the scaffold.'

At the opening of the session of 27th April, the President announced that the counsel defending Madame Bancal had informed him his client was ready to make new revelations. He called on her to speak.

She was heard with great attention – but she only added a few details to the deposition she had already made, the most significant being that she had seen Monsieur Bastide make Monsieur Fualdès sign the documents sometimes in the margins and sometimes at the foot. This was so obviously designed to correct Bax's *faux pas* when in answer to the juryman's question he had said Monsieur Fualdès signed in the margins, that it was impossible not to believe that the authorities had dictated her 'new revelations'.

THE PRESIDENT : Accused Bastide, you have just heard the woman Bancal. What have you to say ?

BASTIDE : That they copy from one another. *Mon Dieu* ! I was certain this woman would also give birth to some of the details produced by Bax. All the 'revelations' are alike. They repeat what the others have said. Put a little Spanish music under them, let each perform his part! It will be as good as *Iphigenia in Tauris*.*

Here Bax and Madame Bancal shouted at him together that he was the cause of all their troubles. Bastide commented, 'What are we to make of this pair of scoundrels?'

The *curé* of Thioullières was called: he had been sent for on the insistence of Bastide who wished him to testify to Jeanne Janny's integrity – she was still under police surveillance, threatened with a charge of bearing false witness. The President addressed the *curé*:

THE PRESIDENT : It has been said that Jeanne Janny, on entering your service, showed you a promissory note from Bastide and that you advised her to cash it as soon as possible because the court would seize all his assets for legal costs?
THE CURE : That is correct.

He was then questioned by Maître Romiguière :

ROMIGUIERE : Do you believe Jeanne Janny was speaking the truth when she affirmed that on the 20th March at eight o'clock in the morning she saw her old master, Bastide, at the domain of La Morne?
THE CURE : Jeanne Janny has constantly told me the same thing. She has never varied it. I am absolutely sure that everything she has said is true, and that she has obeyed only the voice of her conscience.

Instead of Jeanne Janny's opponent, Mademoiselle Bache, being questioned in the presence of the *curé*, he was dismissed and the prosecutor began his speech :

'Gentlemen, we are reaching the end of these memorable assizes whose result is awaited with as much impatience as confidence. The great number of people who have attended the sessions and the avidity with which every detail is discussed outside the courtroom, show that this is not one of those routine cases destined to be lost to view in the immense book of human perversity.

---

* *Iphigenia in Tauris* is the title of an opera by Gluck, founded on an ancient legend in which the high priest Calchas warns the Greeks on their way to Troy that their ships will be wind bound by a curse that will not be lifted until they have made a human sacrifice. It was produced in 1779.

'The new revelations by three of the accused, the terrible allegations that have been made, allegations that carry the ring of truth, their dramatic form, the audacity of the leading criminals, one of whom has seemed to play with the prosecution as he played with the crime, have intensified the interest and provided a new element in the proceedings.

'Probably in the annals of crime there has never been a case like this, of such barbarity, of such long and cold premeditation, with so great a number of accomplices – for you are aware we are still searching for members of this criminal group. It was the victim's relations and pretended friends who betrayed his confidence. They were associated with the most abject type of human being in the brutal murder of the man who had never ceased to shower benefits upon them. None of them were in need : they killed him to possess his fortune. The same blow robbed young Fualdès both of his father and his inheritance. The heartrending expression of his grief has frequently caused your tears to flow.'

He praised the jury for their fair and religious attitude, and for not allowing their indignation for the crime to affect their calm and impartial judgement. Then, so that it would be engraven on their minds, he summarised the evidence of the 380 or more witnesses for the prosecution and showed how they were justified by the recent revelations. He reminded the jury of the threats directed against Madame Manson, the terrors of Bousquier, the alarm of Théron and of other witnesses; and he gave numerous examples of attempts by Bastide's or Jausion's families to bribe them. He called upon them to fulfil the solemn ministry entrusted to them, and in defence of the rights of their country and of humanity to let their just severity avenge the mortal blow they had received through this atrocious crime. Then he changed his tone, and added :

'There is one other duty, gentlemen, for you to fulfil : one more gentle and more consoling. Let us be happy that in the case for the prosecution, among so many guilty we find one innocent. We experience this happiness, and we allow you to share it. We no longer wish to proceed with the serious charges we have brought against Madame Manson for her refusal to speak the truth we demanded of her in the name of the law. It was not for her to decide whether her testimony was necessary : it should have been sufficient for her that we asked for it. It was her duty to give it to us. It is the first obligation all must render to society : it is the price of public security which depends essentially on the suppression of crime. All other obligations, all affections, must give way to this overriding interest. If, oppressed by an emotion which she abused, and which we represented to her as excessive, she has not entirely fulfilled what her conscience demanded of her, she has nevertheless said enough to satisfy justice.

'Let her now forget her misfortunes, and so conduct herself that they will be forgotten by others. Let her renounce this celebrity that women never attain except at the expense of their happiness. Let her regain this happiness by earning the esteem, and living in the affection of those she loves, and whom she ought to love. Let her glory be in the exercise of those gentle and modest virtues that belong to her sex and that her heart, I know, is capable of appreciating. Let her fly to the arms of her tender and virtuous mother who is calling her. May she find there the consolation she needs. Clarissa listened with tears streaming down her cheeks.

Next morning both Monsieur Olivier and Monsieur de Latouche reported that during the night attempts had been made to smuggle poison to Bastide and Jausion, concealed in raw potatoes that were lowered into their cells on threads of silk. The attempt was discovered and frustrated in the nick of time.

The session of 20th April was devoted to speeches for the defence. First Maître Boudet rose to address the court on behalf of Madame Bancal. He began like this :

'Gentlemen, is it to your justice or to your clemency I must appeal on behalf of this unfortunate woman before you? If I speak of her innocence, immediately the colossus of public opinion crushes her as with a mass of iron : if I appeal to your hearts, you rise and reject with horror the feelings of humanity that are normally awakened by the sight of distress.

'How could she, a miserable old woman, have possibly prevented the assassins from entering her house and doing what they pleased there? She was, in any case, under the authority of her husband. Article 64 of the criminal code says, "There is neither crime nor misdemeanour when the accused is forced to it by a power he cannot resist." Will you be more censorious than the law?'

He explained it was only by chance the crime had been committed in her house. The assassins had planned to kill Monsieur Fualdès in Missonier's stable, and they would have done so but for the accident of the beggar, Laville, having gone to sleep there. No premeditation could possibly be attributed to Madame Bancal, particularly as she had permitted several people to make a rendezvous at her house – Madame Manson, possibly Rose Pierret, and others. (Clarissa here nodded her head, as if to affirm the truth of his conjectures.) Maître Boudet summarised the evidence supporting his argument, and concluded :

'Madame Bancal expected to receive only libertines that night, not murderers : it is certain neither she nor the young people with her expected Monsieur Fualdès to be brought there. It is impossible, gentlemen, for you to accuse her of complicity in a crime in the preparation of which she had no part and which she could not prevent.'

Maître Romiguière was to have spoken next. He was so popular an orator that the courtroom was crowded to capacity. To the great surprise of his admirers he rose only to say, 'The accused Bastide wishes to speak.' They looked at Bastide and saw he had a sheaf of papers in his hand. He stood up and began to read aloud. His stilted sentences at once made it apparent he was no orator, and it was a matter for astonishment that he had not left his defence in the hands of his brilliant counsel. He said :

'Gentlemen, my defender has struggled laboriously against my ill fortune, and helped me with his counsels. I ask nothing more of him for the present. No man can have a deeper conviction of my innocence than myself : it is for me to express it.

'There are crimes of which the authors are unknown : Providence reserves to itself their punishment. There are trials in which Providence, playing with human weakness, allows blind prejudice to cause judicial errors : but, for the wise, perceptions of the truth are still possible in spite of the common error.

'What trial has been so prolific in accusations? What trial offers so vast a field for the defence? The general points will be dealt with by the counsels for the rest of the accused : their justification will justify me also. I will deal wtih the facts that concern me personally.

'Few men of my age have furnished so little excuse for old wives' gossip. The single malicious story about my youth, reported by the witness Boudin, has been indignantly refuted by my father. And yet I am accused of having cut the throat of my old friend, Monsieur Fualdès! We had a close friendship, in spite of the difference in our ages.

'What are the proofs? Two witnesses, de Parlan and Labro, thought they saw me on the 17th or 18th drinking in public with Bax and Colard in the Café Ferrand : this was impossible on the 17th because Bax was not yet in Rodez : it was impossible on the 18th because, at the time mentioned, one of the witnesses had already left the café.

On the 19th I am supposed to have given Fualdès a rendezvous for eight o'clock : Cazals deposed thus in his written version. Ursula Pavillon gave another version of this that she said she had forgotten in her earlier deposition. Today, three new witnesses attest the same fact, and the scoundrels don't realise that the more their number increases, the more their absurdity increases also. Who can believe that five different times, in five different places, at almost the same moment, I assigned to Monsieur Fualdès a fatal rendezvous in a voice loud enough for them all to hear?

'But why, you may ask, trouble about what led up to the crime when six persons saw me carry it out and complete it? I answer that to give a passing mention to these six persons, auxiliaries of the prosecution, is to exaggerate the consideration they deserve. I shall take them in turn:

'Bousquier. He is one of the accused who is justifying himself at the expense of the rest. He is a man skilful enough to cover the truth while pretending to reveal it: an imposter who first denied everything, and after turning King's Evidence only arrived by degrees at the version in which I am accused. Is such a man to be the arbiter of my fate?

'Bax and Bancal. The walls of their cells have not given up their secrets. One day they will, and they will tell us of the intrigues and conspiracies that have been going on to force these vile creatures to shamefully save their lives through lying testimony. . . .'

The President here interrupted indignantly, and said, 'Make known these intrigues and conspiracies you suppose have been going on in the cells! Tell us what their walls will reveal one day!'

Bastide ignored him, and continued to read his defence: '. . . today it is evident that the happy example of Bousquier has encouraged them to copy him; it is evident their declarations are incoherent; and that not one of them admits to having done anything wrong himself while their 'confessions' about others present a thousand instances of baseness and improbability. They all leave us in ignorance of the causes, the preparations and circumstances of the crime.

'Clarissa Manson! My defence against this woman, witness, accused, accuser, whom the prosecution alternately blame and caress, humiliate without pity or exalt beyond measure: against this person who, in order not to be degraded by justice forces justice to be degraded for her. . . .'

Again the President interrupted: 'Bastide! Is the defence you are reading your own work?'

BASTIDE: These thoughts are my own.
THE PRESIDENT: Don't add to your misdeeds! Don't increase the indignation already strong against you!

Bastide made an impatient gesture, and continued to read: '. . . my defence against this woman is summed up in these words: Clarissa

Manson admits she lied at Rodez: is this your reason for saying she must be believed now when she states, 'At Albi I speak the truth!'?

'Théron! His deposition is palpably false. To believe it we must assume that there were intervals of daylight in what was a very dark night. Must I reply to it? Surely not! Any credence given to it is more an insult to the good sense of the judges than an addition to my misfortunes. He claims that in this very dark night he recognised me, and also – though we are told he was shivering with cold and fear – Colard, Bancal, Bax and Jausion whose face was masked by a scarf! He claims to have seen two guns, and the direction in which they were pointing, he saw a blanket . . . a body. . . . Oh no! It is really too much! What is the answer? Théron saw nothing!

'Madeleine Bancal! This girl, examined by the magistrates on 24th March knew nothing. Since then she has become the principal instrument in the horrible intrigue that in time will come to light. Its authors have already betrayed themselves. Do you recall the deposition of Canitrot? Is it not suspect? They wanted to confront Madeleine with Bastide, but first they showed her Bastide in his cell!

'Why do you think I continue to deny my presence in Rodez on the morning of 20th March? For no other reason except that it is the truth. I did not appear in Rodez until that evening, and all the rage of the accusers and a thousand of their witnesses will not make me say I was there that morning although I could do so without danger. The truth has only one language, and it will be made manifest in spite of all attempts to distort it.

'According to these witnesses for the prosecution, I have been seen at the same time in several different places, and dressed differently, that I was hiding, that I crossed the principal square again and again: all of them say they recognised me; only one claims to have spoken to me, and he was the servant of Fualdès! . . . What subtlety of mind can make all these discordant statements agree? A reasonable man can see only an obvious confusion of dates and times.

'To this jumble of false and contradictory impressions, I oppose the clear and positive statements of twenty-nine people who knew me well: they are not people who merely imagined they had seen me somewhere among the shadows; they spent the evening with me, they talked with me, they worked with me in the fields, they served my meals, they attended to my horse. They do not mistake times and places. You affect to despise their evidence because some of them are servants – what is wrong with being a servant? Although they were bullied here, accused of false witness and threatened with arrest, they were courageous enough to risk their own safety to testify to the truth. They did not betray their old master.

'There was another kind of servant among them, a servant of God, the *curé* of St Mayne : is he not to be believed? Or Madame Vernhes? Or Monsieur de Courland? Or the miller of Cascame? These are witnesses for the defence. The law has called them to my assistance. No magistrate has the right to disparage them.

'Who dares say that twenty-nine witnesses for the defence are to carry no weight in the scales of justice? Who dares to incur the reproach of having doubted a fact attested by twenty-nine witnesses? No one. You prefer instead a perfidious silence. You prefer to cast discredit on them.

'And why this homicidal scepticism by which you arbitrarily decide that I assassinated Monsieur Fualdès? I had no motive for vengeance. Find someone who had. I was his friend.

'You pretend I killed him for his fortune : he had none. Do you think a man who was constantly borrowing small amounts from here and there could have lent me 10,000 francs? I was not his debtor : he was mine.

'And if this "cupidity" you talk of could have impelled a man like me, sober, industrious, well-off, to attack an old man who had nothing to offer to cupidity, would I have called upon these obscure, contemptible, useless and dangerous hired assassins to assist me? Would I have lured the victim to a frequented quarter of the town, to a house open to all the world? Had I ever had such an intention, there were better opportunities: he frequently invited me to his table, he walked with me in perfect security through the darkest woods. These men, these women, whom you pretended were my accomplices, I do not know them. Either I planned it without them, or they without me. It is impossible that we should have acted together.

'I understand that you need a victim. Here I am. But do not associate me with Bax and Bancal.

'And above all, do not envelop my old parents in my disgrace. My family, which has always lived among its fields and loved simplicity, has been represented as a centre of intrigue, as a nest of brigands. Three of my family, overcome by shame, have died in the flower of their youth : three more are groaning in your dungeons. So much for your justice. You barbarians!'

Bastide now turned away from the judges and faced the jury : he addressed them in very calm and gentle tones :

'You see me, gentlemen, thrown into this ocean of misfortunes. Do you think I care for life? I am justifying myself to God who judges me, not to man : to the God who has given me the strength of soul that my enemies are incapable of understanding. I dispute here not for my life : only for my honour. The impediments put in the way of my defence, solitary confinement for thirteen months, inhuman treatment, the refusal to combine the trial of my relatives with this one making it a supplementary trial although they are essentially indivisable, the fear installed into some of those whom I would have called as witnesses, have delivered me into the hands of my persecutors. I appeal to you to imitate the rare prudence of the ancient judges with all the light and with all the conscience that your duties demand of you : listen to the Roman orator who commanded : "You shall judge the witnesses before you judge the accused."

'If I must still suffer the injustice of the living, I call upon posterity that will engrave upon my tomb : "Bastide is innocent." '

He sat down. There was stony silence. The authorities had certainly laid themselves open to his reproaches, and none of these skilled practitioners of the law found a word to say in their defence. Bastide was indeed unanswerable. Everyone turned to the prosecutor but he sat rigid and spellbound. At last the President called upon the next speaker, as if the whole thing had been merely a matter of routine. The uncomfortable moment passed, and the public settled down to listen to the polished eloquence of Maître Dubernat, defender of Jausion :

'To be accused of a crime is always distressing, and it is even worse when the crime is so atrocious that it appears in the light of a threat to the whole of society : there are agitated cries of alarm, the public imagination is inflamed, demands for vengeance are heard on all sides : and although the wise man waits for the truth to appear, the crowd are aware only of the enormity of the crime : their hearts are closed to pity, and they demand that the sword of justice should fall immediately upon any man who arouses their slightest suspicion. This torrent of public opinion draws with it everyone who is incapable of reflection, and the unfortunate suspect is condemned even before he is heard. Such, gentlemen, is Jausion's deplorable situation. Father of a family, irreproachable till now, he stands before you accused of this horrible crime that plunged Rodez into fear and mourning.

'Jausion, his tearful wife and his young famliy, came to me asking me to represent them. I looked at the evidence, and I saw alleged against him nothing but presumptions, conjectures, and denunciations only too suspect and marked by prejudice – a mere construction of possibilities that I was certain must collapse before a critical examination. And yet I feared, such is the power of prejudice that menaces innocent and guilty alike, that the mere fact of the prosecution bringing charges against him would cause his basic right as an individual to be forgotten – the right, shared by each one of us, to be considered innocent unless, and until, the contrary is proved. I foresaw that if it were not observed, the defence would be hindered in its task of demonstrating that the charges could not be justified. This is precisely what has happened. I have even had to remind the court of this sacred right. From the very first moment of this trial I have seen this deadly prejudice working against the accused, the horror the crime inspired working against them : I have seen them trying in vain to make themselves heard and finding on all sides men turning a deaf ear to them, insensible to their distress. But now we are in the sanctuary of the law where errors and prejudices vanish; where truth is sought with an upright heart, with love and an ardent thirst for justice.

'I have no hesitation in submitting my defence to this jury chosen from the *élite* of this great Department of France : all of them are examples of generosity and virtue : they are accustomed to carrying out their duties with honourable fame. I am sure the case for the accused will be heard with strict impartiality.'

This opening of Maître Dubernat's defence, containing the usual flattery of the jury, was heard with greater pleasure than Bastide's unvarnished statements. Having gained their attention he proceeded to lay the case for Jausion before them. He began by dealing with the alleged motive of theft for the murder, with the object of establishing that there had in fact been no theft at all : the sum of 20,000 francs found in Jausion's possession, received from Monsieur de Seguret for the sale of Flars, was in fact a repayment from Monsieur Fualdès whose debt to Jausion had been reduced in consequence by that amount. The 12,093 francs missing from the amount received from Monsieur de Seguret on the eve of the murder had in fact been replaced by bills payable to Monsieur Fualdès and credited to the account of his inheritors. Of the two missing brief-cases, one had been found. There was no reason to believe there were any securities in the other. The money Jausion was accused of having taken was found in Monsieur Fualdès' desk, or in the wall cupboard of his room. Then he claimed the existence of the journal supposed to have been taken had not been established. The existence of letters of exchange also was nothing but a false supposition : they could never have existed. Therefore, he said, there had been no theft, and consequently Jausion had no motive for the murder.

Then he dealt with the murder itself and with the facts that preceded, accompanied and followed it. The facts preceding it consisted of the depositions of witnesses claiming to have seen Jausion entering the

Maison Bancal – tardy recollections, unworthy of the confidence of the jury, and nothing precise or positive. During the murder, nothing proved Jausion's presence in the Maison Bancal – the revelations of Bax could not be accepted : he was a wretch trying to save himself by accusing others.

Next he embarked on a tortuous analysis of Clarissa's contradictory depositions, and reminded the jury that in any case she had stated later her behaviour on that occasion was not to be interpreted as being un-favourable to the accused. She had always declared she didn't recognise Jausion among the assassins :

'Do you doubt whether the truth is obscure for me? Do you imagine I can admit her half-confessions, her reticencies and her convulsions as evidence against the accused? That I will allow this innocent man to be dragged to the scaffold because of her enigmas, the expressive altera-tions in her features, the wanderings and exaltations of her imagination?'

He dismissed Théron's deposition as unworthy the least consideration, and he claimed those of Bousquier and La Bancal were favourable to his client. He concluded :

'Gentlemen, you are about to return to the bosoms of your families. There, in the midst of all that you hold dear the memory of this trial will come back to you. If you have pronounced a verdict of guilty with-out the sole justification for doing so – that the proofs of guilt are un-answerable and as clear as daylight – the peace of your consciences will have gone for ever; the widow and the young orphans will demand of you a reckoning for the man you have condemned to die in opprobrium and infamy. Let your decision be a new guarantee to society that an unhappy man unjustly accused will find shelter with you against pre-judice and suspicion. The proofs of guilt have not been established. My client implores your justice.'

At the end of this speech, when it was thought the session was about to end, the prosecutor rose and addressed the court as follows :

'Gentlemen, we cannot let this session end without directing your attention to the written defence you have heard the accused Bastide read. From a natural respect for the rights of the defence, which cer-tainly in this instance have been pushed beyond all bounds that have ever been known before, we thought the reading of this defence should not be interrupted.

'As you heard, it was teeming with expressions injurious to the trustees and representatives of the law. He did not scruple to say that Madame Manson "forced justice to degrade itself for her". Have we violated justice? And who on this earth has the power to force it to degrade itself? Can one stygmatise as degradation the opinion expressed by the public minister of the innocence of Madame Manson? Of her non-participation in the assassination of Monsieur Fualdès? If the public minister is to be accountable for his opinion and for his conscience to anything except the laws, we shall ask whether there is a single man or woman in this attentive audience, or in the whole of France, who believes Madame Manson dipped her hands in the blood of Monsieur Fualdès? We ask also if there is a single one of the accused who thinks so?

'Bastide stated also that impediments were put in the way of his defence: has one single formality prescribed by the laws in favour of the accused been neglected? If it has been, let them say so. If we cast a glance on what happened in this session, has there ever been more latitude given to the defence, more facilities both for the accused and for their counsels to be heard? The most minute objections have been listened to, discussed and debated, as well as the most serious: it was enough that they had some importance in the eyes of the accused, and we made it a duty to verify them. We appeal with confidence to witnesses, to the gentlemen of the jury and to the public, to confirm this is so.

'He complains bitterly of the refusal "to combine the supplementary trial with this one, although they are essentially indivisable." This is a new insult to the Court of the Assizes, and to the Supreme Court of Appeal that confirmed its decision.

'One thing is certain. It is that the expressions of which we have reminded you are foreign to Bastide's style, and it would be so unfitting for him in his present situation to express them, that we cannot regard them as his own work. Let us add that did we think they were his, we would keep silence about them and give way to that pity which misery and despair inspire in us, even in criminals.

'It is evident, and you will certainly be convinced also, these lines were traced by a different hand, by a hand as reprehensible as outrageous. We must know whose hand it was. We ask, first, that *Monsieur le Président* has this written defence delivered up this instant by the accused Bastide; second, that he be asked where he got it; third, that he be submitted to interrogation with a view to discovering its perpetrator; and that the questions and his answers should be recorded.'

THE PRESIDENT: Accused Bastide, what have you done with the defence you read?

BASTIDE: I've sent it to my father.

MAITRE ROMIGUIERE: I handed it to one of the court writers.

The document was passed by the court writer to one of the ushers who took it to the President.

THE PRESIDENT : Do you wish to number and initial the pages ?
BASTIDE : No. I have it by heart.
THE PRESIDENT : Who wrote it ?
BASTIDE : I have no more to say.

There was evidently some mystery about all this, for Bastide had frequently complained he had been denied pen and ink to write his defence, and several attempts by his family to smuggle them in to him had been frustrated. There is no doubt, however, that the defence was his own work : it was the essence of the man in its outspokenness and in its abrupt and somewhat homely phrasing : certainly no practised orator had written it : it was entirely without grace or flourish, or logical development of ideas. The prosecutor, in stating he could not have written it himself, was probably only trying to discredit it, to lessen its impact and to divert attention from its contents to the question of who wrote it. He seemed to be implying it was Maître Romiguière's work which he was cunningly passing off as Bastide's so that outrageous things could be said by a man condemned in any case to die : but the style bore no resemblance to that of the brilliant orator who had aroused the enthusiasm of the audience at Rodez for his talents, if not for the cause he represented.

CHAPTER SIXTEEN

'These you are to Believe?'

O the following day, 29th April, it was the turn of the young barrister, Maître Bole, to defend Colard.

He began, 'Gentlemen, I have long debated whether I should simply give you my own conclusions, or explain to you the facts that clearly show the innocence of my client according to the evidence. I admit that without the self-assurance the exercise of my profession has given me I might have allowed myself to be intimidated by the tyranny of public opinion which in this affair condemns all the accused without listening to their defence. That is how public opinion works. But you, gentlemen of the jury, will listen, I know, only to reason; and I address you with all the more confidence because the cause I plead is also the cause of justice, the cause of humanity; and it is therefore, your cause also. It is essential for all of us that no person should be condemned without convincing proofs of guilt. Jean Baptiste Colard stands accused of the premeditated murder of Monsieur Fualdès. . .'

He made a rapid résumé of the facts as they concerned his client, trying to destroy the adverse impression made by the prosecution, and by what he called 'the miserable calumnies' which had secured his conviction at the assizes at Rodez:

'There was no evidence at all of premeditation except an allegation, which has been proved false, that he had been seen with Bax and Bastide in a café two days before the murder. It was alleged also he was in the pay of the assassins: this too cannot be justified: there is no evidence to support it. A careful search of his room has revealed neither money nor valuables of any kind.'

He dealt one by one with the depositions of the witnesses who claimed to have seen him near the scene of the crime, and he objected particularly to the arguments of the prosecution founded upon the depositions of gaolers and of other prisoners:

'In England it became a felony, by a statute of Edward III for the concierge of a prison to attempt to penetrate any secrets of the prisoners,

238

or to divulge them. But in France the unhappy prisoners are spied upon, and even their sighs heard through locks and grilles are recorded against them : he who gives way to his misery is lost : his fugitive words, however divorced from his thoughts, will be used against him before his judges as pretended admissions of his guilt.'

He pointed out that the room in the Maison Bancal shared by Colard and Anne Benoît was above a stable separated by a courtyard from the Bancals' kitchen, and that he was not on speaking terms with Monsieur Bancal. He reminded the jury Colard was in Rose Féral's tavern at the time the murder was committed : he was only accused of being present by the recent revelations of Bax and Madame Bancal. He attacked Bax's deposition point by point; and he maintained that Madame Bancal had had to mention Colard as being present among the assassins or the prosecutor would not have accepted her 'confession' as authentic : but she had left him a way of escape. She had testified he was there for only a quarter of an hour, and that on entering he had said, 'Where have you brought me to?' thus proving he was innocent of premeditation.

Both the President and Maître Bole himself had begged Colard to confirm this was in fact the case, and so save his life, but he had insisted he had not been there, and had had nothing to do with it. 'You tell me,' he had said, 'that I must confirm her story or die. All right, then, abandon me. I shall continue to proclaim on the scaffold that I am innocent.' In view of these protestations, how could one doubt that if they condemned Colard he would die innocent?

'I now come to a part of my plea,' continued Maître Bole, 'where I know I must control myself. I shall stick to facts. When he was condemned at the assizes at Rodez, his unhappy mistress cried out in her despair, "Had it not been for me he would not have stayed in Rodez, he would be living happily with his own people; it is I who have plunged him into this abyss of misfortune!" Have you no tear for these unfortunate lovers? Do not her words touch your hearts? But the prosecutor chose to use them as an argument to. . .'

Immediately the prosecutor interrupted him and requested the President to call him to order. Maître Bole retorted he had cast no reflections; he had pointed out shocking disparities in the system of the prosecution. After mentioning several statements of theirs that could hardly be reconciled with the truth, he said he would suppress his reflections. Then he continued his plea :

'Examine all the charges made by the prosecution, and if you are not convinced of the innocence of the man I am defending, at least you must admit you are not convinced of his guilt. Everything concurs to demonstrate his innocence : the absence of any motive, his presence in the Café Féral while the crime was being committed, the declarations of Bax and Bousquier his accusers, from which it is evident he was not present in the kitchen when it was committed, the silence of little Madeleine about him until after he had been condemned at Rodez, the silence of Madame Manson, the silence of the Saavedra family, his evident poverty : he carries on him all his worldly goods. His family is 200 leagues from here – he could have fled : his conscience caused him to remain. "No, it was love," you may say. But Anne Benoît also has no inheritance except her industry. Why didn't both of them fly? unfortunate young people! You stayed here because you hoped to be married, because you hoped to stand before the altar and consecrate your love before God and man : you stayed . . . O God! I cannot look. . . Before what altar do you stand today, you who are innocent? . . . I weep for humanity; and for you. . . Turn your eyes to the image of Christ, and be consoled.'

He sat down, unable to say more. Although he had defended Anne Benoît equally with Colard, her own counsel, Maître Foulquier, now added his own plea. He said he did not wish to excuse the immorality of the liaison between her and Colard, but it should not be used to substantiate a capital charge; and he complained of the stupid and imprudent censoriousness displayed by some of the witnesses and also by some newpaper reporters. Then he tried to prove that her handkerchief, found in the rue de Hebdomadiers had not been used to gag Monsieur Fualdès but to tie up her bundles of laundry, as she had said : and he reminded the jury that neither Bax nor Madame Bancal had named her as being among the assassins. Her sole accuser was Bousquier whose account, as far as it concerned his client, did not agree with the others.

Maître Dupuy, another young barrister, then spoke for Bax. He said that, following the dictates of his conscience, he frankly supported the revelations of his client : he tried to disprove the objections that had been put forward to them. 'Bax was not afraid,' he said, 'even at the peril of his life, to unveil in the interests of justice all the details of this frightful crime that was never conceived in his heart but in which he unhappily became involved. He maintained that Bax was not an accomplice and had not acted with premeditation. He concluded an eloquent discourse by reminding the jury of the prosecutor's words, 'Bax was not born for crime!'

Maître Grandet followed with a plea for Missonier whom he warmly defended, saying : 'Gentlemen, I'm sure we all share the opinion of Monsieur Didier Fualdès who has assured us there is no crime without a motive. What possible motive can be found for the imbecile Missonier to take part in it? He has no passions: he vegetates rather than lives. If he has some bread and water he is at peace with all the world. Ask the concierge of St Cecile he will tell you of the stupidity of this poor man who cannot even defend his miserable ration from the voracity of the other prisoners. Had he not been protected like a feeble animal he would have died of hunger.

'The stable in which he lives was first designated as the scene of the crime – on what grounds? Only that, apart from the Maison Bancal, it was the most miserable place in Rodez. The eloquent Maître Tajan has told you it was the haunt of brigands: he doesn't know what he is talking about. Missonier comes from a respected family of artisans, a class into which I myself was born, and I don't think any the less of myself for that. An orator should respect everyone's rights even at the cost of a phrase losing some of its colour.

'The prosecutor pretends Missonier's answers prove his intelligence, but to such questions as 'Were you in the café?' and 'When did you leave it?' there is no difference between the answers of a wise and a stupid man. He has told us, 'This accused consented to lend his stable to serve as a retreat for the perpetrators of the crime.' One would imagine from his positive tone he had some trenchant proofs of what he alleged. What was his proof? Only that a beggar, Laville, who happened to be sleeping in it, said he heard someone push against the door: therefore Missonier had lent his stable to the assassins! Now, isn't that a fact well proved? . . . He alleges also Monsieur Fualdès was lured to a rendezvous to make him sign letters of exchange, so obviously a table and a lamp would be required. Missonier has neither.'

He then provoked a murmur of resentment from the public by questioning the truth of Bousquier's deposition, the only one in which Missonier was accused.

He continued: 'You don't need to murmur because I propose to undertake a serious examination of this subject: you can't judge of my reasons until you have heard them. I am not accusing Bousquier of imposture, but I find in his declaration errors and manifest contradictions which prove to me that he is a frighteningly irresponsible witness.'

He proceeded to analyse Bousquier's deposition, contrasting it with those of Bax, Madame Manson and Madame Bancal, and pointing out contradictions. He ended his plea: 'This trial holds many mysteries: it is a Gordian Knot which you would not be justified in cutting to unravel.'

At last it was Clarissa's turn. Her counsel, Maître Esquilat, said that since she had informed justice of the horrible secret of 19th March, the charge of complicity no longer existed against her, and the prosecutor had pleaded her cause in advance : therefore he intended to concentrate on trying to remove the unfavourable opinion of her that still existed in some sections of the public. He claimed she had been haunted constantly by the fear of sharing the fate of Monsieur Fualdès : she had frequently been threatened by the assassins who were both numerous and powerful, and who were not all under arrest. She had suppressed the cry of her conscience, which was in accord with justice, because she dared not face the shame of confessing she had been found in a house of ill fame. For a long while she could not articulate the name of the man who wished to be her executioner, because she would have uncovered by doing so her personal shame : neither could she name the man who liberated her. She had witnessed the crime, she had been powerfully affected by it, it was always in her mind : the secret was a burden too heavy for her to bear. When all the world was talking about it and false conjectures were being made, could she any longer have kept silent? The witnesses to whom she spoke about it were not in accord with each other : everyone wanted to have the glory of having contributed to the manifestation of the truth. . . .

Maître Esquilat continued in this style for a long time and it is doubtful whether he succeeded in removing any of the misunderstandings about Clarissa. It was probably at this time that Rodat, strong in the consciousness that he, more than anybody in the whole world, knew her and understood her, conceived the idea of writing and publishing an intimate account of all that had passed between them since he left Paris to return to Rodez, for he believed that in no other way could she be restored to the esteem and affection of her fellow citizens.

After getting involved in a complicated analysis of Clémendot's deposition and memoirs, Maître Esquilat turned to his client and suggested, 'Madame, if you feel you have the strength, add your observations to mine. I am sure the court and the gentlemen of the jury will listen to you with great interest.'

Clarissa, relieved from the serious charges against her, was at her most brilliant : she spoke with a firmness and an assurance that immediately captivated her audience :

'My counsel has just outlined in a clear and precise manner the evident proof of my innocence : this proof is based upon the documents themselves, records of the trial, and on the depositions of witnesses : is there a single one of them who accuses me? I am well aware I have not the ability to hold your attention for very long, after my counsel has expressed himself with such force and energy. I shall therefore add nothing to my defence; I shall content myself by giving you a brief description of my suffering. . .

'I have been in prison for seven months under the weight of an unjust accusation. But what is that in comparison to what I experienced during that horrible evening of the 19th March? . . . An imprudence had brought me to the house in the rue des Hebdomadiers, the most cruel chance held me there in spite of myself. I search in vain for words that can convey all the anguish I suffered while the unhappy Fualdès was being tortured to death : his efforts to escape his executioners, his prayers for mercy, his lamentations, his groans, his agony, his last sigh . . . I heard them all, and the sound of his blood flowing close to me.

'At every instant I expected to suffer the same fate : it was, indeed, intended for me, but Heaven that watches over me, and which does not permit a great crime to go unpunished, gave a striking proof of its divine providence.

'You know, gentlemen, that in trying to find a way of escape from the assassins, I attracted their attention : one of them appeared before me, his hands still smoking from the blood he had shed : he seemed to me to be covered with it. . . . His frightful air froze my soul with terror. I no longer saw anything but a body, and my own death. . . . But one of them, more merciful, saved my life. Without him my son Edward would have been motherless. . . Can justice reproach me with what I did? Am I forgiven in the eyes of the world? Assuming my liberator is among the guilty, is he less my liberator? Bound by an oath I considered irrevocable, paralysed by the fear of being one day a victim of their vengeance, over-whelmed by a feeling of gratitude, overwhelmed too by the thought that my confession would cover me with shame or that I would be suspected myself of an infamous complicity : all these considerations combined – do they justify my silence? I kept my own counsel – is that a crime? I appeal to those with delicate sensibilities.

'Heaven is my witness that except for the son of the unhappy man I saw massacred, no one wishes more intensely than myself for the detection and punishment of his murderers : and without the enormous mass of evidence which left no doubt that they were guilty I don't know how I could have contained myself for so long from expressing the just indignation I felt. It seemed to me the rest of the proofs were sufficient without my evidence.

'It was five months after the murder that I began to be regarded with suspicion. It was thought I was an essential witness. I defended myself half-heartedly, I appeared to be troubled; and Monsieur Clémendot made a deposition founded upon my tacit admissions.

'Then, pressed by the Prefect of Aveyron, I let out part of the truth: and if I retracted it soon afterwards it was because I was subjected to a power too strong for me: I was surrounded by terror. With Macchiavellian cunning, new methods of oppression were tried against me. My soul lost all its energy, and I promised at last to retract my deposition. I was made to believe I owed this promise to friendship and gratitude, but in spite of myself the truth became known through me. You haven't forgotten the famous session of the 22nd August? My involuntary actions betrayed my words, they contradicted what I was saying. Instead of satisfying everyone, as I had hoped, I made everyone dissatisfied, and I was lost.

'Since then, constantly menaced by violence, the disastrous example of Fualdès ever before my eyes, haunted day and night by his terrifying image, until at last, fearing for the life of my son, I adopted the regrettable system of denial that has made me the horror of well-meaning people, has lost me my liberty and my child, an brought me to the bench of the accused. It would have caused my utter ruin had I not abandoned it.

'Now I have repaired my fatal error! I was far too long obsessed by its dangerous fascination. Now that I have no longer to struggle against my conscience, which reproached me for denying what I owed to justice, my fears have vanished. Attempts to discredit my belated deposition were all in vain: the truth that dictated it compelled its acceptance.

'There, gentlemen, is a short account of what I suffered for a whole year. Do not think my intention in presenting it to you is to arouse your sympathy: it is not pity I am asking for, but justice. To be the object of pity is degrading, but justice is honourable both to those who render it and to those who receive it. The guarantee that you will render it to me lies in the homage your fellow citizens have delighted to pay to your intelligence and to your virtues. Were you not specially chosen for this task by the worthy Prefect of the Department of Tarn?

'I believe I have amply justified myself, not only in your eyes but in those of the whole of Europe whose attention, unhappily, is centred upon me. But if I am deluding myself, if you still have doubts, if I appear guilty to you. . . . Let no consideration hinder your condemnation. Forget my respected father who for many years has occupied with unblemished honour the office of magistrate in the Department of Aveyron; that my brother who wears the French uniform, is covered with glorious wounds. Turn your eyes from the bed of grief upon which my unfortunate mother groans. Close your ears to the cries of my infant son. . . . Strike, gentlemen! Strike if you must! My innocence, and the force to support misfortune, cannot be torn from me!

'Forgive this pride : it is part of my character! it is inseparable from my being. It causes me to forget I am on the bench of the accused, that I am speaking to my judges, that I am a prisoner. She who is innocent of crime does not know how to ask for pardon.

'It is upon you, gentlemen, my fate depends : if you believe the evidence of my conscience, you will absolve me, and give me back my life in giving me back my honour and my freedom. I deny even the suggestion of complicity. But however impartial you may be, and however enlightened, it is not in the nature of man to be infallible : it is still possible I may become the victim of an illusion. In that case I shall know how to resign myself to my fate, how to be silent and console myself in the knowledge that God sees into the depths of all hearts, that His judgements are irrevocable, and that one day He will judge me.'

There was no denying that Clarissa's speech made a deep impression on the audience though the end was too melodramatic considering she was no longer in danger : no doubt she had conceived it and rehearsed it when her situation looked more serious. 'It was a great day when she made her speech,' Rodat tells us,

> Although I didn't find again the Clarissa of our spring meadows whom I had proclaimed Queen of the World, and whom I had sought in vain on the throne of green turf which she had abandoned, at least I found a mature woman of firm character, formed for virtue.

At the session of the 1st May, the prosecution were given the opportunity to answer the criticisms of the defence. First Maître Tajan spoke : he made no attempt to answer Bastide but recapitulated at great length all the evidence of the witnesses for the prosecution against Jausion, then enlarged upon his alleged untrustworthiness in contrast to the late Monsieur Fualdès whom he described as a pattern of virtue. This was followed by more abuse of Jausion by Didier, and then the prosecutor spoke as follows :

'If I request your attention once more, it is not to go back to the innumerable facts that have been laid before you, and which have left such profound traces in your minds, but to re-establish the authority of certain principles that have sometimes been lost sight of in these discussions, principles common to the laws of all countries, and upon which rests the security of all, and of the entire social order. Some are relative to the faith due to witnesses, some are relative to the faith due to confessions of the accused in a criminal trial.

The principle regarding witnesses is this : all those to whose deposition no exception is taken are to be presumed worthy of the judge's confidence. In this trial, in which there are over 300 witnesses for the prosecution, in no case has the defence established an ulterior motive. You know it has not attempted to do so, and this circumstance is a precious monument to the exactitude and attention the ministry has devoted to the selection of the witnesses.

'Remember then this certain rule : any witness called by the prosecution to whom exception is not taken by the defence, offers, in the oath he has taken before God and man, a guarantee that he has given his evidence in the spirit of that oath : it is to be accepted, unless the evidence of other proofs demonstrates that he was mistaken.

'Observe now the language of the accused Bastide. He simply asserted that such and such a witness was not speaking the truth : this does not weigh against a witness testifying under oath. He brought no evidence of malice or passion. If assertions of this kind were to be accepted in a court of law, it would mean that any crime could be committed with impunity, and society would return to chaos. It is assumed, unless there is good reason to believe otherwise, that a witness under oath is speaking the truth. This is necessary, and this is universal.

'Of course, in the case of a single fact, and only one witness appearing, and that fact not supported by any other indication, the judge, having to decide between the witness who affirms and the accused who denies, assumes the accused is innocent.

'But when it is a case, like this one that has occupied us for so many months, in which there are an infinite number of facts which support each other, facts which, taken all together as a whole, establish the guilt of the accused, to insist upon several witnesses for each fact would be to render the discovery of the truth impossible. Such a system was consistently rejected by the ancient tribunals although they had to establish legal as well as convincing proof of guilt. We have even more reason to reject it because our laws prescribe only that the jury should have an intimate conviction of the guilt or innocence of the accused.

'With regard to confessions made by a person on trial, the severe but necessary rule, recognised by the criminal laws of all countries with ordered governments, is that we are to believe his accusations but not the denials by which he justifies his own actions. This rule is founded upon knowledge of the human heart. . . . Therefore the accusations of Bax, Bousquier and Madame Bancal, are to be believed : their denials of participation are not to be accepted if in contradiction to the testimony of a witness.

'To save the innocent is a sacred duty; but it is a duty no less sacred to save society by punishing the guilty. We know that sometimes, such is the unhappy fate of the human condition, we are left in a state of painful uncertainty : but in this case both the crime and the criminals are known, Providence itself has enlightened justice, the fearful truth has been brought out into the light of day. You hold, gentlemen, the shield and the sword. Cover the innocent with the shield, and arm yourself with the sword against the authors of a crime at which all nature shudders and which surpasses all the known combinations of human perversity.'

On Monday morning, 4th May, immense crowds filled the courtroom, the corridors, and the streets round the Palais de Justice to hear the verdict : among them were the families and friends of the accused.

The President began his summing up: 'Truth said, "I am the daughter of Time : in the long run I shall obtain everything from him." Applying this maxim to the considerations, both social and particular, that belong to this memorable trial, and which are now submitted to your judgement, we ask you, is the prosecutor justified? He says to the principal accused, "You are the relations of the unfortunate Monsieur Fualdès; he counted you among the number of his friends . . . that was his fatal error! The proofs which the examination of the witnesses have brought forth have dissipated the shadows in which you tried to hide yourselves and have clearly illuminated the crime and its authors.

' "If we study these proofs we find they point to you, Bastide and Jausion, as the contrivors of this outrage which justice in consternation seeks to repress. . . . It is you who conspired against the life of Fualdès, animated by the thirst for wealth, emboldened by the impunity of your past excesses, trampling underfoot everything men respect and cherish, the most sacred laws, the ties of blood, the affections of the heart. . . . It is you who recruited and paid the mercenaries that a little gold rendered amenable to your cruel orders. . . . It is you who organised the trap into which his too credulous confidence drew him . . . it is you who betrayed and assassinated him.

' "You chose the Maison Bancal as the scene of the crime – was it not the resort of your scandalous disorders? Did it not contain profoundly perverse beings, suitable accomplices because they were accustomed to every kind of excess? It was you who, preluding the murder by a crime of extortion in your criminal and insatiable cupidity, despoiled the victim both before and after tearing his life from him. It was you, Jausion, who first struck your unfortunate relative. You, Bastide, followed with other blows, and killed him." This is the case of the prosecutor, the public minister, who accuses you both of this mass of horrors on behalf of the public. With the authority of irrefutable proofs he believes he has demonstrated invincibly that you are guilty under the headings of the assassination, the theft, and the disposal of the body in the Aveyron River.

'But the voice of the prosecutor must not close our ears to the defence offered by the accused. A provision of the law orders us to listen to their pleas.

'This is Bastide's and Jausion's reply to the charges : "We are innocent. Hazard, fatality, a chain of circumstances we could not foresee has brought upon our heads this mass of lies and errors. . . . Everything shows that the dreadful accusations brought against us are untrue. We are not the assassins of Monsieur Fualdès. The proof is that we were with our families and in our homes at the time the murder was committed. If this proof of our innocence is disallowed, is it not sufficient that we were the friends and relations of the victim? Yes, gentlemen, we dare say, and you yourselves must certainly be convinced of this, that our place in this celebrated trial is not that of criminals but of men suffering protracted and very sad misfortune."

'Our task, gentlemen, that the law imposes upon us, consists of presenting to you an analysis, impartial and exact, of the information that has come to light during the course of the trial, to point out to you the principal proofs, for and against the accused; and finally to remind you of the duty you have to fulfil. In this analysis, which must present a faithful picture of the tragic event the witnesses have described, we will discard everything that appears to us superfluous, and keep to the main lines.

'I will deal with the events antecedent, immediate, and subsequent to the crime. Once the material has been classified it will be easy for me to explain the principal charges to you, and the remarkable incidents belonging to each of these successive periods as they concern the accused individually.'

Monsieur de Latouche of *Le Sténograph Parisien* was very impressed with this address to the jury. He wrote :

This summing up gave us renewed proof that the President combined an analytical method with the art of making deductions that caused seemingly unimportant details to shed new light on the questions at issue. He quoted, for example, the evidence of a witness who thought he had seen

Bastide and Jausion violently dragging a girl into the Maison Bancal on the evening of 19th March, and commented, 'But was he in fact mistaken when he declared he had seen a woman among the group dragging the unhappy Fualdès towards the infamous place where he was to find his death? Anne Benoît who had gone to look for Colard in Rose Féral's tavern, and whom Bousquier saw later in the Bancals' kitchen, was she not the woman the witness had seen among the assassins?' Similarly, trying to explain the presence of the imbecile Missonier, whom the assassins had certainly not taken into their confidence. Monsieur de Faydel said, 'Missonier may have been wandering in the rue des Hebdomadiers – he couldn't get into his stable because the beggar, Laville, was sleeping there – he too may have been seen by those on watch outside the Maison Bancal, have been dragged in and forced to participate in the crime to insure his discretion.'

On the completion of his summing up, the President announced the questions the court was putting to the jury :

First question. Catherine Bruguière, widow Bancal : is she guilty of having, during the evening of 19th March 1817, committed murder on the person of sieur Fualdès, retired magistrate ?

Second question. Was the said Catherine Bruguière an accomplice in the murder committed upon the person of sieur Fualdès, or did she knowingly aid or assist the author or authors of the murder in the events that prepared or facilitated or consummated it ?

Third question. Did the said Catherine Bruguière, widow Bancal, act with premeditation ?

He put these three questions for each of the accused, Bastide-Grammont, Joseph Jausion, Jean-Baptiste Colard, François Bax, Joseph Missonier and Anne Benoît.

He put two additional questions for Bastide, Jausion, Bax, Colard and Missonier :

Is the accused guilty of having thrown the body of sieur Fualdès into the Aveyron River during the same evening of 19th March ?

Was the accused an accomplice in the said action of knowingly aiding or assisting its authors in its preparation, facilitation, or consummation ?

The following three questions were applied to Bastide and Jausion :

Is the accused guilty of having fraudulently removed certain effects, such as papers, account books and other things belonging to the inheritors of the late Fualdès; this removal having taken place on the morning of 20th March, in the house of Sieur Fualdès?

Was the accused an accomplice in the removal of these effects, of having knowingly aided or assisted the author or authors of their removal, in the event, in the preparation, in the facilitation or consummation?

Was their fraudulent removal committed by housebreaking?

The questions he submitted with regard to Clarissa were :

Was Marie-Françoise-Clarisse Enjalran, wife of Marc-Antoine Manson, an accomplice in the murder committed on the person of sieur Fualdès during the evening of 19th March, 1817?

Did she knowingly aid or assist the author or authors in its preparation, facilitation, or consummation?

Did she act with premeditation?

Maître Fulquier objected that Anne Benoît had already been declared not guilty of premeditation at the assizes at Rodez, and therefore could not be charged with it. The prosecutor answered that all the verdicts there had been declared null and void by the Supreme Court of Appeal, and so it was in order for her to be charged again.

The jury were absent for five hours : during that time not one of the spectators left his place. The accused were not taken back to their prison but were placed in a room strongly guarded in the Palais de Justice.

At 7 p.m. the jury returned amid profound silence. The leader, with his hand on his heart, read with some emotion the replies to the questions that had been put to them :

Madame Bancal was declared guilty of murder with premeditation.

Bastide guilty of murder with premeditation.

Jausion guilty of murder with premeditation, and both of them guilty of theft with housebreaking.

Colard guilty of murder with premeditation.

Anne Benoît guilty of complicity in the murder, without premeditation.

Missonier, not guilty of murder or of complicity in the murder, but guilty of complicity in the disposal of the body in the river, with Bax, Colard, Bastide and Jausion.

Madame Manson was unanimously declared not guilty.

The leader of the jury then signed the declaration, and the President ordered the prisoners to be brought in. Jausion was so feeble the gendarmes had to support him : he seemed to know already the fate that was awaiting him. The verdict was read to the accused by the Clerk of the Court. Bastide, always firm, had an air of serenity, almost of pride, that was in marked contrast to the despair of his brother-in-law. Colard was perfectly calm, but Anne Benoît displayed grief in every feature. Clarissa could not contain her joy.

The prosecutor asked for those declared guilty to be sentenced. Maître Tajan for Didier asked for his client to be awarded 60,000 francs damages. The court retired to deliberate. Meanwhile Jausion addressed the jury in broken phrases :

> Ah gentlemen ! You did not wish to know the truth ! I am innocent. . . . If we could ask Monsieur Fualdès which of us are his enemies. . . . As soon as I came here the prosecutor determined on my death. . . . On the scaffold I shall speak as I do now. . . . God will judge. . . . They want my money. . . . Let them have it, but leave me my children. I am innocent. Poor children. . . . What will become of them ? Without honour, with nothing to live on, they'll die in the workhouse. . . . I wish a single grave to be dug for me, my wife and my children, and on it let there be inscribed, 'Jausion is innocent !' Let Bax now tell the truth since he too has been condemned : let him say whether I was in the Maison Bancal !
>
> BAX : Yes, you were there. If it wasn't true, I wouldn't have said so.

They both relapsed into silence, and everyone waited quietly until the court re-entered.

The President pronounced the sentences : Madame Bancal, Bastide, Jausion, Colard and Bax were condemned to death. Anne Benoît was condemned to hard labour for life, to be branded and exposed to the public in the stocks. Missonier to two years in prison and a fine of fifty francs.

The sentence of death caused no change in Bastide's expression, but a shadow of darkness passed over his face. Jausion continued to shout that he was innocent. Anne Benoît, when she heard the sentence on Colard, gave a piercing cry, and in a voice that tore everyone's heart, she said, 'Ah sirs ! Condemn me also. I wish to die if he dies.' Colard, who had listened to his sentence unmoved, could not bear her agony : he melted into tears. When her turn came and she was sentenced to hard labour, she moaned, 'No. No. I want to die.'

Finally the jury, 'in the interests of justice and society and considering the importance of Bax's revelations,' begged the court to recommend him to the royal clemency: he had seemed unaffected by his sentence, and half hid his face in a handkerchief.

The President ordered Clarissa to be released immediately. The court rose. The journalists rushed out to send their couriers poste haste to the most distant parts of France. Rodat made his way towards Clarissa but, he tells us, before joining him she went up to the jurors and with ready sympathy told them, 'You have judged well, sirs. Your consciences can be at ease. You have not condemned the innocent.' Then she left the courtroom with Rodat.

'What a judgment!' she said to him. 'It is the voice of God himself! The unfortunate Fualdès will be avenged at last! Every spasm of his agony claims a victim!'

Outside there was a seething crowd, the women more numerous and more excited than the men. Clarissa was prevented from leaving the Palais de Justice by a crowd of journalists who surrounded her, by many notables of the town who wished to congratulate her, and by distinguished strangers who wished to be presented. She sent an appealing glance in Rodat's direction: he forced himself close enough to catch two words, '*Ma mère.*' He nodded, and left at once for Rodez and the Château Perier to let her parents know that at last she was out of danger.

CHAPTER SEVENTEEN

Clarissa's Triumph

The final session of the trial, at which Didier's financial claims were discussed, was held on 5th May. The courtroom was nearly empty : only a few local people attended, and some visitors who had been unable to find horses or carriages to take them away. Maître Tajan, on Didier's behalf, claimed from the condemned men the sum of 97,665 francs – the amount of the late Monsieur Fualdès' debts which, he maintained, would not have existed had it not been for the thefts by the condemned. Maître Romiguière replied that no instance of the theft of any article had been substantiated, and no documents had been submitted in support of the claim. The greater part of Monsieur Fualdès' debts, as the creditors had affirmed, had been contracted before the date of his death. Maître Dubernat spoke in the same sense, emphasising that to claim recompense for theft the civil cause must state what had been stolen. This Didier was unable to do.

'To finish on a point on which the moderation of my client has shone with such nobility,' Maître Tajan said, 'I claim under the heading of damages the above mentioned sum, with the condition that it is to be used solely to pay his creditors.' The court deliberated, and ordered the condemned men to pay 60,000 francs damages to the civil cause.

Meanwhile Bastide, Jausion and Colard had been locked into a dungeon with walls nine feet thick, and they were so heavily loaded with chains that they could scarcely drag themselves across it. Two companies of soldiers patrolled the streets to guard against any possible attempt to rescue them.

On the morning after they were condemned, a large pool of blood was found between four stones that had been set down in the place of execution to support the scaffold, and on each stone there was a cross of blood : they no more resembled Christian crosses than the X in 'X marks the spot'. The crowd flocked to see them, and they gave rise to the most extraordinary rumours. What strange impulse from the depths of the past had made someone slaughter an animal in that place and mark the stones with blood? Some thought they were supernatural phenomena; others thought they were a warning from some group of desperate bandits that they would attack the town if the prisoners were not released.

Reports of the trial crowded out all other news from the leading journals: *The Times* complained, 'The French papers as usual contribute little or nothing to the common fund of political intelligence.' Clarissa's celebrity was at its height. She was awarded a pension of 1,000 francs a year by the authorities with free education for her son. An apartment was provided for her at Albi which she seldom left except to go for walks and attend Mass, but she received counsellors, lawyers, journalists, jurymen, and many other visitors. She was hailed as 'The Heroine of Aveyron'. The proprietors of the Beaujon Gardens offered her a large sum to walk there daily to attract the crowds. There were other lucrative offers all of which she refused, 'because she belonged to one of the most distinguished families of Aveyron and because her son would reproach her one day if she prostituted her name.' 'Is she worthy of her celebrity?' the *Quotidienne* asked, and answered:

> Yes, if it is sufficient to have a lively spirit, an imagination as ardent as varied, the most brilliant and volatile ideas, a retentive memory, a romantic and elevated soul, exquisite sensibility, a good heart, no head for practical affairs, an expression that is good or evil according to the continuing velocity of her rapidly changing thoughts. Added to all this, her dress is fashionable but original, she is graceful, small but well formed, she has a shapely foot, a white hand, beautiful teeth, a magnificent and very expressive voice, she is quick at repartee and carries on the most amicable and lively conversations, etc., etc.

There were columns of this sort of thing, and accounts of her quarrel with Monsieur Clémendot who continued to abuse her in press interviews and refer to her as 'Madame Mensonge' (Madam Falsehood.)

The barristers were allowed to visit their clients in the dungeon. Colard said to Maître Bole, 'You must not regret your effort to defend me. I am innocent. My last request is this: ask *Monsieur le Président* if I can be led out to execution only after Bax, for at the edge of the grave he must admit that he has falsely accused me.'

Bax's defender, Maître Dupuy, supported by Didier, petitioned the King for a reprieve: this was granted both in the case of Bax and of Madame Bancal as their evidence would be required in the next trial.

Jausion said that if he could be allowed a respite for three months he would definitely prove his innocence. His brother, the Abbé Jausion, visited him daily: this was represented in the press as an act of great courage.

Bastide asked if their wives had been informed of the verdict: Romiguière said they had. It was impossible to keep the news from them. They cried all night. 'They know we are innocent,' Bastide said. 'That must be their consolation.' He asked again and again for his brother, unaware that he had been arrested and was also in the prison of St Cecilia. He also sent for his old friend, the Abbé de Mejanes-Veynac, Grand Vicar of Rodez: he came and prayed with him in spite of the Prefect, Monsieur Decazes, who objected to any of the condemned men receiving the consolations of religion. The makers of models pestered the prison authorities to allow them to buy their clothes for the wax-works. Maître Dubernat, who had unsuccessfully defended Jausion, gave the whole of his fee to various charities.

Maître Romiguière again went to Paris to put his case before the Supreme Court of Appeal. He suggested five reasons why the proceedings should be annulled: that all the accused should have been tried together, that once again the oaths had not been taken in the proper form, that a number of witnesses had been heard who only repeated stories they claimed to have heard from the Bancal children, and the fourth was that obstacles had been put in the way of the defence. All these were rejected. The fifth was the gross injustice of the witnesses for the defence being intimidated and penalised: this too was rejected because it did not legally constitute grounds for declaring the trial null and void. The Supreme Court of Appeal was concerned only with the letter of the law. The sentences were ordered to be carried out.

A month after the verdict, Rodat was still at Olemps: he had heard nothing from Albi for some time except that Romiguière had published and circulated seventeen letters written in praise of Bastide, most of them by priests: among them was one from the Grand Vicar who wrote of the uprightness and sweetness of his character. Then he received the following letter from Clarissa, written in a trembling hand and dated 4th June from Albi:

My Dear Auguste – The assassins of Monsieur Fualdès perished at three o'clock. This fatal event has renewed all my anxieties: the day, sombre and overcast, seemed to add to the horror of the moment. They had tried in vain to keep me in the dark about it. . . . Frightful presentiments were tearing at my heart. On 2nd June my suffering began; on the 3rd I was torn to the very soul as cruelly as on 19th March, the anniversary of the crime. You know, Auguste, all I suffered that day, you were close to me. That evening I heard groans, I lost control of my imagination, my heart beat violently. I don't know if it was my heart or my mind that deceived me, but I heard the blood of the victim dripping, a dying groan froze my soul with terror – it seemed about to leave my body. Alas! on the 4th June, on rising from my bed, I felt the same symptoms coming on, as on the anniversary. I was to have gone to the country but I hadn't the strength. I shut myself up at home with my son and a companion. The tolling bell I had heard all morning, rung for the dying, was in tune with my darkest thoughts – my thoughts? No. I had no thoughts. All my faculties were in suspense. I almost envied the lot of the Christian who was dying and who was forcing me to pray for him. I didn't in the least suspect that I was praying for the man who would have murdered me and for the man who saved my life.

In the evening my little son wanted to go for a walk; on his return he informed me of the death of the criminals: did it have to be the voice of innocence that told me they had been punished for their crime? I pressed my son to my breast. All my anxiety was explained. I sighed for Jausion. I owed him my life: I owed him the happiness of holding my son in my arms. Alas! This embrace made me feel all the bitterness of his last goodbye to his children. How the thirst for gold can dehumanise a man! But I found myself greatly relieved that the earth was delivered from a man as coldly criminal, as frightful, as Bastide. The Clerk of the Court told me that when he was informed his last appeal was rejected he gave a great cry; it was that of a tiger dying before having seized his prey. He showed himself as cowardly as he was criminal: he had to be dragged to his death. He was without human feelings. . . . In vain the minister of religion spoke to him of forgivenness of sins – it meant nothing to him. He regretted only that he could no longer do evil. The language of assassins was the only language he could appreciate. With no further possibility to do evil, the ferocious Bastide had nothing left to live for.

Jausion showed more courage. He put his affairs in order with great composure of mind: he listened to the voice of religion: he walked firmly to his death. He was not born to a life of crime. A man who, in the midst of carnage, can listen to his heart and save a woman's life was not, I repeat, born for crime. . . . Alas, my Auguste, why did he take the road that led to the scaffold? If the thirst for gold had not led him to force open a desk, he would still be alive: and I, who endured eight months of prison rather than name him, would have known how to guard his secret, and I would have rejoiced in his return to the path of virtue. Ah! Why did he reject the advice I gave him, to obtain a pardon by turning King's evidence? In spite of the wisdom of my counsel he rejected it. How powerful great criminals are! What influence they exercise over their companions! Goodbye, my Auguste. Only my parents' forgivenness could relieve the torments I suffer. Need I say that your friendship, of which I am so sure, gives me the courage to beg their pardon although I am unworthy of it. You alone can obtain it for me. – Clarissa.

The eye-witness accounts published in the *Quotidienne* are rather different. They tell us the decision of the Supreme Court of Appeal was brought to Toulouse by special courier and thence to Albi where he arrived on 2nd June towards nine p.m. At 11.30 on the third, Sheriff's Officer Cussac entered the prison and the names of Bastide, Jausion and Colard echoed under the vaults. They were brought to him, their arms bound behind them, their legs chained, and he informed them their appeal had been rejected. They were separated and each placed in a different cell. Counsellor Pagan, charged with the duty of securing confessions, went to each in turn and implored him in the name of the sovereign judge before whom he was about to appear to hide the truth no longer and confess to the horrible crime, because their continued imposture added to their guilt without mitigating their punishment. They all insisted they were innocent and had no knowledge of the crime whatever. Bastide and Jausion asked him to write down their final declarations, which he did, and then left the prison, 'stricken to the heart,' according to Monsieur Olivier of the *Quotidienne,* 'having been able to do nothing for justice.'

The news spread quickly that the executions were about to take place, and this was confirmed by the erection of the guillotine in the Place de Manège : people ran to see it from all over the town and others crowded in from the neighbouring villages. A strong force of mounted police guarded all the approaches, and two companies of soldiers waited outside the prison. Anne Benoît was brought out, placed in the stocks in the public square and branded with a hot iron. She wept all day and called incessantly for Colard.

At 4.30 p.m. the three condemned men were brought from their prison and put into their cage on wheels with two priests, each holding up a crucifix and praying for them. They were surrounded by a numerous escort of police, one company of soldiers led the way to the place of execution, the other followed. Bastide and Colard, their arms bound behind them and their feet shackled, were wearing the clothes they had worn in court. Jausion wore a cap and cloak : he sat immobile, bent over a crucifix. Colard had already lost all appearance of life; his head fell from one shoulder to the other, or down onto his breast, as the cage jolted. Bastide's looks frightened the spectators, his livid cheeks and white face contrasted starkly with his long black beard.

Arrived at the Place de Manège, the armed forces thrust the people back and cleared a wide space round the guillotine. Jausion was the first to be handed over to the executioners: in a feeble voice he said to the public: 'I die innocent of the assassination of Monsieur Fualdès. A day will come when my children will no longer be reproached as the sons of an assassin. I ask for the prayers of all good souls . . .' A few moments later his headless body was lying on the scaffold. Colard was lifted up more dead than alive, but he protested his innocence and blamed Bastide for his death. Bastide descended from the cage, and then his strength seemed to leave him; he swayed backwards and would have fallen had he not been supported and dragged up onto the scaffold. After these few moments of semi-consciousness he recovered and went bravely to his death. He cried out, 'My family! What will they think?' Then he fell down onto the block, the knife descended and a groan of horror burst from the crowd.

What did his family think? Their wives had been kept in ignorance that the appeal had been rejected, and for a whole day none dared tell them of the execution. Then, on the following day, Monsieur Chatard, priest and prison chaplain, with the Abbé Pújol broke the news to them. Madame Bastide fell insensible and for a full hour could not be brought back to life; then she awoke in a pitiful state of nervous prostration. Madame Jausion, who was already ill and in bed, lay for many hours in an agony of grief with her ten-year-old son embracing her and trying to comfort her. The Mayor of Albi sent them word that he was taking measures to prevent the crowd from insulting their husbands' bodies. Commissioners were sent to seize the dead men's furniture and valuables towards paying Didier's and the government's claims: they found only the bare walls of their deserted houses.

Justice at last is satisfied and society avenged. These men upon whom the attention of Europe has been fixed for months, who believed because of their credit in the world and their fortunes that they could elude the arm of the law have no longer been able to save themselves from the avenging sword destined for the punishment of great crimes. For them, as for the poor and obscure citizen, the jury was firm, and the magistrates displayed a just and imposing severity. They no longer exist. May this example live, and spare us in the future the spectacle of another crime like this! (*La Quotidienne*, 12 June, 1818.)

The same journal notes the stay of execution for Madame Bancal: 'She is expected to make new revelations in the interests of justice and truth, but the wretched woman has relapsed into her original impassivity: she declares that her revelations will be only to her confessor.

It is believed that if she persists in this attitude she will be executed next Saturday.'

This was Bastide's last declaration :

I am incapable of committing the crime for which I have been condemned to death. Let them look for the assassins of Monsieur Fualdès among his enemies, not among his friends. I know nothing at all relative to the crime. I was at Gros in the bosom of my family on the evening of 19th March : this fact has been established. I declare those who have testified against me are mistaken or are false witnesses. Bousquier, who admits having assisted in the crime, has falsely accused me : he does not know me. I have never been in the Maison Bancal. It is only to escape the punishment they merit, for they admit themselves guilty, that they have accused me. Théron is a false witness; he could not have recognised those who carried the body of Fualdès to the River Aveyron; the night was too dark.

Clarissa Enjalran Manson admitted that she did not know me : I had seen her only once on the road : she could not, therefore have recognised me in the Maison Bancal : and besides, what faith can one have in a woman who has given us so many versions of her story since the trial began?

I declare that no member of my family could have dipped his hands in the blood of Fualdès : I am sure that Yence d'Istourmet left Rodez on 19th March at six o'clock in the evening : for the whole of that day I did not see Bessières-Veynac at all, nor my brother Louis – for some time there have been disagreements between him and myself. Finally I declare that on my way to Gros on 19th March, I found Charlotte Arlabosse at La Roquette, and on the following day I found her there again. I was on my way to my domain at La Morne.

As the last words of a dying man are sacred, I beg *Monsieur le Conseiller* to set them down in writing, and to transmit them to my family. I declare to my wife and to all my relations that I die innocent.

Jausion in his last declaration stated he had no share in the murder : on 19th March he had supped with his family and had not gone out again, and this had been proved. Without actually accusing anyone, he pointed out that Monsieur Fualdès had had enemies among those whom he had persecuted at Espallion during the Hundred Days, and mentioned particularly a Monsieur Laquelhe père of Mur-de-Barre whose eldest son had vowed to take vengeance. He concluded : 'I declare to my wife and to my children that I shall die innocent.'

Thus ended these two memorable trials. The editor of *L'Histoire Complète du Procès instruit devant la Cour D'Assises de L'Aveyron* summed up as follows :

> Celebrity is the reward not only of great virtues and heroic actions : it is given also to great crimes and great criminals. To pay eternal honour to those men who merit the recognition and the veneration of peoples, history cherishes their memory, but it perpetuates also the memory of those monsters who have sullied the earth and brought dishonour to the human race : therefore the names of Jausion and of Bastide-Grammont will be handed down to posterity.

The final judgment had no sooner been pronounced than Edward again challenged Clémendot to a duel : this time the authorities did not intervene. As soon as Rodat heard of it he hastened to Edward's lodgings, hoping to prevent a meeting, for he felt sure that his mother's life was at stake besides his own. He found him safe and well – he had fought and wounded Clémendot that morning, and he assured Rodat he had no intention of pursuing the affair any further : he begged him to go at once and reassure his mother, but he would not go himself to the Château Perier in case Clarissa should be there, for he refused to be reconciled to her, still mourning for his lost love – Rose Pierret's father had taken her, with Edward's full approval, probably at his suggestion, to a distant part of France to begin life over again. Rodat went back alone to the Château Perier and had the inexpressible joy of assuring his mother that her beloved Edward was safe. He showed Clarissa's letter to her parents, as she had evidently intended him to. Her father's severe looks melted when he read the words written by his daughter's trembling hand; his gentler feelings for her revived, and Rodat was able to write and tell her she could return home.

The Enjalran family were not yet free from these terrible events : Clarissa would be required as a witness in the trial of the other members of Bastide's family that was about to open at Albi. Rodat joined her there, and he found with her a closer relationship than they had had before. She told him that when all danger was past, Ferdinand had come back and tried to assert his old influence over her, but she had replied, 'Clarissa can only love her family, and her trusted friend.' He took this as her way of saying there was no longer any obstacle between them, and he was moved to reply, 'O my Clarissa, as my heart has truly loved you in your misfortune, you may count upon my devotion now and for ever.'

The supplementary trial, designed to bring the remainder of Bastide's gang to justice, opened at Albi on 21st December, 1818. It was under the presidency of Monsieur de Miegeville. The five accused were :

Jean-Josef Yence, a retired magistrate, Bastide's uncle.

Bastide's brother Louis : he too had a well-established fortune and lived simply on his own estate. He was a noted expert on agriculture, and also on astronomy.

Pierre-Josef Bessières-Veynac, the son of one of Bastide's sisters. He had studied law at Toulouse, and after an appointment as a teacher had spent two years at the College of St. Louis le Grand in Paris. He was a lay brother of a Catholic order.

Charlotte Arlabosse, couturière.

Marie-Antoine Constans, an ex-Commissioner of Police.

One of the Laquelhe brothers had also been arrested, but he was released on proving an alibi.

Looking at these people on the bench of the accused, it was hard to imagine any of them capable of committing a crime : they were neatly and simply dressed, interesting in their appearance and pleasant in their manner and in their behaviour towards each other : they were not in chains, and nothing suggested they were criminals except that they were surrounded by gendarmes. The most tragic was Louis Bastide : when he was arrested, his two sons unable to bear the family shame had died, it was said, of grief. His sole accuser was Bax who had first identified him as one of the assassins and then failed to recognise him when they were confronted.

Yence was accused both by Clarissa and Bax of having been one of the assassins in the Maison Bancal : three witnesses claimed they had positively recognised him near the scene of the crime : others said it was he who had paid the hurdy-gurdy players whose noise had covered up the groans of the victim; and many others testified that his troubled and distracted air had convinced them of his guilt. A gendarme reported him as having said the proceedings against Bastide were unjust; that he had protested particularly against Théron's testimony; that he had tried to find witnesses for the defence, and it was alleged also that after Bastide and Jausion's arrest he had advised them to sell their property so that they could go to a country where the family was not known – all of which was what any reasonable man would have said and advised, but it was alleged against him as a crime.

Allegations against Charlotte Arlabosse concerned principally her relations with Bastide. It was testified she had gone with him on a visit to Montpellier, that she had met him frequently at night in Monsieur Fualdès' garden, and that she had been friendly with Madame Pons. Only Bax had accused her of being with the assassins in the Maison Bancal, but he had mistaken her identity several times. Many witnesses for the defence testified she was at La Roquette when the crime was being committed – among these were her father who was a farm labourer, her sister, a number of peasants and a big landowner.

Ex-Police Commissioner Constans was accused of having talked to Bastide shortly before the murder, of having entered the Maison Bancal on the evening of 17th March, of having told the gendarmes not to make their usual rounds on the night of the crime. Various witnesses complained that instead of assiduously collecting the evidence, he had discouraged them when they tried to give him information about the Maison Bancal which public opinion had already fixed upon as the scene of the murder. He was also said to have kept up relations with Bastide and Jausion when they were already under suspicion, and promised them his support.

One would have thought that this trial, after all that had happened, would have aroused only mild curiosity, but public interest in the Fualdès murder seemed to be insatiable: the psychological atmosphere, however, had changed. Instead of the verdict of guilty demanded by the prosecutor being a foregone conclusion, as in the earlier trials, the authorities from the very beginning had difficulty in establishing their case. Instead of the counsels for the defence sounding unconvincing, it was the prosecutor: his statements which in the earlier trials would have been accepted without question were now treated with suspicion: statements such as that the witnesses for the prosecution had no conceivable motive to seek the lives of the accused, and therefore they should be believed, whereas the witnesses for the defence were influenced by personal motives to save their friends by trying to establish alibis for them, therefore they should be disregarded. Neither the public nor the jury seemed to be impressed by his arguments: the supporters of Bastide's family took heart, more and more of them came forward to testify until there were about 150 witnesses on each side.

The declamations about outraged society, the expressions of horror by the President, by Maître Tajan and by the prosecutor, were no less than in the previous trial, the oratory was no less brilliant, Clarissa's descriptions of what she had seen and suffered in the Maison Bancal were no less blood-curdling, the witnesses for the prosecution were no less unanimous in their condemnation of the accused, but they carried no weight. Didier, still declaiming about the sacred duties of filial piety and wallowing in the agonies of his grief, seemed less deserving of pity now that he had tasted the blood of his enemies: the audience were getting tired of him, and of the obsequious Bousquier. Even the cold and furtive Bax who was accustomed to denouncing his companions with perfect equanimity and in the confidence that he would be supported and protected by the authorities, seemed to be losing his nerve: when Louis Bastide roundly accused him of having murdered Bastide by his lying denunciations, he went pale with fury and like an animal at bay hissed back at him, 'You may get me to the scaffold, but I'll make sure that you follow me!' and then he shouted to the President that he had positively seen Louis among the assassins.

This little scene profoundly disillusioned the audience: they murmured to each other, and it was clear they had at last divined that Bax was an unscrupulous scoundrel and not to be trusted. The President was evidently aware of their change of mood, for he announced forthwith that Louis Bastide had no charge to answer, and ordered him to be set at liberty. He had been forty-eight days in prison.*

Madame Bancal was brought in to repeat her testimony against Bessières-Veynac: she looked wizened and dishevelled like a harassed bird of prey. She was confronted with her eldest daughter Marianne, now partly recovered from her illness: they fell into each other's arms and sobbed for several minutes. This startled Rodat: 'I could not have been more horrified if I had seen the Eumenides embracing . . .' but when he glanced around at the audience he saw that many of them were in tears also. When she was able to speak, Madame Bancal retracted her accusation of Bessières-Veynac: she said she had only accused him to make her story more convincing when she was in the shadow of the guillotine. This seemed quite possible: she had twice heard herself condemned to death, and a coffin had been made for her. Her retraction was heard with favour by the public. In this emotional climate it was becoming more and more doubtful whether the authorities were going to succeed in obtaining convictions.

Even their star witness, Clarissa, had lost her appeal: her straightforward denunciations of Bessières-Veynac and the rest of Bastide's family had nothing like the same effect as her earlier half-statements, retractions, emotional outbursts, and silences heavy with implications.

* Soon after Louis Bastide's return to his now desolate home, he went insane.

'How do you know they are guilty?' the President asked her.

'Because I was there!' she answered.

Bessières-Veynac objected that in the previous trial she had stated that she had not seen him in the Maison Bancal.

'Yes,' she said, 'but I was on trial for my life then, and not under oath. I could say what I pleased. But now I am telling the truth.'

Bessières-Veynac was a gracious youth of twenty-seven, very like his elder brother who had been Rodat's early rival with Clarissa, except that he was not so tall. Five witnesses claimed they had seen him near the scene of the crime, one that he was in the Maison Bancal just before the murder was committed, three that he was there while they were killing the victim, and one that he helped to transport the body. Many others testified he had been seen frequently in the company of Bastide and Jausion and their families, and that he had tried to find witnesses for their defence. He was reported to have said that the magistrate who ordered Bastide's arrest ought to have been shot. On the other hand he had a well-attested alibi – he had spent the evening of 19th March at Laborie in the company of a doctor, a lawyer and a justice of the peace, and many others had seen him there.

Again Clarissa was sent for and asked, 'You are quite sure you recognise the accused? You have not the slightest doubt in your mind?'

'No, Monsieur,' she answered, 'I have not the slightest doubt he was among the assassins.'

'What gives you this assurance?'

'It is the force of truth and the blood of Fualdès crying for vengeance!' Her words left the audience unmoved.

She was still treated by the court with deference and by the public with respect because she had atoned for her previous silences by months of imprisonment and a heavy trial, but it was the calm and gentle Charlotte Arlabosse on the bench of the accused who now carried the sympathy of the audience, her fair hair glinting in the sun that slanted in through the tall windows. Months of imprisonment and the tragic death of her lover had saddened her bright features, but her manner had not changed.

Clarissa was now saying what Rodat, her family and the authorities had always wanted her to say – but somehow she was different: her voice sounded harsh at times, almost inhuman, and her appearance, although she was always perfectly dressed, had changed also: she had aged, and there was no longer any play of emotion on her once sensitive features.

How could it be otherwise? Rodat asked himself. How could she

have passed through her terrible experiences, the shame of the prison
cell, the humiliation of sitting on the bench of the accused with the
vilest malefactors, her months of indecision and mental torture and
remain unchanged? The public, who understood nothing of what she
had suffered, sensed the change in her also : although she was always
regarded with interest, and everything she said was eagerly publicised
in the newspapers, she was openly accused of being a celebrity hunter,
of playing for effect : her great, though variable popularity was turning
to mere notoriety. Rodat sensed that now, more perhaps than at any
other time, she needed his help, and he pressed on with the writing
of his book which he hoped would re-establish her in the affections of
her fellow men and women. He wrote in his introduction :

> I flatter myself that the public, always indulgent towards
> one who has captivated their attention and excited their curiosity, will
> thank me for giving back to them Madame Manson such as they have
> always desired her to be : a woman of great fortitude with a high sense
> of honour and a sensitive and generous heart : and I flatter myself
> also that they will trust in my good faith and in the certitude of the facts
> that I report.'

It was not only of Clarissa he was thinking, but of her whole family :
he wanted to establish also her father's severe but upright character,
her mother's tenderness, and Edward's gallantry and generosity.

The trial ended on 14th January 1819, with a verdict of not guilty
on all of the accused. The audience started to applaud, but the President
sternly reminded them that all expressions of approbation or of impro-
bation were strictly forbidden. As soon as the prisoners were set free
they left the courtroom escorted in triumph by their friends and
relatives. Their opponents proclaimed that the still powerful Bastide
family had been able to engage a sufficient number of false witnesses
to sway the jury in their favour.

Rodat's manuscript was nearly ready for the printer. One final scene
he still had to record, illustrating the integrity of Clarissa's character : as
a result of the unavoidable publicity she had brought upon herself, the
representative of a Parisian newspaper made her a financially advantageous offer to go with him to the capital where, he assured her, she
would be a sensation. She rejected his offer with scorn, telling him she
had acted as she did purely from love of justice and not from any
commercial motive or self-interest : and she sent him about his business.
When Rodat had got her away from the importunate crowds they still
had to endure a reception given in her honour.

Next day on the way home she burst into tears and said, 'Ah Auguste! I did not think I had brought such shame upon my head. I was prepared to be rejected by my fellow citizens, but these humiliating commercial proposals overwhelm me.'

An English traveller reported :

Toulouse; March 31st 1819. The woman concerned in the murder of Fualdès was brought before the Court of Assizes to hear her Pardon read. When this was over, she was exhibited as a Spectacle, to the Gentlefolks of the Town, French and English.

She conversed on the subject of the murder, and persisted in maintaining the Guilt of Yence and Bessières-Veynac, who were lately rescued from the hands of Justice by a host of Perjurers.

CHAPTER EIGHTEEN

The Veil Torn Aside

When Rodat had escorted Clarissa to the Château Perier and seen her happily reunited to her father and mother, he completed his manuscript and sent it off to his publisher in Paris. To add to the general air of mystery that had always surrounded the case, he signed it E.E. by which he seems to have intended to convey that he was *Equites Enjalran,* Knight Defender of the Enjalran Family, suppressing his own name which, as he rightly says, may easily be discerned by the reader, and he added that love of mystery seemed to be a *mal de famille.* He adopted as an appropriate title, *Le Coin du Voile Levé,* The Corner of the Veil Lifted, the words Bastide had used when Madame Bancal confessed in court that the crime had in fact been committed in her house, implying (according to Rodat) that more revelations would follow.

He continued his old habit of going over to the Château Perier almost daily : Clarissa always received him so kindly that he again began to hope she would at last consent to unite their lives and destinies that were already so closely intertwined, for he was sure there was a deep attachment between them and that if she had accepted him when they were young, none of these misfortunes would have come upon her. Her mother was overjoyed when he consulted her about it.

One evening as they sat in the lengthening shadows of the walnut-trees, they turned their thoughts to the future. 'Clarissa has made mistakes,' Madame Enjalran said, 'but we can always learn from our experiences. You must be humble, my child, after the terrible things your impetuous and uncontrolled behaviour has brought upon you, and upon us all. I feel certain that true happiness and a modest and virtuous life are still possible for you.' She looked fondly on them both and left them alone together in the garden.

In the little summer-house, half overgrown with roses and honeysuckle, Rodat told her that since his return from Paris he had offered her his friendship only, not wishing to take advantage of her distress, but now he offered her his heart. She replied it was too late : too much had happened to come between them, and she had gone too far ever to come back to him : but he pleaded with her, hour after hour, and finally she relented. He said she had only to entrust herself to him, and he would help her to forget the terror that had been inflicted on her; and she would be the queen of his heart and of his beautiful domain at Olemps where they would allow no evil thing to enter.

She sobbed for a while, and then was silent. It was quite dark now, and he could see her only by the light of the stars. The sorrows of the past year seemed to roll away and they stood again on the brink of a new life such as he had imagined when they played together as children.

He had not expected his task to be an easy one : he understood that no one could have endured the mental strain of the past months without being affected by it, for better or for worse, and he realised with grief that Clarissa had changed in some ways for the worse. But he still believed his quiet devotion and gentle companionship would heal her wounds, and that eventually he would find again the Clarissa he had once known and always loved.

For a while she was content : she listened to the wise words of her mother in a humble spirit, and she frequently asked for the assurance of Rodat's unchanging love for her. Then she began to grow restless, and to all their questions she returned evasive answers. She absented herself more and more frequently from the château without saying where she was going : they learned by chance that she was having her portrait painted in Rodez.

They feared she was returning to her old irresponsible behaviour, but she explained it by saying, 'I want my face to be well known so that any woman feeling she has similar traits of character to mine, and finding herself in similar circumstances, may be warned not to act as I have acted, and to imitate only my repentance.' Rodat had doubts, but her mother listened to her words with approval : 'Misfortune is a school,' she said, 'in which one makes rapid progress.'

Next day Clarissa had gone. She had after all accepted the tempting offer of the journalist and left with him for Paris, taking Kleinking with her. That she could treat her mother like this opened Rodat's eyes at last to the truth : he had been mistaken in her all along : she was cold, she was heartless, she was insensible to the suffering she inflicted on others. Clarissa was interested only in Clarissa. Her situation in the trial had enabled her for months to be the centre of attention and this was, after all, what she most desired. It had enabled her to assume the role of the heroine she had always dreamed of being; and although it broke her mother's heart she would not forego the last act in the drama – her triumphant entry into the capital.

Soon after her departure, the page proofs of his book arrived : in his distress he had entirely forgotten it. He re-read it and realised he could not possibly allow this justification of her actions, this hymn of praise for her virtues, to reach the public. He tried to withdraw the book, but the publisher was adamant : it had to come out, and as soon as possible while the affair was still news. He did allow Rodat, however, to add footnotes commenting adversely on her character and behaviour : they contradicted in important respects what he had said in the main body of the text. He had extolled her sensitivity and her love for her child; in a footnote he said that nothing gentle, nothing peaceful, could enter her strongly constituted heart, and that her tenderness for her child was convulsive, it came upon her suddenly between long spells of ignoring it altogether. He had tried to arouse pity for her imprisonment and for her appearance on the bench of the accused : he now added that she had deliberately brought these upon herself because they made her the centre of attention. He had condoned with her because of the evil things said about her; in his footnote he pointed out that she cared not whether it was praise or blame so long as she was talked about.

After the chapter in which he described how she had told him of her love for Ferdinand, he commented she had never known the happiness that is shared between two generous souls but only the forced expression of love with violent agitation beyond what was natural. Finally he drew a comparison between her mother who constantly forgot herself to think only of the happiness of those around her, and Clarissa who constantly forgot those around her to think only of herself.

In Paris Clarissa's celebrity was brief and quickly eclipsed by new sensations. Soon all that was left of it was a bust of her in the Curtius Waxworks set up beside a gory representation of Monsieur Fualdès' body; and there was a doggerel version of her ordeal in the Maison Bancal, written by a coiffeur of Toulouse and sung to the air of '*Le Maréchal de Saxe*', going the rounds of the provincial fairs. With the Parisians she had little success; they found her clothes and her manner definitely unattractive, and the rough Provençal voice that had so enthralled Rodat grated upon them. There was just sufficient notoriety attached to her name to get her a job as cashier in the Café de

Foy in the Palais-Royal district, one of the centres of Parisian night life.

Rodat had to come to terms with the fact that the woman he had loved so devotedly cared nothing for him in return – and after all it was not her fault that he had endowed her with virtues she didn't possess. He had to understand also that after the frightful scenes she had witnessed, and the intense drama of the trials, it was impossible for her to reconcile herself to the simple pleasures of country life: she needed the tempo and variety of the great city.

On 4th September 1821, three years after the executions, Bousquier being at the point of death in the workhouse at Rodez, solemnly retracted his deposition and requested that his retraction should be made public. On 4th January 1822, the Registrar at Rodez took note of his declaration which had been taken down at his bedside by the Abbé Carcence, vicar of the parish of St Amans: in it Bousquier described how he had been frightened into making accusations against men whom in fact he didn't know, in a desperate attempt to save his own life. Now that everything was past and done with, the provost, le Marquis de la Salle, made no secret of how he had succeeded in getting Bousquier to 'confess':

Bousquier had been put into a cell with another prisoner who was, in fact, a police agent. This *mouton* impressed upon him that his only way to escape the gallows would be to say he had been paid to assist in carrying the body from the Maison Bancal to the river, thus representing himself as an unwilling accomplice terrorised by Bastide into becoming an accessory after the crime. The result was that in the morning he asked to see me. I sent for him; but when he stood before me he was so frightened that he didn't succeed in uttering the least sound. To give him courage I questioned him, saying, 'Come, now. You were in the Maison Bancal on 19th March, weren't you?' He tried in vain to answer: he could only shake his head and make a gesture of denial. 'Ah! Scoundrel!' I cried, leaping to my feet and drawing my pistol, 'So you won't talk?' I fired at him point blank. The bullet whistled past his ear and lodged in the wall behind him. He fell in a heap. At first I thought I had killed the brute, but we managed to bring him round with restoratives. He was unhurt. After that it was easy. Shaking with terror, he agreed sentence by sentence to the deposition we required, and signed it.

And the deposition they required was an eye-witness account that would make the stories of the Bancal children appear to be true. The funeral procession taking the body to the river was constructed on the deposition of the *hôtelier*, Albene, in which he described his fears while going home late in the dark night of 19th March and imagining he had seen the shadows of men under the trees of the boulevard d'Estourmel which, he decided later, must have been the assassins of Monsieur Fualdès! This was the shadowy basis upon which Bousquier's 'confession' and the entire story of the funeral procession from the Maison Bancal to the river were constructed.

The discovery that Bousquier's deposition had been faked, and consequently those of Bax and Madame Bancal were not true either for they had been founded on it, must have been a shattering blow for Rodat, destroying both his own self-confidence and his belief in Clarissa – as if he were gazing once more into the dreadful chasm that had so alarmed him and filled him with foreboding on his journey through the mountains when the conviction that Clarissa was in some way connected with the crime had leapt into his mind and refused to be rationalised out of it. 'O my prophetic soul!' he could have cried with Hamlet: did it know what would happen if he went blindly on through life, and was trying to warn him? Knowing now that the confessions were faked, he had to face the probability that Bastide and Jausion were innocent and that Clarissa with her double tongue had murdered them.

What was the reason for her hatred of Bastide? A statement he made during the trial at Albi holds the key to the mystery: 'Madame Manson persecutes me because I prevented her from marrying a young relative of mine.' The remark had not been taken seriously – but Bastide did not make unfounded statements, and Rodat should have realised, for he knew the whole history of the affair, that the young relative must have been the elder Bessières-Veynac, his youthful rival in the garden for Clarissa's hand, whom her mother was expecting her to marry and was astonished when she did not. This would explain her serious illness, probably hysterical, while she was still in the Bessières-Veynacs' house, and then her insistence on marrying the highly unsuitable Monsieur Manson, saving face by taking the first man who offered. Clarissa was not the innocent victim dragged into the scene of the crime, as she pretended, but a vindictive woman burning with resentment against the man whom she believed had ruined her life and happiness: what crime could be greater than that? What crime more worthy of condign punishment? 'My great secrets . . . only the Devil knows them,' was her enigmatic remark to the examining magistrate, Bertrandi, at Rodez. What were the great secrets she could only share with the Devil? No one had understood her then, or asked: now all was clear: she was slowly murdering Bastide for preventing her from having the man she wanted, and plunging into tragedy and ruin the family into which she had hoped to marry.

Being the intimate friend of Bastide's sister, she probably understood from the beginning that he was innocent; and that the mysterious veiled woman everyone was talking about didn't exist and therefore could not appear and expose her as a fraud. She probably first played for a while with the idea of assuming the role, let herself be tempted by it, allowed her resentment to gloat over the terrible revenge she would be in a position to take; and also enjoyed in anticipation the emotions it would excite in the crowd, whom she despised. For three months after the crime had been committed she made no accusations but confined herself to learning every possible detail reported about it, and about the Maison Bancal. She then tried it out on her lover, Clémendot, whom she found rather a bore and who needed a jolt: the result was most gratifying: when she told him that she was the veiled woman in the case he sobbed, he cried, he pitied her – and he was tremendously intrigued. She knew he would repeat it, but as she had told him in the intimacy of her room and when he had been drinking heavily, she could easily deny that she had said anything of the kind. Later, she half withdrew her statement: from her youth up she had loved mystery, and had learned that if she told only part of a story her hearers would want to know the rest: it helped to focus attention on herself. The effect of her disclosure was sensational, and of her denial more so, but the reaction of the hostile crowd at the theatre must have shown her she was playing a dangerous part. When she had been bullied sufficiently by the prefect, by the examining magistrates and by her father – so that she could say afterwards, if necessary, that she did so only under pressure, she signed a definite statement incriminating Bastide and Jausion.

Then the good and gentle Madame Pons showed her the enormity of what she was doing and persuaded her, with the help of her confessor, to repent and withdraw her statement. But alas! no one, Rodat included, would believe in her retraction, and before the court she could not resist playing the part of the mysterious veiled woman that for so long had occupied her mind, conveniently fainting when she was at a loss what to say and was in danger of being found out and denounced as an imposter – a very real fear: had not Jausion suggested she should be branded as a false witness? At the same time, trying with one part of her mind to keep her promise to Madame Pons, she was denying that she had seen anything of the crime; and so the strain became more and more unbearable until she felt only a confession from Bastide could relieve her from her painful situation : therefore she had cried out, 'Why don't you confess, you wretch?' Unhappily it was taken as proof that she knew he was guilty. The more she struggled to escape, the more she involved herself, and the accused : for them her confusion and her contradictions were deadly, not only because it was assumed they were due to her terror of the assassins, but because her behaviour riveted all attention on the great question of whether or not she was the mysterious veiled woman who had witnessed the crime, instead of on whether such a woman had ever existed. Naturally the authorities were patient and supported her : Bousquier was the lowest type of scoundrel, and here was a high-class witness whose father was a magistrate apparently confirming the children's tales.

As the trial went on she gradually perfected the role she had played but clumsily at first : her confidence grew with her fame, her nature seemed to change until the character she had assumed became more real to her and to her audience than her previous daily drab existence from which she was finding an escape : probably in her more exalted moments she really believed she had witnessed the murder, and even that she was an avenging angel sent from Heaven to confound the assassins – the role that the self-deluded and hysterical Didier, who so exactly expressed the emotions and beliefs of the crowd, had assigned to her : she was at last playing the heroine of a romance, and everything that contributed to its effectiveness she felt to be justified. But even if she lost herself in her part from time to time, she must always have known what she was doing; just as an actor in the theatre may lose himself in the character he is portraying though he is still perfectly aware that he is himself and that the events of the play did not happen to him personally.

The brilliant abilities nature had lavished upon her made her a star of the first magnitude. For months she held the stage alone, and what a performance it was! Accompanied by the acclamations of the audience she deliberately murdered three men in full view of the public and in the glare of national and international publicity – and no one even suspected her! She became an instrument of destruction, for others and for herself, because one element had been stifled in her – love, in its deepest and broadest sense, conscious love and compassion for humanity. In this she was entirely lacking. In order to be avenged on Bastide, she could not avoid condemning Jausion to death as well, and Colard; nor could she avoid utterly destroying the Bancal family, nor letting Anne Benoît be branded and imprisoned for life with hard labour against whom there wasn't even a shred of a piece of evidence that would have been accepted by an impartial court.

All this did not deter her in the least, nor trouble her. It wasn't her fault that Bastide had ruined her life, and because he had done so, he must bear the blame for everything that had happened as a consequence of his interference. It is possible also that she worked off on him, with a good conscience, some of the resentment she had felt since her earliest youth for her father's neglect. All these elements she worked up into a dramatic role and clothed them in the marvellous glamour of a great star who can play on the emotions of a vast audience : and what star of the theatre, that was her passion, had ever taken the risks that she had taken, and finally brought the villain of the piece actually to the guillotine? It was an unheard of triumph with only one disadvantage : she could not share it with a living soul without going to the guillotine herself. Only in the final trial, after the execution of Bastide and Jausion, did she err through over-confidence : when she abandoned mystery, nameless terrors and contradictions, she lost her public and her appeal for the jury.

To believe that Bastide and Jausion were innocent, it is necessary to believe that more than 300 of their fellow citizens bore false witness against them. It seems impossible : so many of them recognised Bastide or Jausion on the fatal night near the scene of the crime – but could they have done so? Bearing in mind the strange appearance of faces glimpsed by torchlight or the flash of a lantern in the dark streets of an ancient town, we have to admit that positive identification would have been extremely difficult; and also it was fatally easy to let their imagination play tricks in retrospect once it was known assassins had been abroad. Such was the hypnotic effect of the people's fears and prejudices that they deluded themselves into imagining they were telling the truth, and at the same time feeling self-righteously that they were serving the cause of justice when in fact they were indulging in the unholy joy of rending a fellow human being who had got into difficulties as wolves rend an injured member of the pack.

Probably in the far distant past, at a very early stage of our civilisation, these primitive impulses served a useful purpose : a herd of animals suddenly taking fright could perhaps save themselves by all running madly together in one direction or another, though they might also destroy themselves; and famished wolves might possibly survive another winter by tearing and devouring one another – but to be swayed by the herd instinct in modern times is to be in the power of the primitive forces symbolised in ancient Rodez by the goddess Rhea. The accused were sacrificed to the blind instinct of the mob, not only of the ignorant and brutish part of it, but of the community as a whole; and in this the Rhutenians were in no wise different from any other community in any other part of the world.

The infantile stories of the Bancal children were also the fault of the townspeople : they had impressed upon the children that the crime must have been committed in their house because it was the most disreputable in the quarter – which was no proof at all – and the children had responded with lurid details in exchange for coins and sugar cakes. The judges should not have accepted any of this testimony; but they seem to have merely counted the numbers of the witnesses on either side and, as a result, disallowed the perfectly sound alibis put forward by the accused; just as they weighed up in their scales of justice the arguments of the learned counsels, ignoring their false premises, until the balance had inclined heavily in favour of the prosecution. With all their pretence of searching for the truth and administering justice, they had wanted only a verdict of guilty, as if to show their superiors in Paris that the investigation had been efficiently carried out and that victims had been thrown to the hungry mob. Bastide was a particularly suitable one : how spectacular, and how useful for their careers to make out that he was guilty! How painstaking, how conscientious, how courageous they appeared in their efforts to break such a well-connected gang of malefactors as Bastide's inoffensive family! Little wonder they made no effort to find the real criminal : any trail leading in a different direction might have spoiled their plan.

Because the jury had to give their verdict not on any logical consideration but on their general impression of the guilt or innocence of the accused, the authorities deliberately encouraged and exploited the general prejudice – at the same time deceitfully praising the public for being unbiased when they were most viciously biased. Their methods were deplorable – the endless interrogations, the misrepresentations, the threats, the employment of police spies disguised as fellow prisoners, the open encouragement of those witnesses who were eager to speak against the accused, and the persecution of those who tried to speak in their favour. When a witness was expected to make a deposition in favour of Bastide or Jausion, their regular practice was first to get other witnesses to say he was unreliable or he had told them precisely the opposite, so that when he made his deposition before the court it was received with incredulity. And we cannot exonerate the prosecutor at Albi from a charge of tampering with the evidence for the defence by bullying the witnesses before they appeared in court : his treatment of the old peasant woman Albresbi is a typical example : 'I represented in vain to this woman the authority and number of the witnesses who had established the falsity of what she was saying. . . .' And all the time in the courtroom at Albi, above the heads of the accused and while they should still have been presumed innocent, there was the large map displayed on the wall, certified by the signatures of the Prefect of Aveyron and the Mayor of Rodez that it showed the route taken by the assassins carrying the body of Monsieur Fualdès through the streets from the Maison Bancal to the river. It was utterly false and misleading. Without Bousquier's deposition, and Théron's statement of what he had seen, and could not possibly have seen, what proof was there that there had been such a procession ? There was none.

It is dreadful to contemplate Bastide's situation. He was snatched away from his daily tasks, his family, his friends, his business, the tilling of his fields : it was as if he had fallen into a nightmare where sense and truth were no longer valid. He had been thrown into prison without a cause and loaded with chains : from being universally respected, he had been execrated and insulted. His protests fell upon deaf ears; his most reasonable explanations of his past conduct met with no acceptance or response : he was surrounded by dream figures who had lost the dimension of common humanity. Goodness, justice, duty to society, were hollow words that were used incessantly but which meant nothing, or they meant their opposites. There was no escape. And yet he had borne it through to the end with courage and dignity, even with good humour. How many of his persecutors would have done so – or of us ?

Madame Bancal, with commendable resolution, had denied all through the first trial that the crime had been committed in her house : she had only broken down after she had been condemned to death, and when it was obviously impossible for her to save the rest of the accused. The retired Spanish magistrate, Saavedra, who had occupied the room immediately above the kitchen, stated positively that nothing unusual had happened there : why was his statement not accepted ? Why had he and his wife been threatened by the President, and his wife put under arrest, for speaking the simple truth ? Rodat himself had been manoeuvred into saying something derogatory about him that was mere hearsay. Of all the allegations of theft no evidence was produced : they were all Didier's invention because without them he could not justify his obsession that the accused had murdered his father.

If there is any satisfaction to be got from a reappraisal of the facts, it is that Monsieur Fualdès did not die in the horrific manner described by Clarissa and the Bancal children and so often repeated by the presidents and the prosecutors, but most probably by the sudden stab of a footpad, Bax, Bousquier, or another, for his bag of money : but what is that satisfaction compared to the knowledge of the agony unrighteously inflicted on Bastide and Jausion and their families, on Colard, Anne Benoît and the Bancal family? Society in trying to get rid of the stigma of a crime had committed an infinitely greater one.

Are we to blame 300 witnesses under oath for lying? It was indeed impossible that they should have done anything else. No one under the sway of destructive emotions, suspicion, resentment, fear, vanity, or with the desire to show off or to be like all the rest, is capable of conveying the truth : he will betray it by suppressing part of his testimony, or by adding to it, or merely by an intonation or a gesture; and his memory will misremember if it has the slightest encouragement or ulterior motive to do so. Or should we blame the presidents, the prosecutors, the advocates-general and the barristers of the civil cause? They were mere puppets representing the functions and prejudices of the law, cogs in the machine. Their individual human content was so small that although they were different persons and had different names, they were hardly distinguishable from each other, except perhaps that some had more rasping voices than others. Bastide the perverted murderer was in them all : the doing of the good man Bastide to death was a blind attempt to get rid of their own nastiness. All this is sad enough to contemplate, but the most frightening thing is they were all helpless in the matter : being as they were, they had of necessity reacted to the circumstances as they had done. Being as Rodat was, he had done the same. Bastide alone, in some strange way had raised himself in the scale of existence and taken his life back to the source of all life, strengthened and purified. Clarissa, in trying to destroy him, had descended to the depths.

What remained then of 'most virtuous Rodat', as the judges called him – a description he accepted with complacency? He had believed himself to be a wise counsellor, more civilised and intelligent than his fellow Rhutenians. It looked at first as if he had been specially sent to Rodez to intervene in and prevent this appalling tragedy – a fitting errand for one who believed the world could be redeemed by chivalry.

Why had he not done so, even after experiencing a sort of vision in the mountains warning him that Clarissa would be involved in it?

Instead of finding out everything he could, he had avoided learning anything at all about her, except from her mother and herself, in case he should suffer the loss of his illusions. Coming from the outside he was in a better position than anyone else to take an objective view of the situation in Rodez and not to be influenced by the intense excitement prevailing at the time; and indeed for a day or two, perhaps for three days, he had succeeded in doing so, which was not a record to be proud of for a man who believed himself capable of balanced judgement.

Then he was put to the test, and he failed miserably: Jausion came to see him and wanted to talk with him privately: he received him coldly and refused him the opportunity because it was already being whispered that he was involved in the case – and yet Jausion was the one man who could have enlightened him, and he was the one man who might have saved Jausion: he might have proved his innocence and he might have warned Rodat of Clarissa's hatred of Bastide and its cause: he must have known of it for he had been intimately concerned as the go-between in her marriage negotiations. With this knowledge he might have interpreted quite differently the brief conversation overheard by moonlight, he might have saved Clarissa from herself, he might have worked on behalf of the accused instead of against them.

One more opportunity he had been given to distinguish truth from falsehood – when he met Madame Pons. She had impressed him immediately and aroused his sympathy, but Clarissa had told him, and he had never doubted it till now, that she knew her brother was guilty and in spite of this had come to implore her to withdraw her evidence: therefore he had used all his influence to counteract hers. A few minutes' quiet talk would have opened his eyes, but Clarissa took good care he should never be alone with her. Why had he loved and trusted the deceitful Clarissa, and not the clear-spirited and equally beautiful Madame Pons?

Then when they were at the hospice, the other Bancal children had warned him Madeleine had a wicked tongue: why had he not followed this up to refute her stories? He might at least have questioned them further. Why had he shut his eyes to every indication that Bastide might have been innocent? It was because, like everyone else, he wanted to think of him as guilty. Life had brutally demonstrated that through the complacency that was his besetting sin he had not only allowed this terrible tragedy to occur, he had actively furthered it by blindly supporting the murderess and assuring the court of her high sense of honour and kindness of heart: and it was through his lips, when she had retracted her statements, that false accusations were made, particularly against Jausion. He had imagined he was helping a damsel in distress, but what chivalry had he shown towards Bastide, towards Jausion, towards Colard? For their deaths he was as much to blame as everyone else : he could neither escape nor answer the dread accusation of the prophet Nathan : 'Thou art the man !'

One after another those who had made false accusations recanted. Perhaps the most callous was the mill-hand Théron : he confessed that he had offered to testify he had seen the accused men escorting the body of Monsieur Fualdès to dump it in the river, only because he had been told the witnesses were being sent at the government's expense to Albi, and he thought it a good opportunity to travel and see the country. Madame Bancal, who out-lived all her children, sent for the *curé* of Cadillac where she was in a penitentiary : he took down her statement and passed it on to the public prosecutor of Toulouse, Monsieur de Bastoulh :

> The woman Bancal has made a declaration saying that during the trial at the tribunal of Rodez she consistently adhered to the truth when she declared she never witnessed the crime and knew nothing about it or where it could have been committed. At Albi she made a statement to the contrary, hoping to save her life. . . .

Only the thoroughly discredited Bax did not recant. From his prison in Toulouse he persistently appealed to the Fualdès family for help – he seemed to feel they were under an obligation to him.

Clarissa soon lost her job as cashier in the Café de Foy – her disdainful airs didn't suit the clientele : and although at first she had attracted some attention as a minor celebrity, the gentlemen had lost interest in her when they found she wouldn't sleep with them. The grant from the government together with a small allowance from Monsieur Manson enabled her to live and support Kleinking while he was studying at the Ecclesiastical College. In the autumn of 1831 she was working as a cashier at the café Véron, close to the Bourse : she lost this job too, and ran a seedy tavern in the rue Copeau behind the Jardin des Plantes. Spending little on food, and more than she could afford on clothes and on the theatres, she moved into poorer and poorer lodgings, first in the rue des Quatre Filles and then in the rue de Grenelle where she was known only as one of several elderly eccentrics inhabiting the quarter.

At last, in March 1833, she fell ill, and having no hope of living longer, or any desire to do so, she sent for her son and the Abbé de Villiers, Vicar of St Thomas d'Aquin. She solemnly told them that she had seen nothing and knew nothing of the murder of Monsieur Fualdès : 'and this you may swear,' she said, 'to all who may wish to know.' And so she died, admitting her guilt : and something must have died in Rodat also. But the massive total of human agony and grief created by the Fualdès trials stood as a monument to Clarissa's useless and misspent life – and to his.

Bibliography

Bibliography

1. Histoire Complète du Procès instruit devant la Cour d'Assises de l'Aveyron relatif a l'Assassinat du Sieur Fauldès. . . . Troisième Édition, Paris 1817.
2. *La Quotidienne.* September 1817–June 1818.
3. Histoire et Procès Complet des Assassins de Monsieur Fualdès, par *Le Sténographe Parisien.* Procédure d'Albi. Paris 1818.
4. Procès des Prévenus de l'Assassinat de M. Fualdès, ex-Magistrat de Rhodez. Paris 1817.
5. Mémoires de Madame Manson explicatif de sa Conduite dans le Procès de L'Assassinat de M. Fualdès, écrite par elle-même. Paris 1818.
6. Memoirs of Madame Manson explanatory of her conduct on trial for the assassination of Monsieur Fualdes. Translated from the French. London 1818.
7. Lettres inédites de Madame Manson, publiées par elle-même. Paris 1819.
8. Fualdès, Didier. Clarissa Manson, ou Le Voile Noir de Rodez dechiré a Albi, suivis des discours prononcés par Maître Didier Fualdès. . . . Paris 1818.
9. Madame Manson Expliqué, ou Refutation de ses Mémoires par Monsieur P.L. Paris 1818.
10. Le Sténographe Parisien, ou Lettres Écrites de Rodez et d'Albi sur le Procès des Assassins de M. Fualdès. Paris 1818.
11. Confidences de Victoire Redoulez, ancienne Femme de Chambre de Madame Enjalran et Nourrice de Madame Manson. Paris 1819.
12. L'Intrigue de Rodez, infanticide imputé a Jausion. Aveu de Monsieur Bancal Mourant. Épisode Oublié dans les Mémoires de Madame Manson. . . . Paris 1818.
13. Cour d'Assises du Département du Tarn. Débats Publiques sur la Procedure instruite contre les Prevenus de L'Assassinat de M. Fualdès Ancien Magistrat de Rodez (Aveyron) Edit : Vieusseux, Toulouse 1818.
14. *Le Gazette de Lausanne,* 9th January 1818.
15. *Le Journal de Toulouse,*
16. *The Times,*
17. Esquillat. Plaidoyer pour Madame Manson et discours composé par Madame Manson et prononcé par elle-même à l'Audience de 29th Avril. Toulouse 1818.

18. Mémoires de Monsieur Clémendot en réponse à ceux de Madame Manson. Paris 1818.

19. Mémoire pour servir à la Défense de Madame Manson devant la Cour d'Assise d'Albi, avec Pièces de Procès, et quelques observations en réponse à un libelle signé Clémendot publié contre cette dame; par M. Lenormand, avocat à la cour royale de Paris.

20. Le Coin de Voile Levé sur l'Affaire Fualdès. Confession et Aveu de Clarisse Enjalran, Madame Manson. . . . Par un habitant de Rodez. Paris 1819.

21. Mathews' Diary of an Invalid for March 31st 1819.

22. Mrs. Manson. Letters, translated from the French, London 1819.

23. Causes Criminelles Celèbres du XIX Siècle par une Societé d'Avocats. Vol. I 1827.

24. London Library. P.2826 N.D.

25. Alfre, H. Biographie l'Aveyronnaise.

26. Cruppi, Jean. La Cour d'Assises, Deuxième Édition, 1898.

27. Praviel, Armand. The Murder of Monsieur Fualdès. Trans. Doris Ashley. (This is fiction, but founded on the documents.) 1923.

28. Wright, F. A. The Love Poems of Joannes Secundus. 1930.

29. Fornairon, Ernest. L'Affaire Fualdès. Oeuvres Libres N.S.166. Paris 1960.

30. Une Brève Évocation de L'Affair Fualdès. Discours de Monsieur Bernard. 1962.

Index

Index

Albene, Monsieur, hôtelier, 28,
  122, 171-2, 225, 271
Albi, 145-8, 151-2, 154-61, 183-4,
  196, 205, 213, 231, 252, 255,
  257, 260, 275, 279
'Albigensian Heresy' the, 155
Alboni, Monsieur, 120
Albresbi, Marianne, shepherdess,
  207, 212, 215, 276
Albui, Sabine, 184
Aldebert, A., gardener, 100
Alibert, Monsieur, 174
Ambergue, rue de, 84, 99, 184
Andromache, 122
Altier, Madame, 203
Anglade, Monsieur, 184
Anglade, Madame, 106
Annonciade, monastery, 44, 55, 58,
  93, 96, 130, 178, 185
Arlabosse, Charlotte, *couturière*,
  100-1, 146, 168, 209-10, 217,
  224, 259, 261-2, 264
Arsaud, Maître, 83-4, 128
Auvergne, 15
Aveyron, district, 53, 74, 95, 137,
  139, 141, 143, 145, 153, 156,
  216, 244, 254
Aveyron, river, 21, 25, 29-30, 118,
  139, 192-3, 201, 218, 225, 248-9,
  259

Bache, Mademoiselle, 213-4, 226
Bancal, Maison, 26, 28-30, 46-53,
  56-60, 62-4, 66, 69-71, 73-6,
  80-2, 88-95, 97, 100-1, 103-6,
  113, 116, 118, 129-30, 133-4,
  146, 149, 154, 161-2, 164-6,
  168-9, 173, 175, 178, 180-2, 184,
  187-9, 192, 198, 203, 206, 216,
  221, 224-5, 235, 241, 247, 249,
  259, 261-2, 264, 269-72, 276
Bancal, Monsieur, 21, 32, 43-4, 66,
  75, 78, 82, 85-6, 103, 105-6, 116,
  176, 192, 196-8, 231-2; his death,
  43, 66, 121
Bancal, Madame, 26, 32, 57, 71,
  75, 79-80, 82, 85, 86-8, 91,
  103-5, 118, 125-6, 130, 134-5,
  137-8, 142-3, 147, 156-7, 163,
  175, 181, 190-2, 195-9, 201-3,
  206, 209, 213, 217, 221, 223,
  225-6, 228-30, 235, 239, 240-1,
  246, 249-51, 254, 258, 263, 267,
  271, 274, 276, 279; her
  appearance, 79-80, 163, 263;
  and Clarissa, 149-50;
  condemned, 143, 251;
  denounces Bastide, 196-8;
  reprieved, 258; withdraws her
  deposition, 279
Bancal, Alexis, 67-8
Bancal, Madeleine, 32-3, 44, 54,
  610, 66-8, 84-6, 130, 150, 191-2,
  196-7, 224, 231, 240, 278; her
  'wicked tongue', 67, 278
Bancal, Marianne, 67, 71, 75, 82,
  103, 126, 135, 142-3, 191, 263;
  and her father's death, 66
Bancal, Victor, 67
Bancal, Children, 30, 53-4, 67, 70,
  80, 84, 86-7, 104, 125, 146, 162,
  169, 175, 185, 191-2, 221, 223,
  255, 271, 273, 275, 277-9
Bastide, or Bastide-Grammont, 14,
  24, 28, 30, 32-3, 39, 54, 57-8,
  60-1, 63, 68-9, 71-3, 75, 79-81,

83-4, 90-3, 96-9, 102, 111-3, 115,
117, 119, 127, 130, 137, 140-3,
146, 153, 158, 162-5, 167-70,
173-9, 181-98, 201-2, 204,
207-12, 214-8, 221-9, 235-8,
245-52, 255-65, 267, 270-9;
description of, 33, 81-2, 97-9,
148, 257; suspected of murder,
17, 21, 26; arrested, 27; his
trial at Rodez, 71-143 *passim;*
attempts to escape, 107, 147-8;
transferred to Albi, 156-7; second
trial, 162-265 *passim;* denounced
by Clarissa, 91, 182, 189, 224;
Romiguière's defence of, 119-24,
255; his own defence, 229-33;
humour, 183-5, 187, 201, 276;
courage, 276; tries to save
Clarissa from herself, 201; and
Clarissa's marriage, 189, 270;
compares truth to the corner of
a veil that rises, 197; and
Charlotte Arlabosse, 110-1, 146,
209-10, 262; and Madame
Vernhes, 207-9; the verdicts,
142-3, 250-1; the appeals, 143-5,
255-7; last declaration, 259; his
end, 255-9

Bastide, Madame, 98, 137, 148,
170, 185, 195, 214, 255, 258

Bastide, père, 99, 123, 229, 232,
236

Bastide, mère, 232

Bastide, Louis, 168, 221, 255, 259,
261, 263, 263N

Bastouhl, Monsieur de, 279

Batut, Maître, 103, 126

Bax, François, smuggler, 71-2,
74-6, 82, 106-7, 115-6, 118,
122, 127, 142, 147, 151, 156,
159, 164, 169, 175-7, 183, 185,
192, 194, 196, 198-9, 203, 206,
209, 216, 220-6, 229-32, 235,
238-41, 246, 249-52, 254, 261-3,
271, 277, 279; Appearance, 106,
condemned, 143, 251; turns
King's evidence, 174-5;

reprieved, 253; accuses Louis
Bastide, 263

Beaujon Gardens, 254

Benoît, Anne, laundrymaid, 32, 71,
82, 105-7, 116, 118, 127, 142-3,
147, 151, 156, 158, 163, 170,
175, 177, 191, 193-4, 196, 198,
239-40, 249-52, 257, 275, 277;
pretence that her handkerchief
was used to gag Monsieur
Fualdès, 76, 78; her love for
Colard, 105, 118, 147, 158,
239-40, 251; life sentence, 143,
252; branded, 257; pleads for
death, 252

Bertrandi, examining magistrate,
150-1, 154, 272

Besse, Madame, known as de la
Bessote, butcher, 26N

Bessières-Veynac, Louis, 20-1, 35,
41, 44, 63, 271

Bessières-Veynac, Pierre-Joseph,
71, 83, 122, 128, 146, 168, 172,
175, 216-7, 259, 261, 263-5 :
appearance, 264

Boccaccio, 62

Bole, Maître, 199, 220-1, 238-40,
254

Bon, Marianne, 103

Bonnes, Marianne, 100

Boudet, Maître, 190, 228-9

Boudin, A, 99, 229

Bourget, 99

Bourrine, Jean François Blanc de,
180-1, 215

Bourse, the, 279

Bousquier, smuggler, 44, 53, 71-2,
74-6, 82-4, 94, 98-9, 101, 104-5,
107-8, 113, 115-8, 121-2, 125-9,
142-3, 146, 157-8, 162, 169-70,
175-6, 183, 191, 194, 196, 198-9,
206, 223, 227, 230, 235, 240-1,
246, 249, 259, 263, 270-1, 277;
turns King's evidence, 30;
appearance, 82; retracts his
deposition, 270

Bousquier, Madame, 169

Boyer, Maître, 159
Brast, Abbé, 97
Brast, tailor, 78, 173
Brast, Madame, 173-4
Bress, mill of, 29, 75, 192
Brugière, known as Pistolet,
 police spy, 105
Bruyère, Monsieur, assistant court
 usher, 101

Cabrioler, Jean-Antoine, saddler,
 102
Cadillac, *curé* of, 279
Caesar, Julius, 15
Calcas, high priest, 226N
Calmals, François, police agent,
 103
Calvet, police official, 112, 169,
 172
Camboulazet, *curé* of, 108
Canitrot, gaoler, 169-70, 195, 199,
 231
Capuchin Prison, 147, 154, 156
Carcence, Abbé, 270
Carrère, Monsieur, 179
Carrier, Monsieur, 111
Casal, Pierre, stone mason, 98
Cascame, the miller of, 232
Caston, Advocate-General, 72, 95,
 135, 138-40
Caumont, Councillor Cambettes
 de, 106, 261-2
Cazals, 229
Cervantes, 203
Chalies, groom, 99
Charivari, 26N
Charlemagne, 123
Chatard, prison chaplain, 258
Chaudes-Aigues, 17-20, 24
Chronos, 15
Clémendot, aide-de-camp, 42-7,
 50-1, 65, 69, 92-3, 96, 133, 135,
 157, 162-3, 172-3, 216, 242, 244,
 254, 272 : wounded by Edward
 Enjalran, 260
Code, d'Instruction, the Criminal
 Code, 102, 144-5, 168N, 183,

207, 211-2, 228
Colard, Jean-Baptiste, ex-soldier,
 71-2, 74, 76, 82, 104-5, 107,
 115-6, 118, 126, 142-3, 147, 151,
 156, 158, 164, 168, 170, 174-5,
 191-6, 198-9, 220, 229, 232,
 238-40, 249-52, 254, 257-8, 273,
 277, 279; Appearance, 104, 164,
 257; tried for murder at Rodez,
 71-143 *passim;* tried again at
 Albi, 162-265 *passim;* proclaims
 innocence, 239, 258; his last
 request, 253; and Anne Benoît,
 71, 76, 118, 147, 239-40, 251-2
Combarel, Maître, père, 125, 198
Combarel, Maître, fils, 127
Comeiras, de, Maître, 128
Constans, Monseiur, merchant,
 130
Constans, Madame, dressmaker,
 69, 130-1, 134, 161, 216
Constans, Marie-Antoine, Police
 Commissioner, 106, 261-2
Copeau, rue, 279
Coq, café, 51
Corday, Charlotte, 27
Cordeliers Prison, 147-8, 156
Cossacks, 43-4
Coudère, Catherine, 103
Cour de Cassation, see Supreme
 Court of Appeal
Courland, Monsieur de, 232
Curtius Waxworks, 269
Cussac, sheriff's officer, 257

David, Jacques Louis, painter, 158
Daubusson, Jeanne, 105-6
Decazes, Baron, Prefect of Tarn,
 154, 164, 244, 255
Destampes, Guillaume, servant,
 108-9
Desperières, General, 71, 88, 90
Doitre, Canon, 203
Dornes, le sieur Jean Josef, 84,
 102, 121
Drak, poltergeist, 16, 101
Dubernat, Maître, 181, 186, 192,

194, 223, 233, 253, 255
Dubock, Monsieur, 99
Duclos, Mademoiselle, *fille de joie,*
    202-3
Dupré, Monsieur, 17
Dupuy, Maître, 240, 254

Edward III, 238
Enjalran, Monsieur, magistrate,
    President of the Provost's Court,
    18, 35-7, 39, 45, 50-2, 56, 64-5,
    69, 88-9, 132-3, 149-50, 164,
    186, 222, 244, 260, 265, 267,
    272-3
Enjalran, Madame, 34-8, 43, 45,
    65, 162, 244, 252, 260, 265,
    267-8
Enjalran, Edward, 34-5, 37-8,
    42-3, 45, 47, 50, 65, 69, 244,
    265; his duel with Clémendot,
    69, 260
Esquilat, Maître, 169, 201-2, 242
Espalion, 259
Estourmel, boulevard de, 28-9,
    83, 99, 107, 122, 271
Estourmel, Marquis de, Prefect of
    Aveyron, 46, 50-2, 64-5, 68-9,
    71-2, 95, 122, 131, 133, 154,
    161, 165, 192, 216, 244, 272,
    276
Eumenides, the, 263

Faydel, chevalier de, President of
    the Court at Albi, 164-189,
    passim, 217, 220-3, 230, 233,
    236-7, 239, 247-52, 254, 277
Febry, Marianne, 103
Féral, Rose, 30, 126
Féral Tavern, 30, 74, 76, 82, 104,
    127, 169, 239-40, 249
'Ferdinand', 55-60, 260
Ferrand, café, 229
Flars, domain of, 70, 75, 111-2,
    114, 234
Fontana, jeweller, 83
Foulquier, *le sieur,* priest, 102
Foulquier, Maître, 126, 240, 250

Foy, café de, 270, 279
France, Monsieur de, 222-3
French Revolution, 17, 74
Fualdès, Didier, 16, 69-70, 72-4,
    90, 93, 95-6, 102-3, 108-14, 117,
    134, 139, 141, 143, 157, 164,
    167, 171, 177-9, 182, 188, 194,
    204-5, 217-9, 221, 223-4, 227,
    240, 245, 251, 253-4, 258, 263,
    273, 277, 279; his Act of
    Intervention, 72-3, 167;
    appearance, 73, 164; and
    Romiguière, 79, 123, 179; horror
    of Jausion, 108-9; refuses to
    consider Jausion's accounts, 205
Fualdès, Jean-Baptiste, 16-7, 21,
    23-8, 38, 43-5, 50, 54, 57-8, 66-7,
    69-70, 72-8, 80-1, 84-5, 88-9, 92,
    98-9, 100-6, 108, 110-6, 118,
    120, 126-30, 137-8, 143, 146,
    165-8, 170-1, 174, 179-85, 188-9,
    191-4, 196-7, 199, 201-2, 204-6,
    217-8, 221-5, 227-32, 234, 236,
    240-5, 247-50, 252-3, 255, 258-9,
    262, 264, 266, 269, 271, 277,
    279; his career, 16, 27; his body
    found in the river, 25, 29, 44-5,
    201; the mystery of his death,
    passim
Fualdès, Madame, 70, 108, 218,
    276

Gallibert, Monsieur, 112, 204
Galtier, Madame, 39, 61, 71-2, 76,
    108, 110, 114-6, 119, 127-8,
    142-3, 170
Garde des Sceaux, le, the
    Chancellor, 71, 77
Gary, Baron, prosecutor, 167-8,
    174, 177, 180, 185, 187, 190,
    193-5, 198, 200, 203-4, 207,
    210-6, 220-1, 226-8, 235-7, 239,
    241, 245-8, 263, 276
Gazette de France, la, 154
Gazette de Lausanne, le, 156
Geniers, Madame, 195
Gévaudan, 21, 172; beast of, 172N

Ginestet, Madame, hôtelière, 84, 121

Ginesti, Monsieur le chevalier de, juryman, 223

Ginesty, officer, 50

Gipson, Miss, 54

Girard-Duplessis, Maître, *Avocat-Général*, 144

Giraud, Thérèse, 195

Giron, Madame, hôtelière, 101, 105-6

Glandines, court usher, 130

Glausy, hotel, 103

Gluck, Christoph Willibald, composer, 225N

Goudalie, Monsieur de la, 172

Grammont, chevalier de, 17

Grandet, Maître, 127-8, 159, 164, 240-1

Grenelle, rue de, 279

Grenier, Monsieur, President of the Court at Rodez, 72, 74, 78-9, 80-3, 86-95, 102, 104-5, 107-8, 110-1, 122, 128-35, 137, 140-4, 149-50

Gros, domain of, 26, 80-1, 99-102, 120-1, 207-8, 210, 259

Guitard, F., dealer, 98

Hamlet, 123, 271

Hebdomadiers, rue des, 25, 53, 56, 60, 74, 78, 81, 83, 100, 146, 173, 193, 143

Hérail, Foreman of the Jury, 142

Horace, 151

Hurdy-gurdy players, 56, 74, 78, 80, 100

Innocent III, Pope, 155

Inquisition, the, 155

Iphigenia in Tauris, 226, 226N

Janny, Jeanne, manageress, 210-14, 226

Jardin des Plantes, 279

Jausion, Abbé, 255

Jausion, Josef, 14, 24-6, 32, 68-9,
71-3, 76, 78, 81-2, 84, 89-92, 94, 96-7, 101, 108-12, 114-5, 122, 128, 130-1, 137-40, 142-3, 148-9, 153, 158, 162-3, 165, 167-8, 170-1, 175-7, 179-82, 185-6, 188, 192-4, 199, 204-5, 216, 218, 221-4, 227-8, 245, 247-52, 255-62, 271-4, 277-9; visits Rodat, 24; goes through Monsieur Fualdès' papers, 26, 28, 256; 'That woman has killed me!' 96; Appearance, 24, 81, 149; arrested, 28, 37; on trial at Rodez, 71-143 *passim;* on trial at Albi, 162-265 *passim;* last declaration, 259-60

Jausion, Madame, 39, 61, 71, 76, 83, 108, 114-6, 119, 128, 142-3, 148, 170, 205, 233, 255, 258

Jolicoeur, gardener, 104, 174

Journal de Paris, le, 163

Julien, Monsieur, examining magistrate, 53

Junot, General, 36

'Kleinking', see Edward Manson

Labro, Monsieur, 229

Laborie, 264

Lacombe, Jean-Louis, bootmaker, 102

Lacombe, Louis, carpenter, 167-8, 174

Laggarigue, Françoise, the widow Solonat, 99

Lagoudie, René de, 99

Languedoc, 18, 155

La Morne, domain of, 81, 98, 100, 102, 121, 207, 210, 214-5, 226, 259

La Mouline, village, 24

Laquelhe Brothers, 170, 259, 261

Larouche, père, innkeeper, 22

La Roquette, village, 100, 146, 109, 210, 259, 262

La Salle, chevalier de, Provost of Aveyron, 169-70, 270

Latouche, Monsieur Henri de, journalist, 148, 151-4, 162-4, 178, 180, 189
Layole Mountains, 17
Leconier, Councillor, 114
L'Homme des Morts, 93
Les Ternes, village, 172N
Lilo, Colonel Roque, 203
Loiseau, Maître, 143-4
Lot, river, 185
Louis XVI, 74
Louis XVIII, 254
Loubière, Alexis-Etienne, chief usher, 221
Loubière, Amans, blacksmith, 104
Lyons, 18

Macbeth, 79
Mainier, Monsieur, prosecutor, 72, 77, 90, 117-8, 132-3, 137, 140, 143
Mallarme, Madame Marcame de, 101
Manège, Place de, 257
Manson, Edward, 'Kleinking', 37, 40, 52, 147, 149-50, 244, 256, 268, 279
Manson, Lieutenant Marc-Antoine, 35-7, 60, 133, 149, 250, 154, 271, 279
Manson, Marie-Françoise-Clarisse, née Enjalran, 13, 28, 32-40, 44, 50-3, 66, 74, 116-7, 121, 125, 128, 136-7, 140-4, 146-7, 149, 159, 163-5, 168, 172-3, 175, 178, 180-3, 185-92, 195, 201-5, 209, 216-7, 221-5, 227-8, 230-1, 235-6, 240-2, 250-2, 255-7, 259-74, 277-80 : childhood, 18-22; appearance, 40, 87, 122-3, 163, 165, 264; her portrait, 268; and Louis Bessières-Veynac, 19-21, 35, 83, 160; and her father, 18, 41-2, 51-3, 89, 132-3, 149-50, 163, 260, 273-4; illness, 35-6; marriage, 37, 39-40, 189, 270-1;

and 'Kleinking', 37, 52, 147, 149-50, 269, 279; and her ideal lover, Ferdinand, 55-60, 260, 269; love for the theatre, 42, 54, 68, 186, 189-90, 273-4; scandals concerning, 39, 62; claim to have witnessed the murder of Monsieur Fualdès, 45-50; statements to the Prefect, 46, 50-2, 64, 76; visit to the Maison Bancal, 53; confesses to Rodat, 55-60; accuses Bastide, 57-8, 91, 181, 189, 224; involves Rose Pierret, 69, 132; friendship with Madame Pons, 39, 61-2, 87-8, 97, 273; withdraws accusation, 64; meeting with Madeleine Bancal, 66-8; summoned to appear in court, 87-92; and Clémendot, 42-3, 45-6, 50, 162, 172-3, 242, 244, 254, 272; applies to be heard again, 97, 129; 'You have not arrested all the assassins!', 140; accused of complicity, 143; interrogated, 150-1, 159; in the Capuchin Prison, 149-52; and Henri de Latouche, 152-4, 162, 164, 180; her memoirs, 153-4, 156-8; growing fame, 135, 137, 152, 254, 265; transferred to Albi, 154-6; her trial, 162-265 *passim;* and Charlotte Arlabosse, 109-10; refuses to name Jausion, 178, 182, 186-8, 235; her defence, 242-5; the verdict, 251-2; reconciliation with parents, 36, 260, 267; accuses Pierre-Josef Bessières-Veynac, 263-4; goes to Paris, 268-9; hatred of Bastide, 271-2; last confession, 280
Marthy, Marianne, 98
Masson-Latieule, Monsieur, Mayor of St Felix de Lunel, 142
Mayor of Albi, the, 159-60, 163, 220, 258
Mayor of Rodez, the, 106, 192,

276

Mejanes-Veynac, Abbé de, Grand Vicar of Rodez, 255

Merlin, Maître, 72-3, 102, 112-7, 126, 131, 135, 141, 143, 167

Miegeville, Monsieur de, President of the Court at Albi, 261-5

Migoule, Monsieur, 202

Milhaud, 206

Ministre Publique, 72N

Missionier, Josef, cutler, 32, 71-2, 74-6, 82, 100, 104, 107-8, 115-6, 127-8, 142-3, 147, 151, 156, 159, 175, 182, 196-9, 205-6, 228, 240-1, 249-51

Moisset, Monsieur, 121

Moniteur, le, 163

Montegnac, 209

Montfort, Simon de, 155

Montepellier, 61, 143, 262

Moses, 127

Moscow, Retreat from, 34, 36, 42

Mur-de-Barre, 259

Nathan, prophet, 279

Naves, *curé* of, 108

Nebuchednezzar, 36

Neuve, rue, 56, 64

Notre Dame Cathedral, Rodez, 22, 64, 71

Olemps, 22, 25, 33, 37, 44-5, 93, 255, 268

Olivier, Monsieur, journalist, 163, 183, 228, 257

Pagan, Councillor, 190, 194, 257

Pal, Madame, 54

Pal, Mademoiselle, 201

Palais-Royal district, 270

Palayrot, Monsieur, 126

Palous, *le sieur,* Mayor of Magnac, 108

Pampelone, 155, 157

Paris, 15-6, 20, 23, 26, 33-4, 38, 62, 69, 108, 111-2, 143, 157, 164, 199, 242, 261, 267-9, 275

Parlan, Monsieur, 229

Pascal, Anne, 184-5

Pavillon Ursula, 84, 121, 184, 227

Perier, château, 22, 34-5, 69, 149, 252, 260, 267-8

Persico, Monsieur, painter, 158

Petit Champ, Rodez, 175-6

Pierret, Monsieur, commander of police, 147, 260

Pierret, Rose, 38, 42, 45, 69, 132-4, 147, 163, 228, 260

Pillet, publisher, 154

Pinaud, councillor, 176-7, 185, 188, 190, 200, 216-7

Place d'Armes, 99

Place de la Cité, 84, 102, 146, 184

Place de Manège, 257

Pomayrols, village, 184

Pons, Monsieur, 61

Pons, Madame, 39, 44, 56, 60-5, 69-70, 87-9, 93, 95-7, 118, 133, 143, 151-2, 154, 181, 210, 262, 272-3, 278

Pont, Faubourg du, 155

Prades, 98, 101

Princes, hôtel des, 99

Provence, 15, 19, 34, 152

Pujol, Abbé, 258

Quatres Filles, rue des, 279

Quotidienne, la, 26N, 137, 163, 183, 253, 258

Racine, 122, 190

Rami, bookseller, 161

Raymond, Madame, 99, 210-2

Raynal, Monsieur, farmer, 111

Redoulez, Victoire, nurse, 56, 58, 68-9, 93, 96

Regnes, Madame, 101

Rhea, goddess, 15, 274

Rhutenians, 15-6, 23, 30, 43, 73-4, 141, 155-6, 219, 274, 277

Rodat, Amans, known as Auguste, 13, 27-8, 32-9, 44, 47, 50-4, 157, 162, 164-5, 178, 180, 197, 201,

203, 209, 225, 242, 245, 252,
255-6, 260, 263-72, 277, 280 :
leaves Paris, 15; journey to
Rodez, 15-22; the deep gorge
in the mountains, 21, 271; his
youth with Clarissa, 18-20;
opinion of the Rhutenians, 15-6;
and Bastide, 17, 33, 81, 278;
calls on Clarissa's mother, 34-9;
finds Clarissa again, 40; her
confession, 55-60; and Talliarda,
27-34, 39, 61-2; testifies in court,
93-5, 131, 188, 190-1, 203;
'Most virtuous Rodat!', 131,
277; and Madame Pons, 60-1,
63-4, 151-2, 278; and
Clémendot, 42-3, 45, 50, 97,
172; writes book to win
sympathy for Clarissa, 13, 242,
265, 267; qualifies it with notes,
269
Rodez, 13, 15, 20-1, 23, 27, 29,
42, 46, 56, 60, 62, 64, 69, 71-3,
80-1, 83, 86, 98, 100-2, 108, 113,
118-9, 121, 136-9, 142, 146-7,
152, 156, 159, 161-2, 165-9,
172-4, 176-9, 181, 183-4, 186,
188-9, 195-7, 202, 204-5, 207,
209, 212, 216-8, 220, 222-3, 225,
229, 231, 237, 239, 240-2, 250,
252, 259, 268, 270, 274, 277-9
Rodier, Maître, 78, 84, 108, 112,
128-9, 140, 143, 173
Romiguière, Maître, 14, 72, 86,
102, 118-24, 126, 129, 138,
140-1, 143, 164, 168-9, 172, 177,
179, 188, 193, 198, 207, 210-3,
223, 226, 229, 236-7, 253, 255;
appearance, 79; and Clarissa,
122, 140; demands free access
for counsel to the prisoners they
represent, 183; protest against
persecution of witnesses for the
defence, 211-2
Reuvellat, police spy, 105
Rous, Maître, 127
Rozier, Antoine, 99

Rudelle, *le sieur, curé* of Prades,
101

Saavedras, Senor, retired
magistrate, 146, 202-3, 240, 277
Saavedras, Senora, 146, 202-3,
240, 277
St Amans, parish, 270
St Anne, hospice of, 66-8, 130
St Cecilia, church, 155, 157, 160,
163
St Cecilia, prison, 156-60, 209,
241, 255
St Flour, 16-7, 21, 38, 172N
St Louis le Grand, college, 261
St Mayme, *curé* of, 121, 231
Salvanhac, Marianne, 105
Sasmayous, Monsieur, 179
Sauveterre, village, 155
Secundus, Joannes, poet, 18, 18N
Seguret, Monsieur de, 75, 83, 111,
114, 204, 234
Serres, de, judge, 72
Solignac, Anne, 105
Solonat, widow, see Françoise
Laggarigue
Spain, 16, 36, 55, 60, 137
Sténograph Parisien, le, 148, 151,
248
Sudre, Monsieur, painter, 158
Supreme Court of Appeal, 168-9,
236, 255, 257

Talliarda, Monsieur, 28-30, 32-4,
37-40, 61-3, 67
Tajan, Maître, 164, 167, 177, 187,
219, 224, 245, 251-2, 262
Tarn, district, 154, 157, 164, 168,
244
Tarraux, Maître, 159
Terral, rue de, 25, 78, 99
Teulat, Chief Superintendent,
26-7
Théron, mill hand, 192-5, 199,
220, 227, 231, 235, 259, 261,
276, 279
The Times, 254

Thioullières, *curé* of, 213-4, 226
Touat, rue de, 56, 74
Toulouse, 14, 16, 145, 147, 257, 261, 266, 269, 279
Tremouille, 194
Torquomeda, Madame, 203
Troy, 226N

Var, river, 155
Verlac, Maître, 107, 129
Vernes, Marianne, servant, 210
Vernhes, Madame, 101-2, 207-8, 231
Véron, café, 279

Versailles, 17
Victoire, concierge's daughter, 178
Vignes, Professor J., 83
Villiers, Abbé de, Vicar of St Thomas d'Aquin, 279
Viola, Martin, hôtelier, 107

Wagram, battle of, 38
Wautré, General, 69, 172

Yence, Jean-Josef, d'Istourmet, public notary, 111, 168, 170, 217, 221-2, 259, 261, 266